Dedicated to Les the Cat,
Shirl the Pearl, the Oul Boss Man
and the Minister for Edumacation.

Contents

About the Contributors

JEFF KING lives in Barcelona and is a regular contributor to *Goal*, *World Soccer*, *Total Sport* and *Match of the Day*. He is co-author of *George Graham: The Wonder Years*, also published by Virgin. He was an associate producer on the BBC's *Fantasy Football League* and the Terry Venables documentary, *The Man Who Would Be King*. In the autumn of 1997, Virgin will publish his *A Year in the Life: Bobby Robson at FC Barcelona, 1996–97*.

JOHN KELLY is a freelance writer for the *Daily Express Sport*, *World Soccer*, *90 Minutes* and *Loaded*, among others. He is author of the *Sky Sports FA Premier League Official Fans Guide*. A denizen of fortress Portman Road, he is also available for pantomime.

KEIR RADNEDGE, the editor of *World Soccer*, is the author of *The Ultimate Encyclopedia of World Soccer* and many other books on international football. He was publications consultant to the FA for Euro 96, has collaborated on videos and documentaries, and regularly contributes to radio and television.

DANNY KELLY is a writer and broadcaster. He is editor of *Total Sport*, managing editor of *Q*, presenter of *Baker & Kelly Up Front* on BBC Radio 5 Live, and presenter of Channel 4's *Under the Moon*. Some plumbing attempted, no job too small.

STEPHEN WAGG is a lecturer in sociology at London's Roehampton Institute. He is author of *The Football World: A Contemporary Social History*.

DAVE COTTRELL is deputy editor of *Goal*. He is a regular guest on Talk Radio.

JOHN COLQUHOUN, the former Hearts and Scotland footballer, is now a writer and broadcaster. He is a columnist for *Scotland On Sunday*.

ELEANOR LEVY is the editor of *90 Minutes*.

GAVIN HAMILTON is the deputy editor of *World Soccer*.

IAN EDWARDS is football correspondent at the *Nottingham Post*.

GRAHAM CARTER is a sportswriter on Swindon's *Evening Advertiser*.

MICHAEL HODGES is staff writer on *Goal*.

ADRIAN THRILLS is a freelance writer.

Acknowledgements

Our thanks to some great writers and good fellas: Graham Carter, Dave Cottrell, John Colquhoun, Ian Edwards, Gavin Hamilton, Michael Hodges, Danny Kelly, Eleanor Levy (definitely not a fella, but thanks anyway), Keir Radnedge and Stephen Wagg.

Special thanks to Bobby Robson and Michael Robinson (if everybody handled success like these two guys, Planet Football would be a much nicer place). Thanks also to Paul Hawksbee at *Goal*, José Miguel Teres at FC Barcelona, Alex White of the Association of Football Statisticians, Javier Corbat at Videocomunicación, Cristina Pestonit at Canal Plus, and Hannah MacDonald and Wendy Brown at Virgin Publishing.

To kindred spirits Steve Ford, Antoni Closa, Juan Pedro Martínez, Alex Simpson, Tony Willis, Oliver King, Don Rogers, Gabs, Colin Levine, Steve Lewis, Vaughan Joseph, Roger McGuinn, Dave Fletcher and Lloyd Butler.

Finally, very special thanks to Olga Rubio and Ayesha Cotobally . . . they know who they are!

Foreword

By Keir Radnedge

The setting was Goodison Park, Liverpool, and the Everton boardroom. The date was sometime in the early 1970s.

The occasion was a confrontation between Bill McGarry, manager of visiting Wolverhampton Wanderers, and one of the travelling contingent of Midlands newspaper reporters. McGarry had paused at the door to berate one particular journalist for describing Mike Bailey, Wolves' right half, captain, driving force and inspiration, as being 'injury prone'. The fact that Bailey had missed a third of Wolves' League matches over the previous three seasons was apparently immaterial. McGarry was standing up for his skipper as if his own personal integrity had been questioned.

I know . . . because I was that reporter and because that incident has always remained in my mind as a prime example of the conscious schizophrenia that a man must apparently adopt if he chooses to enter that most peculiar of occupations: football management.

Managers come in all shapes, sizes and styles. On the one hand he is guru, commander and father figure (or mother figure) to his players; on the other he is expected to be the dispassionate dispenser of erudite wisdom about football in particular and life in general. All must be delivered from a foundation fractured by the absolute certainty that one day, amidst screaming headlines and dramatically overstated radio and television bulletins, he will suffer that ultimate humiliation – the sack.

Tommy Docherty was first credited with the cynicism that 'you can tell when a manager is lying – his lips move'. But a football manager's professional life is built on what our parliamentarians would diplomatically describe as 'dissembling'.

You discover the truth sitting, relaxed, in the corner of some off-duty press room or social event with any one of the dozens of managers and coaches who spin on the roundabout of football power; you discover the same truth in an off-the-record corner of Terry Venables' West End club; or in some Continental restaurant or café in the company of a Bobby Robson or Arsène Wenger.

Doesn't the manager realise, thinks the fan or reporter, what a poor player he picks week in, week out? Take up the private conversation and you find, more often than not, that the manager will offer an even harsher private assessment of the same player. You discover, perhaps, that the player wants a transfer but won't command any sort of reasonable fee unless he is playing first-team football; or that the international-fringe man possesses just the right personality to be invaluable, socially, to the squad; or that the player concerned needs encouragement because of an un-reported family trauma.

The more you discover, the more complicated appears the world in which the manager must sink or swim.

Why, for example, do managers insist on sitting in the touchline dugout, where the view is one of scarred knees and flying feet? For any strategist, such a view of a match is akin to being blindfold.

Ask any football reporter, for example, which is the poorest press-box view in the Premiership and most will reply Tottenham – because the Spurs press box is at pitch level ... alongside the Spurs' manager's dugout.

Every fan remembers the shock of the first time he or she moves out of the pitchside front row and up into the seats high in the stand. The game takes on a new dimension. No longer is it about foreshortened physical contact; suddenly it becomes a glorious, live chess match. You see the shapes and the patterns.

Graham Taylor, in his early successful days at Watford, appreciated the point. He would spend the first half of a match sitting up in the stand, 'seeing' the overall picture. Then he moved down onto the bench in the second half, to be able to mastermind his substitutions and shout any necessary instructions in the decisive, closing phase of a match.

Many managers dare not even do that. They find sitting in the directors' box too oppressive. For one thing, they are a sitting target for fans' fury when things go wrong. Secondly, managers do not enjoy sitting adjacent to their chairmen – particularly chairmen who may be apt to throw out their arms in horror when the centre-forward shoots over the top of an open goal from the edge of the six-yard box. The contemptuous implication of the gesture is all too painfully obvious: 'I didn't pick that carthorse – HE did!'

Other managers choose to sit on the bench so as to shout away the weight of nervous tension. Keith Burkinshaw was one such boss. In fact, players will tell you they hear very little of the manager's high-decibel ranting coming from the bench. But it helps the manager's stress level.

Johan Cruyff, during his controversial but highly successful years at Barcelona, sometimes used technological assistance – having a small television set installed alongside his bench in Nou Camp. That way he could study the game from all angles. The only surprise is that so few managers and coaches have followed his example; but then, as player and coach, Cruyff always was years ahead of his time.

Cruyff's success demonstrated vividly another shift in the relationship between manager/coach and player. In the early years of the century the likes of Jimmy Hogan and Arthur Pentland crossed to the continent of Europe – the one to Austria, the other to Italy and Spain – to teach the game. But the teaching role was already forgotten at home in Britain, where the manager was the man in the collar and tie who spent most of his time in his office, watched his players occasionally as they lapped the pitch in training, and the day before a game – on the basis of such arm's length appreciation – duly selected his team.

Such was the image of the great pre-war managers such as Herbert Chapman at Arsenal, the Austrian Hugo Meisl and the Italian Vittorio Pozzo. Indeed, in many clubs in the interwar years it was the manager/secretary who both ran the administration and selected the team. In Britain the tradition lived on with the manager carrying far wider and heavier responsibilities than his cousin on the Continent, where the roles of administrator and first-team coach were separated decades before the English came, slowly, to appreciate the point.

True, European and British games demanded a different managerial approach. The tradition on the Continent – which is changing rapidly in the wake of the Bosman judgement – was for transfers to be permitted only in the summer close-season. (A 'hidden' implication of the Bosman judgement is that timed restrictions on player movements from one employer to another must be illegally restrictive.) In Britain, by contrast, transfer activity goes on all year round, with the briefest hiatus between the end of March and mid-May.

On the Continent this left the coach with 'only' the in-season task of turning out his team week by week to the best of his, and his players', abilities. By contrast the British manager not only had to turn out his team but keep one eye open for opportunities to strengthen it as the season went along.

Those would-be modernists who complained that British clubs should long ago have adopted the Continental system of dual managerial responsibility ignored the demands of a basic difference in transfer structure. The manager as remote father figure was the rule until the mid-1960s. The manner in which Sir Alf Ramsey masterminded England's World Cup victory in 1966 marked the watershed between old and new managerial labour. But while Ramsey was considered socially aloof from his players, he was a tracksuit manager on the training ground – bridging the change in style towards a younger generation.

Managers, suddenly, became higher-profile than their players. In the late 1960s and 1970s the likes of Brian Clough, Tommy Docherty, Malcolm Allison, Ron Atkinson and Don Revie completed the transformation of the manager from back-room shadow-man into up-front performer. Indeed, some of their press conferences were more entertaining than the matches. Clough, then bossing Derby, was the archetypal darling of the new media; his outspoken views very nearly turned him from football manager into full-time television pundit. Clough learned to use the media to ruthless effect. For most of his latter years at Nottingham Forest he eschewed the standard post-match press conference, having become (understandably) bored with the predictability of the questions. But when there was a story 'on', Clough was highly adept at dropping the right hint in the right media ear.

No harm in that: media manipulation would become an occupation in its own right in the 1990s. Clough was his own 'spin doctor' long before that particular job description had been imported into British politics.

Much of the change of managers' image had to do with the end of the traditional acceptance of class barriers. A generation grew up free of the restrictive social force-feeding of armed service ranks, implying levels of superiority and inferiority. In the second half of the century young people cast aside their parents' and grandparents' assertion that authority had to be obeyed *per se* and demanded that authority and respect should be earned.

Much of the contempt into which politicians have fallen may be traced to this new awakening. And, as in politics, so in every other walk of life – including football.

In English football it was surely no accident that player/managers such as Kenny Dalglish, most notably, and Bryan Robson emerged at the highest levels. Dalglish took over a ready-made team (developed by Joe Fagan) at Liverpool and turned them into League and FA Cup double-winners. The other players respected his authority because he had proved himself out with them on the pitch – he led and inspired with the authority that stemmed from personal, exemplary achievement.

How Dalglish would have developed as a manager at Liverpool we may only surmise. The weight of the Hillsborough disaster took a mental and psychological toll that led to his retirement. His ability to inspire footballers was evident again in Blackburn's remarkable revival. By the time he went to Ewood Park he was a proven achiever not merely at playing but at managerial level.

Fabrizio Ravanelli, when he tried to explain why he had joined Middlesbrough on leaving Juventus, recounted how he knew Bryan Robson as an inspirational player and thus accepted his ambitions to turn Middlesbrough into a sort of British Parma – a provincial also-ran with European trophy-winning capabilities.

So much for inspiration. That leaves three other managerial categories: the motivators, the intellectuals and the theorists.

Clough and the late Bill Shankly rank among English football's greatest motivators. It may also be argued that a motivator/manager is more likely to succeed as a national coach than a theorist. Clough would have loved the opportunity to prove the point with England. When a national coach has his squad together for only a few days a month the pragmatic approach is to choose a simple tactical framework and instil in your players enormous self-belief. The trick is knowing which players respond best to the stick and which to the carrot. Clough had it worked out; so did Shankly; so, of course, did Jack Charlton, who took a basically ordinary Republic of Ireland team to the finals of the World Cup and European Championship for the first time in their history.

None would be described as among the great intellectuals of management. Such a mantle is more easily worn by the coaches of central and eastern Europe who have had to study wide-ranging college courses on their way to obtaining formal qualifications to coach and manage a football team. Not for a Czech or German club the lottery of appointing a manager simply because he scored (or saved) a hatful of goals. Such countries have raised football to the status of a cerebral rather than merely a physical science.

Clearly the theorist managers succeed to a far greater extent at club level, where they have daily contact with their players and are thus blessed with all the time they need to expound their ideas and drill them into the players' heads. The national manager – save, usually, for host nations approaching World Cups or European Championships – has no such luck. Don Revie, Bobby Robson and Graham Taylor were all sadly surprised by the time it took them to adjust to life as England boss after intensive years as club managers. As Robson put it: 'People take up management because it's the next best thing after playing, it keeps you close to the game. As a national team manager you lose that closeness to your players. You see them once a month. Then again, as a club manager if you lose on Saturday you tell yourself: "We'll put that right on Wednesday – or, at worst, next Saturday." But, as a national manager, you carry the weight of a defeat for a month or more. It takes some getting used to.' Revie's formula for coping was to try to turn England into a club team. His departure for the Gulf in the middle of a World Cup qualifying campaign was an all-too-obvious admission of failure.

As for the theorists, consider the case of Arrigo Sacchi. He may one day be considered, with the perspective of history, as a successful manager of Italy after taking them to the World Cup final in the United States in 1994 . . . but it's doubtful.

Sacchi had been the obvious choice, after his successes with Milan, when the Italian Federation appointed him in the autumn of 1991. But Sacchi the theorist was an increasingly controversial national coach. Critics felt that Italy finished runners-up to Brazil at USA 94 despite Sacchi rather than because of him. The theoretical castle duly collapsed around his ears two years later when he rang disastrous wholesale changes between matches at Euro 96 in the over-confident misconception that systems were more important than players. Perhaps that explains why so few coaches have proved successfully creative in the realm of tactical shapes.

Herbert Chapman, transforming the old WM into the third-back system, was one; Karl Rappan, developing the so-called Swiss Bolt, also in the 1930s, was another; Gustav Sebes, who made the withdrawn centre-forward work for Hungary in the 1950s, was a third; Rinus Michels, who unearthed Holland's 'total football' generation, was a fourth; Carlos Bilardo (much to his own surprise), who perfected the use of 3-5-2 with Argentina at the 1986 World Cup, a fifth.

Many more imitated them: Helenio Herrera perfected *catenaccio* in Italy in the early 1960s – yet *catenaccio* was only a defensive variation of Rappan's Swiss Bolt. Even Sir Alf Ramsey admitted that he killed off wingers, with England in 1966, because the wingers at his disposal (Peter Thompson, Terry Paine and John Connelly) could not deliver the performance level he demanded. In Holland it took the Romanian, Stefan Kovacs, to bring Ajax to their 'total football' perfection after Michels had left for Barcelona.

At the end of the day, as so many managers delight in saying, it's all about players, and managers are at their mercy.

Perhaps that explains everything . . .

Introduction

The Cult of the Manager: Do They *Really* Make A Difference?
By Jeff King and John Kelly

The Argentinian Jorge Valdano, in his still-embryonic career as a manager, has already won a Spanish championship with Real Madrid and coached Tenerife into Europe for the first time in their history. He is also one of the few football managers to go on record and question the myth of managerial absolutism. 'The figure of the coach is assuming far greater importance than it merits,' insists Valdano, a World Cup winner as a player in 1986. 'It's the curse of a new age. Maybe I've got to accept it, but it's not a trend I agree with. When I'm watching football on the television and the editor suddenly cuts to a shot of the coach sat on the bench, it strikes me as an absurd and irritating interruption; even if it's me!'

Many managers spend their whole careers delivering the 'I'm totally in control' sales pitch, but Valdano, now in charge at Valencia, rubbishes the notion that any man can deliver results *per se*. 'No coach can guarantee results, the best you can do is guarantee a way of playing; results are in the hands of fate. It's ridiculous to pin the label of success or failure on a coach just because a coin comes up heads or tails.'

Not surprisingly, managers who question their own contribution are few and far between. Everton's Joe Royle, a refreshingly honest presence in the English game, is another dissenting voice: 'The importance people attach to the manager has always amazed me. When teams win we get too much praise, when they lose we get too much criticism.' Despite the high-octane rhetoric that surrounds the contemporary game, there is, indeed, little debate about the real influence of the manager/coach. Three decades on from the cult of the manager's TV-assisted birth, it takes a brave soul to suggest that the all-pervading influence of football's men at the top is not all it's cracked up to be.

The Cult of the Manager

Whoever said that life is not a spectator sport had obviously never been a football manager. For the 90 minutes a week that really matter, managers are indeed little more than impotent bystanders. 'I always thought managers were more involved,' observed Kevin Keegan, shortly after taking over at Newcastle, 'but when it comes down to it, I just sit there and watch like everyone else.' Bertie Mee, manager of Arsenal's 1971 double-winners, once said, 'I am not important, only the players are important.'

Naturally, the guys on the pitch are only too happy to claim most of the credit. 'I simply haven't got time for players who say "I couldn't do this, or I couldn't do that" because they were carrying out orders from the coach, or waiting for instructions from the bench,' says Diego Maradona, a man who clearly does his thinking with his feet. 'In reality it's always the footballer who decides games. It's ridiculous hiding behind the coach, or using him as an alibi. Football matches are won, or lost, by the players.'

'As a manager you're like a prostitute; you depend on other people for your living,' says Steve Coppell. But it's not just a team of has-beens, never-has-beens and never-will-bes that the average manager has to contend with. Referees, directors, journalists, fans, the groundsmen, his dog; if you believed some managers, we're all part of a huge plot to sabotage their best-laid plans. So given the odds, why do we persist in referring to Kenny Dalglish's Newcastle ... Alex Ferguson's Manchester United ... or Glenn Hoddle's England?

Why indeed? There are plenty of books about football managers. *The Cult of the Manager* is the first to address questions that are normally ignored or buried under lavish layers of hype. Do we exaggerate the manager's influence? Are they just another cog in the machine? Is there really such a thing as a good manager? Are the best managers necessarily the winners? Are prevailing circumstances as important as a manager's ability?

The successful manager is often an enigmatic figure. How often did you hear Brian Clough say anything profound, or Bob Paisley, or Kenny Dalglish? Equally, the new breed (Bryan Robson, Glenn Hoddle) rarely stray beyond the realms of cliché. And that's just the way football's insiders would like to keep things – it's called self-preservation. As interested parties, managers can be excused their unwillingness to raise questions about their *raison d'être*.

However, players, football club directors and the media also have a vested interest in reinforcing the 'managers really do make a difference' party line.

Many footballers harbour managerial or coaching ambitions, and are hardly likely to jeopardise a possible new career route by questioning the gaffer's influence. Chairmen and directors are happy to perpetuate the myth of managerial accountability-cum-culpability in order to prevent fingers pointing their way when things go wrong. The media need managers to hook their stories on; in the age of the identikit footballer they have to get their soundbites from somewhere, after all. Off the record, journalists may criticise Alan Shearer for being bland, but as a footballer he is not obliged to deliver on quotability, nor is he judged on his lack of charisma. By contrast, the media's relentless attacks on the similarly taciturn Kenny Dalglish are an example of what happens when a manager refuses to, well, play the game. *The Cult of the Manager* is also about personality; the likes of Ron Atkinson and Terry Venables, men who have thrived on their ability to 'manipulate' the media. The more recent high-profile harassment of the latter is simply a case of 'if you live by the sword . . .'

Football managers themselves are clearly not going to ask questions about the real extent of their influence. Hugh McIlvanney once observed that managers dealt in generalisations clothed in cult jargon. It's a familiar recipe; lots of platitudes about hard work and discipline, backed up by a liberal dose of the nudge, nudge, wink, wink, 'you wouldn't understand anyway' attitude. In this age of high-tech, high-yield business and streamlined, consumer-defined capitalism, is there another British industry that finds itself 'managed' by men who, for the most part, left school long before they were old enough to form a solid opinion about anything other than footie, ale and girls, much less explain it? An alarming number of managers do not have the self-confidence, clarity of mind or eloquence to be too specific about what they really do. As for the genuinely intelligent and articulate, as a rule they prefer to throw a shroud over the tricks of their trade. And why not? When was the last time *you* told your boss that you were surplus to requirements, or simply not as influential as people made out?

The real influence of most football managers may be exaggerated, but you'd need a pretty suspicious agenda to deny the legacy of the few truly great bosses. The likes of Bill Shankly, Sir Matt Busby, Jock Stein and Brian Clough are managers who clearly made a telling difference (see John Colquhoun's 'The Scots Clan', Chapter 3, on why so many of the all-time greats are from north of the border, p. 52). These are men who imposed their character and style on their own clubs, and left some kind of legacy to the game in general. But few managers have such a lasting effect. And even the best managers still make decisions that defy logic.

Terry Venables has been slaughtered for his financial acumen, but even his detractors tend to give his tactical errors a wide berth. Your FA coaching badge starter for ten (no conferring): you are manager of England, you are in the semifinal of the European Championship, Wembley is packed to its Olympian rafters, your team is playing its second period of extra time in just five days, the opposition defence – already ravaged by injury and suspension – is knackered, several of your own attacking players are out on their feet, the opposing manager has used up all his substitutions, you have Les Ferdinand and Robbie Fowler (65 goals between them in the 1995/96 season) straining at the leash on the bench. Do you (a) play out time with your eleven starters and lose to the Germans on penalties as *everyone* does, or (b) go for the bloody jugular? And afterwards, do journalists (a) ask what the hell was going through your mind, Tel, or (b) decide not to rock the Euro 96 feel-good factor and/or not kick a man when he's down?

Everybody makes the odd howler, but do managers make that much difference even on their good days? Bobby Robson, another man to suffer at the hands of Germany from twelve yards, certainly thinks so. No other British manager has enjoyed such a lengthy and varied career. It's a long way from Ipswich to Barcelona, and after eight years as England manager and Championship triumphs in Holland and Portugal, football management holds few secrets for the man in the Camp Nou hotseat. Michael Robinson, now Spain's most prestigious TV commentator, and a man who turned down the chance to coach alongside Raddy Antic in his Championship-winning adventure at Atlético Madrid, joins Robson to talk exclusively and at length about the secrets of successful management (see 'Managing Home and Away', Chapter 11, p. 183).

Time and time again, Robinson refers back to his playing days at Liverpool and a philosophy grounded in keeping things simple. It's a lesson passed down to many an Anfield old boy.

'You didn't need to be Sherlock Holmes to work it out,' says Kenny Dalglish of the key to Liverpool's dynasty (see Dave Cottrell's 'The Secret of the Liverpool Boot Room', Chapter 2, p. 39). 'The secret of Liverpool's success was that every employee was good at his job.' But few 'employees' are so exposed to the vagaries of fortune as the football manager, much less other people's fortunes. A good manager can buy the best players his budget allows, organise them superbly and inspire individuals to perform heroics above and beyond anything they had previously considered possible, but, as Graham Taylor puts it: 'once the players have crossed that touchline, they really are on their own'.

Barked instructions lost on the wind and tactical substitutions apart, the manager can no more legislate for what is going on during the game than Joe Public sat two rows behind him. And what can any manager do about faster, stronger and more technically gifted opponents? As for Lady Luck's allies – an awkward bounce, the width of a crossbar, a gust of wind, the whims of a referee; quite simply, we're looking at an interminable list of imponderables that are beyond anybody's control, let alone a manager's. And what of injuries? A twist of his star player's ankle can change a manager's whole career. A succession of England managers might have enjoyed far more glorious careers if it hadn't been for their top talents' knack of getting crocked at the worst possible time (see John Kelly's 'In Defence of the Realm', Chapter 4, p. 64). Ron Greenwood lost his best striker, Trevor Francis, for the 1980 European finals, and had to make do without the experience of Kevin Keegan and Trevor Brooking for all but the dying minutes of the 1982 World Cup finals. Bobby Robson lost his namesake captain at both the 1986 and 1990 World Cup. 'We got to the quarterfinals and semifinals without Bryan,' says Robson, 'but I think we could have done even better if he'd been in the team.'

Graham Taylor was vilified for using Keith Curle, Trevor Steven and David Batty at right back during the 1992 European Championship. But was it his fault Lee Dixon, Rob Jones and Gary Stevens were all injured? And who's to say England wouldn't have made USA 94 if Alan Shearer hadn't missed seven of the ten qualifiers? These days, nobody would rate Graham Taylor's chances of making the pantheon of managerial greats, but what if injuries hadn't robbed him of Shearer and Gascoigne so often, and what if that bloody German referee had sent off Ronald Koeman as he was duty-bound to? That's the kind of rank bad luck no manager can legislate for. Given the mediocre fare on offer at the 1994 World Cup finals, who's to say what England might have achieved if they'd qualified? If fortune had smiled on Taylor just a little more often, he might now be idolised instead of derided. Top banana instead of turnip.

You might argue that for every lucky manager there is an unlucky one, but football is not an each-way bet. The unwavering enemy that is the law of averages guarantees there's only one annual champion, one Cup winner and a few consolation prizes. Arsenal skipper Tony Adams once observed that 'managers manage, the players play, and the board board, as it were'. He might have added, and then Lady Luck flips a coin to decide the outcome . . . as it were.

Admittedly, all sports are unpredictable to some degree. The Chicago Bulls might have failed to make the 1997 NBA play-offs. Well, they might have done; if Michael Jordan had retired again, if Scottie Pippen had mangled his leg in summer training camp, if Dennis Rodman had finally eloped with Eddie Vedder, and if the Mob had finally taken over the Windy City for real. The beauty of football, and one of the reasons it remains the most democratic of sports, is that its *ifs* are less likely to be etched in the third conditional.

In January 1992, reigning League champions Arsenal were knocked out of the FA Cup by Wrexham, the side that had finished the previous season 92nd and last in the old Football League. In many, if not most, sports, the ninth-best team has little chance of upsetting the apple-cart, let alone the 92nd. Paris Saint-Germain RFC to beat Wigan, anyone? Detroit Lions to turn over the Dallas Cowboys? The Mighty Ducks of Anaheim for the Stanley Cup? Glamorgan to win the County Championship? Any takers on Britain in the Davis Cup? The Open University for the Boat Race? Thought not. Admittedly, the Power of the Pound is doing its best to tilt football's balance of power in favour of the big guys, but it'll be a while yet before we live in a totalitarian football state. Just ask Everton, Tottenham, West Ham, Southampton, Blackburn, Chelsea and Coventry – all mugged by lower-division opposition in the 1996/97 season alone.

The David slamming Goliath phenomenon is not only a domestic one. As Euro 96 kicked off, you could have got eighty to one on the Czech Republic to reach the final. Denmark won the 1992 tournament after failing to qualify, goddammit! That's a bit like the Best Actor Oscar going to someone who failed to get beyond the casting session. Bordeaux emerged from the no-man's land of the InterToto Cup to reach the 1996 UEFA Cup final; Italian giants Parma, Lazio and Roma had all waved goodbye to this season's UEFA Cup by October. And practically every time an English club ventures abroad it's 'Surprise, surprise'. The Premiership is now regarded as one of the strongest Leagues in the world, yet Manchester United, Blackburn Rovers and Aston Villa have lost games to teams from Norway, Russia, Sweden and Turkey in the last two seasons alone. Even the most hardened Europhile would never have predicted that chain of disasters.

It's the game's very unpredictability that makes managing a football club such a precarious job; if results suddenly became predictable, most managers would surely kiss goodbye to the stress and make a fat living running pools syndicates. The really keen ones would maybe coach a bit in their spare time. 'Nobody knows anything,' claimed the celebrated screenwriter William Goldman apropos Hollywood. He could have been talking about Planet Football.

Increasingly, the only identifiable studio policy California way is to throw money at star-led vehicles and hope for the best. Sounds familiar, right? Like football managers, Hollywood producers really have no idea what makes a hit. Twentieth Century-Fox, the studio that made *Independence Day*, also made *Jingle All the Way* ... Universal made *Apollo 13* and *Waterworld* ... Paramount made *Mission Impossible* and *Congo*! In reality, overpaid actors are about as predictable as laughing-all-the-way-to-the-bank footballers. Was the (frankly hysterical) Brad Pitt of *Interview with a Vampire* really the same understated performer who stole the show from Morgan Freeman in *Seven*? Is the Andy Cole who shot blanks as Manchester United surrendered the 1995 Championship to Blackburn really the same guy who poached forty goals in one season for Newcastle? You might argue that Cole's goal glut at St James' Park was a flash in the pan, but a consistent track record offers no guarantees either. A score of prestige-seeking film directors have squeezed nothing but wearisome cameos out of Marlon Brando for a decade now. Whatever happened to the award-winning movie don of earlier vintage, they ask? Arsenal probably beg the same question of David Platt. Even when you've got the whole damn package it doesn't necessarily make for a box-office hit. What do you get when you throw Europe's top marksman (Alan Shearer), Colombia's best-ever striker (Faustino Asprilla) and a gifted supporting cast (Ferdinand, Beardsley, Gillespie, Lee, Ginola, etc.) into the same attacking equation? Derisory reviews. Overbooking in attack. Last-gasp Championship surrender. Managerial mayhem.

Clearly, there are good and bad football managers in the same way as there are good and bad butchers, bakers and candlestick-makers. However, the criteria for judging the manager are as inflexible as they are arbitrary; and not necessarily related to his intrinsic ability. Football boasts two great unpredictables: the players themselves (who really knows how they will perform from one week to the next?) and what they produce (the results). Football managers are judged solely on the latter, and are thus at the mercy of the former. 'My brother always said you'd have to be mad to be a football manager,' says Francis Lee on the perils of management. 'What other job is there where your entire livelihood depends on eleven daft lads?' If Kenny Dalglish, Scotland's most-capped player, reckons his international career suffered because of his 'inferiority complex', obviously no footballer is immune to the pressure. Man management is a key factor, but does it go beyond cod psychology? Alex Ferguson has often been described as a surrogate mother; Eleanor Levy, editor of *90 Minutes*, asks if he is guilty as charged? (see 'The Manager as Surrogate Mother', Chapter 5, p. 91).

When critics and pundits talk about good managers they are rarely analysing what he brings to the job; he may be a good judge of players, tactically astute, a good motivator, dedicated to his job and hard-working, but a manager's stature is simply about whether his team won, drew or lost at the weekend (or that same equation multiplied over the season). 'The toughest part is having to win every Saturday,' admits Bobby Gould. 'There's a leather case full of wind, and it doesn't always bounce your way.' Unfortunately for the manager who really does know what he is doing, there is nothing scientific about the relationship between the A-B-C of his input and the 1-2-X on your pools coupon. 'In football, if you win three games in a row, you're a phenomenal manager, if you lose the next two people begin to doubt you,' says José Antonio Camacho, ex-Spanish captain and currently manager of Sevilla. 'Neither posture takes into account the run of the ball – that's all that counts in the end – and the roll of the ball is unpredictable and always decides your future.' In other words, you'd better be lucky if you fancy a career in football management. Faced with appointing a new general, Napoleon would always ask the same question. 'Is he a lucky man?' Football directors could do worse than pose the same question to potential employees.

Amidst all the intangibles that make up a manager's input, his ability to buy well, above all else, stands as a matter of public record. Even then, if you are manager of a Torquay or a Darlington, a lack of resources makes life a cut-price lottery. Top managers seem to agree that being a good judge of players is fundamental. Unfortunately, they must live with one very unpalatable truth; *nobody* really knows how a player will turn out. Proof positive is the Andy Cole saga.

First the facts. Arsenal manager George Graham is faced with a choice between two teenage strikers. He decides to sell Cole to Bristol City for £500,000 after just six minutes of first-team action and perseveres with the pedestrian Kevin Campbell for more than two hundred games (the fact that Frank Clark later squanders £2.2 million on Campbell hardly constitutes mitigating circumstances). Less than a year after arriving at Ashton Gate, the can't-stop-scoring Cole joins Newcastle for £1.75 million. Fifty-five goals in seventy League games later, the same fans that questioned Kevin Keegan's decision to splash out so much on the then relatively unknown Cole are queuing up to berate him for selling their new idol to Manchester United. Cole's performances at Old Trafford soon make Keegan look like a genius for squeezing £5 million out of Alex Ferguson. So, on Cole's Newcastle form, Graham obviously made a howler; on his Man Utd form, it's open to debate. Did Keegan make a mistake selling Cole? On his Newcastle form, possibly. On his subsequent form, certainly not. Did Ferguson pay over the odds? On Cole's Old Trafford form so far, almost certainly. If he recovers his golden touch, perhaps not.

Confused? Well, OK, but there *is* a moral to the story; three of the game's most prestigious managers have played a game of to-have-and-have-not with Andy Cole, but to have *what*? Given the striker's seesaw form, that's anybody's guess.

You could write a book about top managers and their ability to misjudge a player's potential. Graeme Souness, Des Walker and David Platt, three members of the exclusive Brits-in-the-*Calcio* club, were rejected as youngsters by Tottenham and Manchester United. Well done, Bill Nicholson, Keith Burkenshaw and Ron Atkinson (they would no doubt claim the decision was not theirs, but if football management is a collective process why does the manager get all the plaudits when things go right?). Ian Wright was rejected by just about every club in London and the South-East, Paul Gascoigne returned home from a trial at Ipswich a disappointed teenager, while Peter Beardsley had to kick-start his career in Canada after it had stalled on the Old Trafford starting blocks. It's not just an English disease either. Jean-Pierre Papin had to emigrate to Belgium before returning to France and glory with Marseille. Nor is it a phenomenon confined to club level and absolute beginners. With hindsight, anyone can tell you that Gary Lineker was England's most prolific striker since Jimmy Greaves. But he was banging the goals in for Leicester for seven seasons before any of the big clubs plucked up the courage to sign him. A couple of months before his consecration at the Mexico World Cup, Lineker was still competing for an England place with Kerry Dixon and Mark Hateley!

There is not a single big-name manager who is immune to the crass misjudgement syndrome. Brian Clough smashed transfer records buying Peter Ward, Ian Wallace and John Fashanu. George Graham, a man who bought John Jensen, Eddie McGoldrick, Glenn Helder and Chris Kiwomya, once described Eric Cantona as a cry baby who would let you down when the going got tough (see Adrian Thrills on managers and mavericks, Chapter 9, p. 156). Glenn Hoddle's idea of an intimidating forward line is Paul Furlong and Mark Stein. Kenny Dalglish bought Jimmy Carter and sold Peter Beardsley; Alex Ferguson bought Danny Wallace and sold Andrei Kanchelskis. Terry Venables told the Barcelona board he wasn't interested in Hugo Sánchez and bought Steve Archibald instead (see 'El Tel and the Flying Dutchman', Chapter 8, p. 131). Jorge Valdano arrived at Real Madrid in 1994 and immediately declared, 'If I had five centre-forwards on the books, Iván Zamorano would be fifth in line.' The Chilean striker refused to budge and went on to score thirty goals as Madrid won the Championship. Alongside him, Amavisca, a young winger Valdano also tried to discard, scored fifteen goals, played his way into the Spanish national side, and was voted Spanish Footballer of the Year by top-flight managers. All of the above managers are respected names, but it's not a case of setting them up to knock them down. Quite simply, if the guys most people think are the top dogs can make such dumb errors, what does it say about the rest?

When it comes to buying players, things are about to get far, *far* more complicated. At least Hollywood casting directors still get to work with the natives. The repercussions of the Bosman case and the influx of foreigners into the Premiership present the contemporary manager with a whole new world of problems. Legendary control freaks like Don Revie, Bill Shankly and Sir Matt Busby would turn in their graves at the consequences of international free trade.

On signing Wayne Collins from Crewe for £650,000, David Pleat insisted it was important to talk to people that had worked with players in the past. 'I like footballers with solid backgrounds,' said the Sheffield Wednesday boss. 'Hungry players are what I want.' It's the kind of practice you can trace back fifty years. Herbert Chapman, legendary manager of Huddersfield and Arsenal, always asked the same questions before buying a player. 'How does he behave? What sort of life does he lead? Unless the answers are satisfactory, I do not pursue the matter further.' (See Stephen Wagg's 'Organising Victory? A Social History of the Football Manager', Chapter 1, p. 19.) Fair enough, but it's one thing grabbing the phone and picking the brains of a fellow manager, former teammate, scout, schoolteacher or tame journalist in Crewe, it's quite another doing that kind of homework on players from abroad. With that localised old-school networking about to be confined to the dustbin of history, managers will lose even more control over transfers, one of the few tangibles they really can influence.

At least it used to be a case of 'you pays your money and takes your choice'. Now it's 'you pays your money and takes somebody else's choice'. In the post-Bosman era, football managers spend vast amounts of money on players they have barely, if ever, seen perform in the flesh. Welcome to the age of the video takeaway. How many times do you think Pleat saw Benito Carbone play before investing £2 million of Sheffield Wednesday's money on the Inter Milan reserve? How many times had Bryan Robson seen the Brazilians Juninho, Branco or Emerson play except in his living room? Had Harry Redknapp ever seen Florin Raducioiu play before spending £2.4 million on a player who'd spent the last four years in Espanyol's treatment room or on Milan's bench? Three months after buying the Romanian, Redknapp was trying to get rid of him, which proves he knows a bum when he sees one; the problem is he obviously hadn't seen enough of him *before* West Ham flashed the cash. Even big-name players are unknown quantities as human beings. Everybody knows what Ravanelli and Asprilla can do on the pitch, but I doubt if Bryan Robson and Kevin Keegan boast the contacts in Turin or Bogotá to check out their personal backgrounds. The Colombian's turbulent past was hardly a closely guarded secret, so maybe Keegan fell into what Bobby Robson describes as the 'I'm different, I can change him syndrome'.

We've all heard the story about the fantastic black forward at a little English club called Watford, wanted by a wealthy Italian team. One case of mistaken identity later and AC Milan receive a package marked Luther Blissett, instead of John Barnes. Similarly, it is alleged that when Strasbourg bought Michael Hughes from Manchester City, they only got half of what they were after ... *Mark* Hughes, from Manchester *United*. These tales may be apocryphal, but it's the kind of blind-leading-the-blind story that could become increasingly common. No single club, let alone one manager, can realistically monitor every market in the world. After eight years as Johan Cruyff's number two, Carles Rexach has been appointed international football director at FC Barcelona, and the club is considering setting up nursery clubs in other countries. This could be a growing trend in the future, too. Everton have recently sponsored Dublin side Home Farm, with the Merseysiders getting the pick of the Irish side's players in return for their investment. Parmalat, the Italian dairy company, now sponsor more than a dozen clubs round the globe; who's to say they will not use their shared knowledge to move players from one club to another within their 'empire'? Clearly, the wealthy élite have a better chance than most, but even then it's a logistic and linguistic impossibility to monitor foreign markets in the same way as domestic ones.

Managers will perhaps try to alleviate the damage by accumulating players from one country: Bobby Robson has surrounded himself with Portuguese and Portuguese-speaking Brazilians at Barcelona, John Toshack's Deportivo boasts a veritable Brazilian clan, Arsène Wenger's first two signings for Arsenal were French, etc. But as Bryan Robson has discovered, buying in packs is hardly a foolproof arrangement. And a manager's relationship with his players is obviously much harder if they don't share the same language. 'The manager's job in the Premier League has become much more sophisticated and demanding,' maintains Ruud Gullit. 'It's not my case, but I know lots of other managers who go crazy trying to reach an agreement with Brazilians or Italians on technical matters as basic as the way to play offside, or how to mark people. These days you really do need to understand languages.'

Increasingly, football clubs will rely on the much-maligned agents. Indeed, it's a relationship that already exists. Manager A will telephone agent B and say, 'I've got X amount of money to spend and I desperately need a creative midfield player; there's nobody available in England, can you find me somebody abroad?' It's also a very slippery slope because it means agents, with their own very different agendas, will control (manipulate if you like) a club's options. Gone are the days of the all-seeing hands-on manager. Increasingly, the only thing managers will control is the fast forward button on their video and the redial button on their sponsored mobile phone.

Bobby Robson admits he'd never heard of the Brazilian midfielder Giovanni before Barcelona signed him, let alone seen him play. Indeed, nobody at the club had seen the £5 million signing from Santos perform live. 'I obviously didn't watch just the one video, the president threw a whole bunch at me,' insists Robson in mitigation. But who provides the videos? The agent, of course. And does he provide a selection of the good, the bad and the ugly? Ask a silly question. Lest we forget, the agent's considerations are monetary, and getting a good deal for his client (the player) and satisfying the buyer (the club) are clearly not always one and the same thing. Even in cases where an agent has been contracted by a club to headhunt a player he doesn't represent, he will only receive a fee if a deal is secured, therefore the selective highlights video thrives. In most cases, a manager will see just a couple of tapes of entire games. If the player is a forward, he'll maybe get a goals compilation as well. It all adds up to an awfully risky way to spend a huge amount of money.

Even managers who are sound judges risk losing their way when they have to cast their net further afield. Tony Adams, Steve Bould, Lee Dixon and Nigel Winterburn are currently in their ninth year together at Arsenal. Adams came through the ranks, but George Graham bought the other three for barely a million pounds. That's just a million for possibly the best English defence ever: two Championships, the FA Cup, a European Cup-Winners' Cup, two League Cups and longevity way beyond the call of duty. As a rookie manager at Millwall, Graham could have popped over to Wimbledon to check out Winterburn and would have come across Dixon and Bould in games against Stoke. That's the kind of first-hand contact you can never have with foreign players, especially up-and-coming ones. The Scot built a Championship-winning side around that back four and other unsung acquisitions such as Alan Smith and Brian Marwood, players he would never have discovered if they had played anywhere outside the British Isles. When he started to import overseas players, however, he went off the tracks in more ways than one: John Jensen, Pal Lydersen, Stefan Schwarz and Glenn Helder were failures in any language.

Alex Ferguson is the only British manager to have won more trophies than Graham over the last decade, but even with the manpower of Manchester United PLC to call on, he must be buying blind a lot of the time. If Solskjaer and Johnsen are long-term successes, Ferguson will probably get the credit, but they obviously came recommended by somebody else. And how many times had he seen Jordi Cruyff or Karel Poborsky play before Euro 96? And who can guarantee good tips every time? This is Howard Kendall, on why he didn't buy Eric Cantona when he was in charge at Everton. 'I made a number of enquiries and everyone said the same thing: "He's totally unsuitable for English football." Needless to say, I acted on that information and turned him down.' How different his second spell at Goodison might have been but for those bum leads? On such tenuous threads whole managerial careers are forged or destroyed.

The problem for the manager is not just in dealing with unknown quantities, but over-paid and pampered unknown qualities. The huge sums being paid for, and to, players these days will also do little to make the manager's life easier. How, for instance, can a manager earning £200,000 a year control his star centre-forward who earns five times that much? Are we now entering a period where, as in American sports, the players – the club's most valuable tangible assets – hold most of the cards, not the managers? The Bosman case has given far greater power to the players, and the clubs can only protect their huge investments with long-term, highly-paid contracts. Where, then, is the motivation for a player who knows he will earn a million a year for the next eight years regardless of how he is playing? How will a manager motivate such a player if that player simply refuses to listen to the advice being offered? These Bosman-inspired questions will be answered only in the future, but already the signs are ominous. Witness Stan Collymore's refusal to play for Liverpool's reserves. If Stan the Man can pull such a stunt at a club like Liverpool and still regain a first-team place . . .

With just a little help from his talent spotters, Kendall is a prime example of the manager who got it right on the night only to lose the plot in the morning. Graeme Souness, Ron Atkinson, Graham Taylor and Ossie Ardiles are others whose reputations have waned with a change of sponsored motor. Perhaps it's just a case of being in the right place at the right time, or being the right man at the right club. As Michael Robinson argues, 'time and place is everything'. Again, prevailing circumstances. Never has a manager squeezed so much out of so little as Brian Clough did at Derby and Nottingham Forest (see Ian Edward's 'The Life of Brian', Chapter 7, p. 117), but handed the best squad in England he lasted only 40 days at Leeds. In reality, the domineering Clough was always going to have a problem with a dressing room of characters like Billy Bremner, Johnny Giles and Allan Clarke. Jack Charlton, another member of that Leeds side, created his own legend as Ireland boss; yet it's difficult to imagine his style fitting in at Lancaster Gate. And can anyone imagine the Liverpool boot room in London? Nonetheless, many of the all-time greats arrived at clubs in unfavourable circumstances and dragged their charges into the right place at the right time. Don Revie transformed Leeds from a club that was on the brink of relegation to the Third

Division into one of the most redoubtable powers in postwar football; Bill Shankly joined a Liverpool side also languishing in the Second Division; Brian Clough led both Derby and Nottingham Forest from the old Second Division to the League Championship (and in Forest's case the European Cup); Celtic had won nothing for a decade when Jock Stein took over.

The above men all came from similarly humble backgrounds. The spivvish culture surrounding football management is perhaps more sophisticated nowadays – Alan Sugar wooing Jurgen Klinsmann on a yacht in Monte Carlo is about as far removed from the motorway service station ritual of football folklore as you can get – but for the foreseeable future, managers will come from the same kinds of background as their predecessors. Given the sweeping changes in context, are managers equipped to cope with the new world order? 'All good footballers never did any work, they just played football,' says Crystal Palace chairman Ron Noades. 'They became players and then you expect them to be managers and deal with multi-million-pound transfers. Invariably these guys went to a secondary modern school. On the Continent most managers have degrees before they come into the business. Rarely do you find the football side and the directors working together. There's too much suspicion between the two. You don't get much long-term planning because people have short-term agendas in order to further their own ambitions.'

Noades may exaggerate the educational backgrounds of European coaches, but the globalisation of the football manager's patch could indeed demand a more cultured generation; it also means a concentration of power that manifestly affects the influence of the new breed of manager. In a nutshell, the amount of money flowing into the modern game, and specifically into the coffers of a pseudo-cartel of dominant clubs, will make it even more difficult to talk about great managers in the future. In the past, many of the legends had to prove themselves on limited resources: Bill Shankly at Carlisle and Huddersfield, Alf Ramsey at Ipswich and Brian Clough at Hartlepool all knew what it meant to scrape a living. More recently, men like Terry Venables at Crystal Palace, Alex Ferguson at Aberdeen, George Graham at Millwall and Glenn Hoddle at Swindon (see Graham Carter's 'Managing on Limited Resources', Chapter 10, p. 171) have cut their managerial teeth well away from football's corridors of power. Increasingly, though, the trend is for wealthy clubs to go for big-name players with no managerial background whatsoever: Kevin Keegan at Newcastle, Bryan Robson at Middlesborough and John Cruyff at Ajax all avoided football's nether regions; and then there's Franz Beckenbauer and Michel Platini, legendary players who leap-frogged the club experience altogether to manage their countries. (All these men were pedigree footballers, but is it so vital to have played at the top level? For every Keegan or Hoddle there is a David Pleat or Graham Taylor, for every Beckenbauer or Platini a Carlos Parreira or Roy Hodgson (see Gavin Hamilton on 'The Rise and Fall of Arrigo Sacchi', Chapter 6, p. 104).)

The superstar players-turned-managers will never have to survive on a wing and a prayer, so whatever they achieve, there will always remain question marks against their personal contributions. Great managers or just free-spending ones? Kenny Dalglish, the man who kick-started the trend of absolute beginners inheriting top jobs, has won championships at Liverpool and Blackburn. But given his head start, can we really talk about him as a great manager? Even in his own words, 'at Liverpool, I just carried on everything that had been started by Shanks, Bob and Joe', and 'none of Blackburn's success would have been possible without Jack Walker's financial resources'. The sting in the tail as he twice abandoned (a sinking?) ship certainly does his reputation no favours.

'Money doesn't talk, it swears,' said Bob Dylan. In footballing parlance, it says, 'Fuck off, little guy.' The increasing accumulation of all the best players at a few powerful clubs suggests that smaller clubs can no longer aspire to winning Championships, *whoever* and *however* accomplished their manager. 'If your players are better than your opponents, ninety per cent of the time you will win,' says Johan Cruyff. Fair enough if you're manager of Barcelona, but a no-hope scenario if you're in charge of top-flight debutants Extremadura, a club whose annual budget for 1996/97 would barely cover the one-million-pound wages of a Barcelona reserve like Pizzi.

It's probably no consolation to the little guy, but at least football's shifting balance of power means great players have the chance to reclaim the game from the touchline upstarts (and in the process, make Jorge Valdano happy). When we recall the legendary Real Madrid side it's always Di Stéfano's or Puskas' Madrid; nobody mentions the manager. Probably because the side that won the first five European Cups was managed by four different managers. And who managed the great Brazilian side of Pelé, Tostao, Jairzinho and Rivelino? Really who cares? If anybody still harbours doubts about the reason Milan lorded over the European roost in the late 1980s/early 1990s, Arrigo Sacchi's woeful record as Italian manager surely settles the score. In football's new world order, the men who wield the power are those who sign the cheques and their expensive charges. That's Milan's Silvio Berlusconi with Van Basten, Gullit, Rijkaard, Savicevic and Weah, not Arrigo Sacchi or Fabio Capello. That's FC Barcelona's Josep Lluis Nuñez with Koeman, Laudrup, Giovanni and Ronaldo, not Johan Cruyff or Bobby Robson. That's Newcastle's Sir John Hall with Shearer, Ferdinand and Asprilla, not Kevin Keegan or Kenny Dalglish.

The Cult of the Manager can only begin to take on board the real extent of managerial power in a changing environment. In Britain, for instance, are we witnessing the beginning of the end for the old school of top-to-bottom management? Arsenal, after their traumas with George Graham, decided to opt for the 'Continental' model, where the manager looks after the team, and the businessmen look after everything else. Other clubs are watching carefully.

The battle-lines are changing in a way that makes things even more difficult for managers to control their own destinies, but here is the story so far. In a decade's time we may have to edit a companion volume to this, *The Cult of the Manager: Post-Bosman*, or make that *The Cult of the Footballing Magnate*.

1 Organising Victory?

A Social History of the Football Manager
By Stephen Wagg

Former Republic of Ireland manager Eoin Hand put it as well as anyone: 'There are only two certainties in life,' he said. 'People die and football managers get the sack.' Every season around half the members of the 'profession' of football management will be dismissed.

And when a football manager is asked to clear his desk, it is invariably for the same reason: he has failed, in the words of the legendary Herbert Chapman, manager of Huddersfield Town and Arsenal between the wars, to 'organise victory'. He has become the victim of a longing, now virtually universal in urban communities throughout the world, to see the local football team succeed. In this chapter I will look historically at the phenomenon of the football manager, to ask how we came to have them in the first place and to assess in what ways our ideas of managers have changed in the 75 years or so since the 'cult' of the manager attracted its first believers.

Old Boys

The commercialisation of football in the late twentieth century is so unrestrained that it's easy to forget the importance of amateurism in the forging of the modern game. 'Amateur' didn't just mean 'unpaid'; it was a metaphor for 'respectable' and 'upper-middle-class'. Amateurs, both as players and as administrators, dominated Association Football in its early decades. Old boys' teams, composed of young gentlemen, who had learned the game perhaps at an élite public school such as Eton or Westminster or at Cambridge University, invariably won the FA Cup in the 1860s and 1870s, and officials of the Football Association, founded in 1863, upheld a devoutly amateur ethos. Winning football matches was a vindication of this ethos – an ethos which, paradoxically, held that winning was not important.

The Cult of the Manager

Old Etonians and Royal Engineers were among the leading amateur teams of this period. Their football was characteristically carefree and individualistic: the ball would never be passed backwards (if it was passed at all) and training and tactical preparation were shunned – the players of Corinthians, a top amateur side, refused even to meet as a team before matches. Sir Frederick Wall, who went on to become secretary of the Football Association in the 1920s and early 1930s, liked to tell of how, as a player, he'd eaten a huge rump steak before going out to play in an FA Cup tie against Royal Engineers, so unconcerned had he been about the outcome of the game. Among such people, clearly, there could be no notion of a football manager.

By the early 1880s, though, on the field at least, the amateurs knew that their superiority was at an end. The working-class teams were taking over. 'For some,' says the historian Bill Murray, 'the threat of the working classes came with the Chartists and the trade unions. For others it came with the FA Cup final of 1883, the year when Blackburn Olympic won the trophy and took it north, where it would remain, with only a few exceptions, for the next four decades.' Their opponents that day were the holders, Old Etonians.

Thereafter, men of gentlemanly background and amateur persuasion, although they continued to play and to administer the game through the FA, withdrew into their own Leagues and, where possible, avoided direct dealing with the working-class professionals. Indeed, in 1906 a pressure group called the Amateur Football Defence Federation was formed, which was reconstituted the following year as the Amateur Football Association. The AFA immediately tried to affiliate to FIFA separately from the main FA – tantamount, in a sense, to claiming separate nationhood. The AFA did not join the FA until 1914; in the same year, when Liverpool were due to play Burnley in the FA Cup final, *The Times*, organ of the nation's élite, pronounced the event 'of comparatively little interest, except to the Lancashire working classes'.

The northern and midland clubs that now dominated the Association Football scene in England were, however, not governed according to unconstrained market principles. On the contrary, although the drapers, brewers and mill-owners who ran these clubs, and who, in 1888 formed the Football League, were invariably men of commerce, they regarded professionalism essentially as a necessary evil and sought to keep it in its place. Professional players were treated with disdain at many clubs right through to the 1960s; it was often as if the humbler bourgeois of the north were trying to repress the upstart working-class footballer on behalf of their social betters in the south.

Before the First World War, League football clubs were run unambiguously by their boards of directors, who took care of club administration, finance, the recruitment of players, the selection of teams, and so on. Thus, their work encompassed all the things that nowadays are taken care of by the manager. As limited companies, the clubs had secretaries, but these secretaries had no direct responsibility for the team. Team matters were dealt with by the directors, who, because they regarded players as socially inferior, frequently used the secretary as go-between in their dealings with the dressing room. Press coverage of the time, however, when it reported on team matters, generally rendered the executive role of directors in soft focus, seldom mentioning them by name: 'Adams is selected at right half . . .' or 'the directors recall Smith . . .'

However, in the years before the First World War, it appears that, while still clutching tightly to the reins of team policy, club directors were leaving more and more of the assessment and recruitment of players to their secretaries – or secretary/managers, as they were now usually called. There was also a growing likelihood that the secretary/manager might one day be called to account for the state of the club. Time and again, despite his lack of public prominence (he was seldom mentioned in the press), the secretary/manager resigned as a consequence either of his club's parlous financial situation or its poor playing record. In 1902, for example, Frank Heaven, the secretary of West Bromwich Albion, resigned; the club were heavily in debt and the board of directors departed *en bloc* in 1904. Similarly, Arsenal, who had appointed their first secretary/manager in 1897, appointed a further three in quick succession in the early 1900s; it is not a coincidence that, during this period, Arsenal failed to draw large crowds and, in 1913, moved from their Plumstead ground to Highbury. Likewise the *Manchester Evening News* began to stress the role in the success of Manchester United (who were promoted to Division One in 1906) played by their secretary/manager J. E. Mangnall.

Several factors contributed to this new visibility of the secretary/

manager. Firstly, running a football club, especially given the increasingly widespread acceptance of the need to bring in players from other clubs and localities, was now a very time-consuming business, and club directors had other businesses to run. Secondly, this was a period of great status anxiety and sharpening social division in British society. Most directors regarded professional players as their social inferiors and were reluctant to have too many direct dealings with them. The secretary/manager was therefore a useful go-between for them. This was particularly so in the years leading up to the First World War, a time of militancy among the players of the Football League. The recently reconstituted players' union affiliated to the Federation of Trade Unions in 1909 and thereafter threatened strike action against the League's employment structure: specifically, the maximum wage ceiling and the retain-and-transfer system. (The League resisted this militancy with some difficulty but, by 1914, the union had lost 80 per cent of its members.) This idea of the secretary/manager as go-between is strengthened by the evidence of Middlesbrough. When the club turned professional in 1899 Mr J. Robson was appointed team manager, at a salary of £156 per year, but on the specific understanding that the team was to be selected by the club's directors and that he would not travel to away matches. Salary negotiations were also often conducted by the secretary/manager, as at West Ham United in the early 1900s.

Thirdly, and perhaps most importantly, directors were now anxious that some public figure other than themselves should become the focus of the passionate interest that working people, in increasing numbers, now took in their local football club. The volatile nature of supporters' feelings was becoming more and more apparent. Pitch invasions, for example, had been frequent in the early years of professional football and disturbances among spectators, contrary to the conventional view that football hooliganism is a recent development, were far from rare. In the 1882/83 season, after a game between Aston Villa and West Bromwich Albion at Perry Barr, sods of turf and stones were thrown by wagonloads of rival supporters. Three years later, in 1886, when Albion beat neighbours Small Heath Alliance 4–0 in an FA Cup semifinal, the Small Heath goalkeeper was pelted with snowballs by a group of the team's followers. After Aston Villa lost to West Bromwich in the Cup Final of 1892, the Villa faithful blamed the club's goalkeeper, Jimmy Warner, and smashed all the windows of his pub in the Spring Hill district of Birmingham. In 1910, Stoke City supporters invaded the field of play during a North Staffordshire League match between Stoke Reserves and Port Vale Reserves, abducted Vale goalkeeper Roose, whom they believed to be ineligible to play, and threw him into the River Trent. Noticeably, feelings ran highest at encounters between teams who were near-neighbours and this was acutely so in the British cities of the North: Manchester, Liverpool and, particularly, Glasgow, where basic territorial feelings mingled with religious bigotry and organised discrimination against Irish immigrants to the city. But local football rivalries were also a feature of life in cities further south. There were strong local loyalties in Birmingham, as we've seen, and in Bristol in the 1890s the players of Bristol South End (later Bristol City) stood to gain four times the win bonus for beating neighbouring Bedminster as for defeating Tottenham or Southampton. (In the South spectators, ironically, could be just as vociferous in defence of amateur ideals: for instance, at Tottenham in 1897, members of the crowd attacked several of the visiting Luton team, apparently because they were trying too hard to win. Luton were the first club in the metropolitan area to employ professional footballers.)

These often-angry displays of public expectation would have been viewed with some disquiet by club directors, who, because many clubs were now limited companies, bore ultimate responsibility for team performance, but who would be anxious nonetheless to devolve public accountability onto someone else. This, then, was the crucible in which the idea of the modern football manager was formed.

Early Managers: The Men on the Platform

The interwar period was a time of definite, if uneven, developments among football managers. There were signs by the 1930s, thanks largely to the press, that the football manager was being more closely associated with performance on the field of play. In some cases too it's clear that behind the scenes there was a certain substance to this impression, in that managers actually engaged in planning. This was far from universal, though: some clubs merely flirted with the idea of a manager, others patently used him as a front man and still others did not trouble to take on a manager until after the Second World War. At Aston Villa, for example, nobody was to hold the title of 'manager' until 1958, although someone with roughly that responsibility was taken on in 1934 ('for no logical reason', to quote the club's historian, because in his judgement the club had been run successfully by the directors up to then). Everton, like Villa, spent heavily on players, but, unlike them, did not even trouble to appoint a manager figure. The chairman, Will Cuff, ran the team and responded bluntly to public criticism by saying simply that, when games were lost, the players were responsible. Other clubs, such as Preston North End, Blackpool, Newcastle United and Blackburn Rovers, took on managers from time to time during the 1920s and 1930s but were not wedded to the idea and often, when a manager left, it was decided not to replace him.

In other towns, though, the football manager was becoming an established figure, cementing changes already in train at some clubs before 1914. As suggested, the main reason for this, although not the sole one, was that boards of directors preferred a manager, rather than themselves, to be accountable to the local football public.

This wouldn't necessarily be bad for the football manager, at least in some ways. After all, most clubs, given their healthy attendances, had little excuse for not showing a respectable profit, so, provided results were not too poor, a manager could perhaps expect to hold down a job for a long time. This certainly seems to have been the case at some clubs: in the 20 years between the wars, Manchester City had only two managers, Birmingham City had three and Crystal Palace four, two of whom went of their own accord.

Elsewhere, though, the scapegoating of managers could be seen quite clearly. In Coventry, for instance, an expanding town in the 1920s and 1930s, the local club struggled to establish itself as a member of the Football League, having moved from the Southern League in 1919, and attendances were frequently poor. Coventry City had six managers during this period, including three in twelve months in the 1919/20 season. Leyton Orient were even more prolific. Orient, significantly, had had a manager since the early 1900s and were usually in financial difficulty. Between the wars the club changed its manager *ten* times; three dismissals were of the same man, Peter Proudfoot. Nor were city clubs always spared this turbulence. Manchester United experienced difficulties, both on the field and at the bank, during the 1920s and 1930s. In October 1930, three thousand disgruntled supporters met in Hulme Town Hall and passed a motion of no confidence in the board of directors; they also called for a boycott of the following day's match against Arsenal. A few months later, the team manager, Herbert Bamlett, was sacked, part of a pattern of rapid managerial turnover at Old Trafford during this period.

For the managers themselves, there was more than one way of coming to terms with their situation. Many of them – probably the great majority – saw little of their players in the normal course of events. There was usually a trainer to take charge of the team during the week, and mostly he had them running and doing perfunctory exercises. Much of the manager's time would be spent behind a desk. He would likely travel to watch a large number of football matches and he would be involved in the recruiting of players, but having once signed them he would not expect to instruct them in what to do on the field. He simply pinned up the team sheet on a Friday lunchtime and, in general, concentrated on keeping the board sweet. This latter priority is reflected in the fact that, as innumerable sepia photographs show, the managers of the time always wore suits, hats, watch chains and the like: they identified upward, never downward in the direction of the 'shop floor'.

This was so despite the fact that a growing number of League players at this time were beginning to favour tactical preparation for matches. An apocryphal story depicts the typical manager of the 1930s: a First Division team have an important FA Cup match; the players are expecting a tough game and they hope that the manager will be devising some kind of strategy for them, but they haven't seen him all week; with ten minutes to go before the kick-off, they are changed and assembled in the dressing room; the door opens and in strides the manager; 'No messing about in the bath afterwards, lads,' he tells them. 'We've got a train to catch.'

There were, though, several managers who had responded to this nascent professionalism in the dressing rooms. In effect, they seized the logic of the manager's situation: if managers were going to be associated in *the public mind* with the performances of their teams, then it would be better perhaps to strive *in practice* to influence these performances. Two men stand out in this respect: Major Frank Buckley and Herbert Chapman. Buckley and Chapman saw which way football was going. They grasped the changing ideology of the game and, in the context of League football, they wanted to see the amateur ethos buried for good.

To Buckley, who became Wolverhampton Wanderers manager in 1927, football was a serious affair. In a speech at a local hotel, he told his audience: 'Football is a business, a prestige has to be maintained. A football club in a town is an asset. It brings people to it and benefits the Corporation through patronage of tramcars and increased business for tradespeople ...' Chapman took a similar view. 'Football today', he wrote in 1934, 'is too big a job to be a director's hobby ...' Indeed, in a series of articles for the *Sunday Express*, written shortly before his death, Chapman anticipated virtually every facet of modern football management as it was to emerge in the 1960s and 1970s. 'In my opinion', he wrote, 'the club manager ought to pick the team. I would go further and say he is the only official qualified to do so.' Moreover, managers should now try to 'organise victory'. And those followers of the game who felt that football had been stripped of its personalities and who clamoured for more spontaneity were living in a bygone age: 'I have been told that there is too much system, and that those of us who are said to have conspired to bring it about have been responsible for driving out the individual touch. The truth is that the exigencies of the game have left us no alternative. We have been compelled to scheme, to produce the results which the public demand.' Moreover, a manager must no longer be content merely to recruit good players. His team should be seen as a functioning unit and no 'bad apple' should be allowed to jeopardise the overall performance of this unit: '... one of the first enquiries I make when contemplating the engagement of a man is: "How does he behave? What sort of life does he lead?" Unless the answers are satisfactory I do not pursue the matter further. It would not be fair to the staff to do so. Today there is only room for the decent fellow in the dressing room.' In the light of the innumerable scandals that have befallen the football world since the Second World War, this looks hopelessly optimistic. But what it shows is the football manager now actively grasping the reins that had previously only tentatively, and at crucial moments, been dropped in his lap.

Some managers now began to work more closely with the players, and players at most clubs expected as much. Feelings against directors often ran high. For many players, directors enjoyed power without responsibility. Frequently they bought and sold players and picked teams and had the manager, if there was one, in their pocket. Almost none of them had ever 'played' (i.e. been professionals), so they didn't know from experience what it was like directly to bear the expectations of the local football public. There was much resentment of the open difference in status: directors were served first in hotels, treated players with curtness and condescension and called them by their last names. Stories about directors' ignorance of the modern game were legion in the dressing rooms. Players now increasingly wanted an independent managerial figure, whom they could trust and who knew what he was talking about in football matters. They began to complain if nobody at the club appeared to fit this description: in February 1931, for example, the players of Blackburn Rovers signed a round robin expressing dissatisfaction with Bob Crompton, a former England international but now on the board of the club and managing the team in an honorary capacity. There were similar developments at Tottenham and Everton, and at Arsenal, following the death of Chapman, there was open dismay among the players at the appointment of George Allison as his successor. Allison, on his own admission, was a journalist and publicity specialist and he hadn't played football professionally.

Chapman, like Buckley and a number of other managers – Bob Hewison of Bristol City, Harry Curtis at Brentford, Tom McIntosh of Tranmere Rovers and Jimmy Seed at Charlton Athletic – gave players a greater sense of involvement and of their own professionalism. While manager of Leeds City before the First World War, Chapman had pioneered the use of team talks, usually held in a hotel before matches. He regularly denounced uninformed criticism and, in the early 1930s, he succeeded in making the Arsenal dressing room out of bounds to all bar players and team officials half an hour before kick-off.

If the manager was to get the best out of his players, wrote Chapman, 'he must share their troubles, help them out of difficulties, and within the limits of discipline, be their pal'. But, for Chapman as for most managers of this era, the limits imposed by discipline were severe. Chapman was a man of austere authority and others, notably Buckley (who also managed Norwich City and Blackpool before going to Wolverhampton) and Harry Storer, who was at Coventry City in the 1930s, never sought to be a 'pal' to their players. For Buckley and Storer, and others like them, the dressing room was essentially a barracks wherein a constant vigil must be kept for skivers and sissies. Although they were both well versed in football tactics, they were nevertheless primarily not coaches but sergeant-majors. Their stock-in-trade was harsh, unsentimental masculinity. Tales of the toughness of each man abound. Storer (who incidentally was the manager whom both Brian Clough and Peter Taylor cited as their inspiration) often berated his team if they lost. On one such occasion, he singled out a particular player for criticism. 'But, boss,' pleaded the man, 'I wasn't playing.' 'Well,' replied Storer, 'if you can't get in this team, you *must* be useless.' He was also fond of countering the familiar question 'Boss, why am I in the second team?' with the withering 'Because we've got no fucking third team'.

Buckley, while managing Blackpool in the early 1920s, was often out coaching the players himself: he was therefore almost certainly the first 'tracksuit manager'. Nevertheless he was not above milking public anger at his players' expense. Once, after an FA Cup defeat by Mansfield Town, he made the Wolves players parade through the town in their playing kit, receiving abuse from the locals. He followed this up with a training session. The hardness of these men's vocabulary was often matched by the performance of the teams that they sent out onto the field. Both of them frequently lacked funds and might ask their players to compensate physically for a lack of the more intricate skills. Buckley was said to wind his players up with the notion that 'It's easier to beat nine or ten than eleven . . .'

A growing public awareness of football managers and their role in club matters is perceptible at this time, due in large part to the expanding sports press. The popular press showed an increasingly keen interest in the football world after 1919: like crime, sex and horse-racing, the game was soon recognised by editors as one of the surest ways to boost circulation. A concern to have football stories in turn meant a move towards reportage of off-the-field affairs. After all, most papers were printed six days a week, but matches could usually account only for two days: Saturday morning for prospects and Monday morning for reports. Any further news would have to be provided by, or focus upon, a particular figure. Directors and administrators were inappropriate: they were either too high-handed or out of touch or resentful of press intrusion. Players were forbidden in their contracts to speak to the press. Managers were the obvious source of stories.

This suited the managers. They were, for one thing, increasingly publicity-conscious and, for those who actually now enjoyed autonomy in the handling of team matters, there was a satisfaction in placing their own activities on view. And, for the clubs where managers were still powerless clerks, some chastisement on the sports pages for the directors would not be without its populist appeal: why didn't the stubborn meddlers of the boardroom take a back seat and make way for a professional manager?

The *Daily Express* is a good case in point here. In 1925, a football correspondent wrote of the ill-feeling at the Den about Millwall's current performances and raised a polite eyebrow at the directors' stance on this: they replied, he noted, 'that they are quite capable of looking after the team themselves and seem to resent the action of supporters of tendering constructive criticism'. At the same time press coverage increasingly married a team's performance to that of its manager: 'SECRET OF ARSENAL'S SUCCESS,' trumpeted another *Express* headline; 'Miracle worked by Mr Herbert Chapman at Highbury.'

This, naturally, did no harm either to managers' salaries or to their reputation, and pressmen stood to benefit too. They got their stories and were often now chosen by club directors as intermediaries in their dealings with prospective managers.

This mutually beneficial relationship between football managers and the press developed steadily during the 1930s. By this time most football stories were being organised around the manager and the language used to describe his movements was more flamboyant: he was 'swooping' to sign X or Y, 'springing into transfer action', and so on. The managers now began to acquire a special mystique. They became canny wheeler-dealers hanging furtively around railway platforms or hotel lobbies, waiting to conclude secret business. They were implied to be in a permanent battle of wits, trying to sell each other players with undisclosed injuries or vices, conning the parents of gifted young footballers into parting with their sons' signatures, and so on. In the football folklore of the 1930s the manager always had a trick or two up his sleeve. He was no longer so much sacrificial clerk as tactician-horsetrader.

Muddy Boots v. Chalky Fingers

In the postwar period, one by one, British football managers (some of them still called secretary/managers) said goodbye to their trilby hats and watch chains and arranged to be measured up for a couple of tracksuits. This, of course, reflected the changed power relations of the football world. Among these changed relations, three factors were very important: the promotion of coaching by the Football Association; the abolition of the Football League's wage ceiling in 1961; and the growth, from the mid-1960s, in the access of television to the game of football.

Coaching, as we know, was, historically, all bound up with professionalism and with the hated working-class footballers who had proved too good for the carefree, unconniving amateur. From the early 1900s, British ex-footballers had worked abroad as coaches, notably in Hungary, Austria and Scandinavia. At home, though, there was little support for coaching *as an activity*, at least until the mid-1930s and the appointment of Stanley Rous as secretary of the FA.

Rous took over in 1934 from Sir Frederick Wall, and found himself running an organisation quite stultified in its ignorance of political trends in sport. By the 1930s, the political importance and commercial possibilities of modern sport had become clear: public enthusiasm for international competitions such as the Olympics and the World Cup was growing and big crowds flocked to see boxers, cricketers and jockeys compete. The FA had maintained a snobbish distance from all this: it had refused to join FIFA at its inception in 1904, declined an invitation to take part in the first World Cup finals (in Uruguay in 1930) and, when Rous took over, huge numbers of grammar schools were switching from association to rugby football, citing the greater respectability of the latter code.

Rous now immediately initiated coaching courses at the FA, reasoning that formal qualifications would help raise the status of football as a profession, while popularising the game among schoolchildren and providing professional footballers, still very poorly paid at this time, with the chance of extra income. He was also taking the long view. While administrators and popular press alike had clung to the notion that, as the country that had given the game to the world, England had little to learn, Rous was aware of the rapid progress being made in other parts of the world. Significantly, in 1946, he secured the appointment of the FA's first director of coaching; the man appointed, Walter Winterbottom, would also coach the England team.

It was a long time before either the FA or the commentators of the popular press would accept the idea of coaching in relation to the England team. In a bizarre incident in 1933, the FA had seemed to acknowledge the growing importance of football management when they had invited Herbert Chapman to accompany the England team as unofficial team manager at a match in Italy. However, when Chapman had delivered a pep talk to the England players at half-time, he had been reported to the FA selection committee for interference! Similarly, when Winterbottom took over, the England team was selected by FA officials and it was not until the later years of his tenure that Winterbottom picked the side; and even then, the FA selection committee had to rubber-stamp his choices.

The popular newspapers were hostile to coaching at the time. They'd been opposed to the idea of an England team manager and their response to Winterbottom, during the early years of his management, was either to ignore him or to mock him. For example, coverage of the World Cup finals of 1950, held in Brazil, contains little reference to Winterbottom; and when the England team were beaten by the United States in Belo Horizonte reporters generally blamed the players. During the early 1950s pressmen were fond of depicting Winterbottom as an unworldly professor, chalking on a blackboard while the self-tutored exponents of the people's game laughed at him behind their hands.

This, for a time, was a promising populist line to take: readers of the popular press generally don't like 'experts' (or 'boffins', as they are invariably known in the popular prints); English football was still seen as the best and the leading England players – the Billy Wrights, the Jackie Milburns – were still assumed to have learned all they needed to know about the game on the cobbled streets of northern cities; and, perhaps most importantly, the response to FA coaching initiatives among the football reporters' chief informants, the League club managers, was hostile.

The Cult of the Manager

This hostility had partly to do with threats to the club manager's authority from players who had spent the summer on an FA coaching course and had come back thinking that they knew more than he did. But it had rather more to do with the growing fear within the professional football world that coaches who had never played football professionally, but who had gained full badge qualifications from the FA, might now become competitors for the increasingly lucrative management and coaching jobs at the League clubs. This explains why, after the watershed defeat of England by Hungary at Wembley in 1953, hostility to coaching as an activity diminished sharply, but hostility towards people who'd never played professionally and had only 'paper qualifications' was greater than ever.

This resentment of 'outsiders' within the professional football world grew steadily during the 1950s and went hand in hand with an increasing militancy among professional players. Footballers had been earning big money in countries such as Italy since the 1920s. By the time the Professional Footballers Association, led by Jimmy Hill, mounted its final campaign to free the 'Soccer Slaves' in 1960, there was considerable political support for them, not least from the Conservative Party.

When the maximum wage restriction was removed in 1961, the financial life of the League clubs changed irrevocably. Quite quickly most clubs moved from having large squads of players on a few pounds a week each to the employment of smaller staffs of considerably higher earners. These smaller staffs plainly needed more comprehensive 'management' in the modern sense. As well-paid professionals, they increasingly demanded the close attention of someone who 'had played' and who 'knew the game'. Boards of directors, likewise, clearly now wished to see greater general care and tactical preparation accorded to what were now the clubs' greatest assets. The new culture of commercially liberated professionalism in the football world could no longer support the absent manager in his suit and tie. The manager's place was now on the training field.

For some, this adjustment was difficult. Mike Doyle, who joined Manchester City in the early 1960s, recalls how the club manager, George Poyser, turned up at training one day wearing a tracksuit. Poyser, a pipe-smoker of middle age, had drawn gales of laughter from the players. Similarly, it was said of Harry Catterick, who managed Everton in the 1960s, that his tracksuit was only for TV appearances. But many of the younger managers were qualified coaches and disciples of Winterbottom. And the growing pace of managerial turnover in the League was bringing more and more new men into management jobs. The proliferation of tracksuited managers, therefore, helped to strengthen the modern perception of the football manager, begun with Chapman and Buckley, as a kind of Svengali. Now if a team won, it was because of some managerial master plan; if they lost, it was because they'd been badly coached or given the wrong tactics.

This perception was further enhanced by the intervention of television, in two ways. Firstly, television began to show more of the professional game. Television pictures of the World Cup had been increasingly available since the tournament of 1954 in Switzerland, and England matches were usually televised. There was the beginning of BBC's Saturday evening highlights programme, *Match of the Day*, in 1964, and an attendant growth in reportage of football matters: managers were interviewed during the week for the match previews in *Grandstand* on a Saturday lunchtime, and so on. Football people also began to appear in other TV shows – quizzes, magazine programmes and the like. Secondly, the greater involvement of TV further usurped the role of press reporters and made it even more imperative for them to generate their own news. These media trends combined to turn the football manager into a celebrity and, with the possible exception of Chapman, the gallery of 'great' or 'famous' managers is inaugurated here in the 1960s. Most people of a certain age in Britain, whether they interest themselves in football or not, have heard of Matt Busby, Bill Shankly, Don Revie, maybe Bill Nicholson – the major English club managers of the 1960s. But scarcely any of them, outside of the respective communities, could name the men who managed Manchester United before Busby, Liverpool before Shankly, Leeds United before Revie or Tottenham Hotspur before Nicholson. Tottenham's previous managers had included Arthur Rowe, a tactician well known in football for his successful 'Push and Run' team of the early 1950s; but Rowe was never a national figure, simply because he managed before the age of publicity.

The 1960s brought a whole new range of problems and possibilities to the work of the British football manager. Firstly, there was Europe. The parochialism of the Football League had discouraged participation in the European Cup when it was begun in the mid-1950s. However, in the 1960s, with the British Government leaning toward membership of the 'Common Market' and British clubs having bigger wage bills to pay, 'getting into Europe', with the money it brought from television, advertising and the trophies themselves, became a universal aspiration among leading British club managers.

Secondly, since the linking of managerial responsibility with team performance was now unequivocal, managers took greater care to avoid failure. This, in practice, meant, at some clubs at any rate, an increased emphasis on efficiency. Bill Shankly's teams at Liverpool and Don Revie's at Leeds, for example, became known for the rationalised nature of their play: they conceded few goals and rarely scored more than they had to; they worked hard to keep possession of the ball and, when they lost it, they worked hard to get it back. These, of course, are the commonplaces of football coaching in the 1990s, but in the 1960s they represented, to many, an ugly new departure: Jimmy Greaves, one of the finest players of the decade, once said that, although he didn't mind being tackled, he wouldn't want to tackle anyone himself. The new style of play was widely derided and its exponents frequently took refuge behind the word 'professional'. Nobody was more embattled in this respect than Revie, whose club sides were often accused of ruthlessness. (Revie became manager of England in 1974 and, early in his tenure, he was accused of picking a team containing too many 'physical' players. 'It's not a bad side,' he told reporters, 'I could have picked a real bastard of a team.')

Thirdly, because players were now such expensive assets, the balance of power was altered at the clubs, and managers became conspicuously closer to their playing staffs than to their board of directors. This often involved them in extravagant public tributes to their players and a benevolent concern for them as people. Busby, Shankly, Revie and Jock Stein at Celtic, each in his separate way, played the role of *paterfamilias*, throwing Christmas parties for wives and children, organising sing-songs and bingo sessions and providing advice to players on sensible handling of the large sums of money they were now being paid. They worked hard, if sometimes vainly, to keep their younger players out of the new nightclubs and discotheques opening up in many British cities, and away from the glamorous and hedonistic lifestyles to which they might be tempted. Wealth, for this generation of football managers, carried responsibilities, both public and private: players should marry and provide for their families; they should stay out of night spots and off the back pages; on match days they should arrive for work attired in club ties, blazers and pressed grey flannel trousers. Norman Hunter, a Leeds United player in the 1960s and 1970s, was once forbidden by Revie to wear jeans, and has never worn a pair since.

Finally, there were the demands of publicity itself. The managers of the 1960s, some of them with visible reluctance, became used to having microphones shoved under their chins and to having things that they may or may not have said crop up in the sports press. Whether they liked it or not, they were now walking news items.

Faust or Fall Guy? Managers in the Post-modern age

Looking back now on a further 35 years of English football history, two things seem important about the 'cult' of the football manager during that period. One is that the professional, psychological and emotional life of the football manager was very complex and therefore often difficult for the individuals concerned to negotiate. The other is that the circumstances that helped to produce this cult in the first place have never gone away; indeed, they seem in the 1980s and 1990s to have re-emerged.

Football managers today are people of whom big things are expected. The fact that these aims are probably not achieveable is the one thing they cannot admit – perhaps even to themselves. We see this both at club and at national level. Supporters expect great things of their club and of their country. These expectations are the seedbed of most media discussion of football: if a team is near the foot of the League, then, while a regiment of journalists and hosts of radio phone-ins talk about the 'pressure' building upon him, the manager must still meet the media and account for 'his' failure.

In a sense nobody better represents the growing pains of this new 'post-modern' football culture, and the manager's place within it, than Sir Alf Ramsey. Ramsey achieved the two great prizes of football management: his country's national club championship and victory in the World Cup. Because neither Ipswich Town, whom he managed to the League Championship in 1962, nor England, who won the World Cup under his management in 1966, were expected to succeed, Ramsey became the embodiment of all the myths of football management: he stood as the miracle worker, who proved it could be done. But part of Ramsey's public persona belonged to a bygone age. He was pompous and tetchy with virtually anyone who was not a professional footballer and spoke uncomfortably in the manner of a former working-class person now trying to talk like a toff. This made him completely inappropriate for the media age. He hated giving press conferences, but, for the contemporary football manager, life is, in a sense, a press conference. He also found commercialisation distasteful and was bitterly upset when, in 1973, several of his players, against his wishes, agreed to wear Adidas boots in a televised match with Germany in Hanover.

Under Ramsey, England, as well as winning the World Cup in 1966, reached the quarterfinals in 1970. He received a knighthood, but when England didn't qualify for the 1974 finals he was dismissed, dismissal being, arguably, the price of his failure to deliver England's participation to a huge market of advertisers.

The post-modern managers – those, that is, who manage within a forest of microphones, television cameras, flashbulbs and PR executives – know the demands of the job. Sometimes these demands have amounted almost to a Faustian bargain, in which they are given a new identity – as saviour, master strategist, or whatever – only to have it stripped away when things go wrong. In 1978, for instance, when England again failed to qualify for the World Cup, this time being held in Argentina, media attention in Britain switched to Scotland, who had qualified, and to their manager, Ally MacLeod. The Scotland squad endorsed a range of products while MacLeod was promoted as a winner and as the leader of 'Ally's Tartan Army'. When Scotland faltered at the first hurdle, MacLeod immediately became a joke figure, universally condemned as a bungler, and in his subsequent dealings with the media he became visibly confused. Similarly, in the 1980s, England manager Bobby Robson became vilified as a 'plonker' by the English popular press and his successor, Graham Taylor, fared no better, becoming the 'turnip' who suffered defeat at the hands of the Swedes in the 1992 European Championship.

Leading managers in this era therefore have not only to 'organise victory' but to 'manage' an ongoing news story that bears their name. The football supporter of the late twentieth century may expect nothing less. I remember talking to a Leeds United fan the day Howard Wilkinson resigned as Leeds manager in late summer 1996. The fan was pleased, because now he could start going to Elland Road again. 'He's an arsehole,' he said angrily of Wilkinson. 'He's got *terrible* PR.'

Again, the one thing that, historically, a football manager seldom has been permitted to say is that none of this – the string of defeats, the falling attendances, the fractiousness in the dressing room – was his fault. The buck invariably has stopped with him, as the club directors of generations ago intended that it should. But, strangely, in the 1990s the widespread acceptance of managerial responsibility has begun to waver. This wavering has been brought about, indirectly, by the founding of the Premiership (initially the Premier League) in England in 1992 and, more particularly, by the massive infusion of money into Blackburn Rovers by their patron Jack Walker in the early 1990s.

During the 1970s and 1980s Blackburn had been a modest club, more out of the top division than in it. Promoted in 1992, Blackburn were able to win the Premiership only two years later following donations by Walker estimated at between £60 and £100 million. This suggested two things to club supporters around the country. One was that all the tactical guile of the canniest manager in the world might not be sufficient to win the highest prizes in domestic football; the manager needed money. The second thing was that the likeliest source of this money was a private benefactor, a lifelong supporter perhaps, or someone who might be persuaded that investing in the local football club was part of the civic duty of capital.

Around the country, the hunt has been on for such a saviour and impatient calls have been made at many grounds for the present incumbents, now perceived as having access to too little wealth, to step aside. Sometimes a fairy godfather has indeed emerged. At Chelsea the late Matthew Harding, a financier with a nine-digit fortune, became a folk hero for endowing his beloved club. Middlesbrough chairman Steve Gibson is another example.

At Manchester City in 1994 hopes soared with the arrival as chairman of Francis Lee, a former player and now millionaire businessman; by 1996, four managers later and the club an estimated £26 million in debt, there were calls for Lee to depart as well. At Norwich in 1995 angry public protests brought the resignation of Norwich City chairman Robert Chase after he forced the sale of several players in order to pay for a new stand. At Leicester in 1996, after the second manager within twelve months had left to join a financially more powerful club, a group of supporters began smashing windows at the ground and chanting for the board to 'spend some fucking money'. In the autumn of the same year a running battle was being fought by fans of Brighton and Hove Albion against the club's board of directors; matches had been stopped by pitch invasions and calls made for future games to be boycotted.

Everywhere the talk is of business consortiums and football-mad philanthropists waiting in the wings and, of course, there will always be 'money for new players'. But one thing is unlikely to change: whoever takes over your local club will appoint a manager, of whom both the club and the supporters ultimately will expect, well, miracles.

2 The Secret of the Liverpool Boot Room

Myth or role model?
By Dave Cottrell

Now we are 25 or 30 years old. By birthright, we were party to the myth. We read the papers and the programmes and the souvenir editions, and we stared in raptness at pictures of Brylcreemed pensioners who belonged to some other black-and-white time; avuncular types with so many wrinkles on their foreheads it looked like their woolly hats were screwed on. While others their age plodded along the cardiovascular highway in full geriatric regalia, here were men in shrink-wrapped Gola tracksuits and mud-clogged football boots, hands on hips, active, alert and smiling. They called them the Boys from the Backroom, or the Boot Room.

We were the newest recruits to Paisley's Red Army, all innocence and reverence, and because they were justified and ancient, we believed them. Simplicity, honour and humility, a little psychology and a meticulous attention to detail. If there was a secret to Liverpool's wonderful success, that was it. Then we grew up and, like people from other places, we wanted more. Because, when they asked us, we were meant to know. And those old, self-effacing explanations from Anfield's patriarchs, the elders of this great functional family who forever hid their light under a bushel, seemed a little smug. We felt let down. We wondered how, week in, week out, journalists could churn out all that sentimental guff. We remembered what Bill Shankly had written in his autobiography: 'Paddy Crerand was once quoted in a newspaper as saying that when Jock Stein, Matt Busby and myself spoke about football, a six-year-old boy could understand us. We never tried to complicate people . . . the simple things are the ones that count.' Twenty years on, we listened when Sammy Lee said, 'You can't live in the past, but we're thinking of the principles that did us ever so proud back then. Those principles are simplicity and enjoyment. Football is a simple game. Why complicate it?' And we thought, 'is that it?'

We still believe in the Boot Room myth because myths are true if we believe in them. In sport, as in life, we alter the landscape to suit our needs, and we act upon it. But when the myth fails, as it did when Graeme Souness was manager of Liverpool, we look back, ask questions and, for better or worse, deconstruct what we had created. Liverpool's tradition and continuity appear to come at a price. Shankly, all Cagney and charisma, died a sad and lonely man. Bob Paisley and Joe Fagan had an almost phobic aversion to the public eye. Kenny Dalglish wrestled with his sanity. Graeme Souness underwent triple heart surgery. The jury is still out on Roy Evans, who enthusiastically admits that he lives to work for the club in an era when a spate of his contemporaries have cowered amid the stress-related maelstrom of management. The success speaks for itself, but what kind of role model is that?

One day, perhaps, Channel 4 will commission a *Secret Lives* special on Bill Shankly. Aghast, we will learn how the so-called Liverpool legend almost walked out of Anfield after his first season in charge; how his wife sensed that he regretted leaving Huddersfield Town; how he was never happy unless he was threatening to resign; how his first foray into the transfer market ended in farce, with Motherwell winger Sammy Reid arriving for a colossal (in Liverpool terms) £8,000 and returning to Scotland a year later without making a single first-team appearance; how in the early days the gates fell drastically and fans questioned his appointment; how Liverpool failed to win a single trophy under him between 1966 and 1973; how Paisley, who never mixed socially with the manager, secretly resented him for stealing all his best lines; how after his resignation Shankly continued to train at Melwood, where the players continued to call him 'Boss', until the club were forced to ban him from turning up. There will be revelations, recently observed in biographies, about xenophobia, parochialism and eccentricity. This is the man who, on a club tour of the USA in the summer of 1964, stubbornly stayed with GMT, going so far as to hand out team sheets at three in the morning; the man who, on a trip to Italy, insisted that all those vans bearing the VW logo belonged to Woolworths; the man who was painfully class-conscious and terrified of speaking at golf club dinners.

Fast-forward to present-day Anfield and, reading between the lines, we will find similar traits in Roy Evans, a man so acutely shy he hates watching himself on TV. Too phlegmatic to be eccentric – he says his main strength is 'common sense' – he is nonetheless distrustful of foreigners, at least in a footballing sense, and suspicious of change, despite half-hearted remonstrations to the contrary. 'If Shanks had been in the game at this stage,' he says, 'he'd have been a fantastic manager because he would've moved with the times.' Channel 4 would be inclined to disagree.

This is Shankly, the man behind the myth, and he is not alone. In his memoirs, Paisley, a north-eastern bricklayer in his youth, was loath to dwell upon his own personality. 'I knew there was no way that I could establish the rapport with the fans that Shanks had done . . . so I simply said, "I'll let the team do the talking for me."' This is the most successful English club manager of all time, unable to communicate to a wider audience yet covered in greatness. The club have always liked it that way, which is why the wilfully high-profile Graeme Souness was such a shock to the system. It takes a peculiar kind of person to manage Liverpool, or for that matter to graduate into their tight-knit coaching community. Others, often ex-players of the club, have tried and failed to emulate it elsewhere. Like us, they were romanced by the myth. But it is unique to Anfield because, as in a family business, it is bound up with tradition and succession. And, as in a family business, it is struggling to adapt.

In 1978 John Toshack left Liverpool for Third Division Swansea City. He lured several former Liverpool players, among them Tommy Smith, Ray Kennedy and Phil Boersma, to the Vetch Field, plus a healthy smattering of ex-Evertonians. His intentions were obvious, superficial and short-term. In October 1981, after ten league games in the old First Division, Swansea were top. Two years later, they had been relegated to the Second Division. With debts of more than £1.5 million, they put their entire side up for sale. By December 1985, Toshack had resigned and the club were in the Third Division. Owing over £100,000 in taxes, they were eventually wound up and relegated once more. Toshack had failed to create a managerial model along Liverpool lines. He had tried to copy Shankly, rather than Paisley.

There has yet to be a successful ex-Liverpool player at the top end of management . . . with the notable, money-fuelled exceptions of Souness at Rangers, Dalglish at Blackburn Rovers, and Kevin Keegan at Newcastle. Perhaps having learned from the mistakes of his old pal Toshack, the latter, an unashamed Shankly fan, began recruiting a back-room staff on Tyneside in the Liverpool mould, specifically Terry McDermott and Mark Lawrenson. Keegan: part dreamer, part realist. Aware that the Anfield original was twenty years in the making, he realised that he could use Newcastle's millions to institute the next best thing to the Boot Room – a Sporting Club, financing its own production line of players and coaches. Shankly, the irresistible but essential extrovert whose arrival was the chance Big Bang of Liverpool's universe, was anything but a Boot Room man. 'Occasionally he'd show his face,' recalls Evans, 'but it was Bob and Joe Fagan and Ronnie Moran, they started that side of it, it was their domain. We were there every day. Going back ten years ago, we used to come in on Sundays regularly, from ten to twelve.'

It was, of course, 'nothing fancy ... just a little room that we had to hang our coats and chat about football over a cup of tea or sometimes a beer.' It was also, of course, strictly private, although opposition managers were always welcome for a post-match drink in the true spirit of Liverpool kidology. Even the players were prohibited. Any caught loitering outside suffered the wrath of Moran.

It was opium for the Kop's masses. While we, the disciples, could only wonder what secrets this most sacred of sites underneath the Main Stand might contain, the select few who gained access described a shabby room 12 feet by 12 feet reeking of dubbin and liniment; its floor space occupied by tatty kit hampers which doubled up as seats, its walls plastered with faded photographs and tit calendars; its cupboards stacked with notepads, Rothmans Yearbooks and drinks. Like its patrons, it was deliberately unremarkable. Ill-fitting tracksuits, muddy boots, mundane meeting places. Its demolition in 1993, acknowledged by those who were left to pick up the pieces as an act of arch-vandalism by Graeme Souness, was simply legend fodder.

In 1974, Paisley, the inner sanctum's Jesuit priest, saw something of himself in Roy Evans, and persuaded the 26-year-old left back to forsake playing for a career in coaching. 'I didn't have to retire through injury, that's a fallacy everyone writes about,' says Evans, who at the time was publicly earmarked as a future

Liverpool manager by the club president, John Smith. 'There was no injury. I could have played on. I was just offered the job. When Shanks retired, Bob said, "take the reserve-team job on." I said no for weeks and weeks. Bob, Ronnie Moran and Joe Fagan were all trying to persuade me. In the end I took it. I'd always been a good trainer and I'd always been enthusiastic about the game.'

Inevitably, he was also humble and unassuming, qualities that were not lost on Paisley and remain with Evans to this day. Mr Average, the man with the nondescript name. 'The club you manage is high-profile, and that makes me reasonably high-profile because I'm going to be in the public eye on a regular basis. But, as far as my own personality being bigger than the club, I don't see the point in that. I'm here as their spokesman, really. It's only part of the job, but if you've got one voice then there's no mix-ups, and we try to keep it that way.'

As a player at Anfield in the late 1960s and early 1970s, Evans became a close friend of Chris Lawler, another full-back and an ever-present in the first team for six years. Lawler had originally joined the club as a member of the ground staff in 1959. Like Evans, he was Liverpool-born and had come through the ranks. And like Evans, he was a thinker, and eager to learn. Dubbed 'The Silent Knight' by the Kop and 'the quiet man of Anfield' by Paisley, he let his football do the talking. He was dependable, dour, even. He had potential. 'You wouldn't know whether Chris was excited or not,' recalls Evans. 'He had a great passion for Liverpool, but it was on the inside. You don't judge players from the outside alone.'

After 406 League games, injury forced Lawler to leave Liverpool for Portsmouth and Stockport. Then Liverpool brought him home. He replaced Evans as reserve-team trainer in 1983, a classic year of Boot Room progression. Joe Fagan, formerly reserve-team trainer then first-team trainer, and a fixture at Anfield for 25 years, had been appointed manager. Evans succeeded him as first-team trainer. Ronnie Moran remained the chief coach, a position he had held since 1974 and retains to this day. He is the resident caretaker manager, and Liverpool's great miseries have been his miseries. Like Shankly, he is a motivator, but his psychology is ogrish rather than articulate. Generations of players have grown to hate rather than respect his ability to wring every last ounce of effort from them. Possessed of a face that blocked too many free kicks in its playing days, he is, to coin a phrase, a source of little visible delight, but necessary; the pot-walloper who obliterates the swank and vanity of the first team, the 'Big Heads'.

When Fagan took over in 1983, Evans was effectively first in line to the throne. Lawler, just behind him, was sacked by Kenny Dalglish when the latter leap-frogged out of the first team, over Evans, and into the manager's seat two years later. Dalglish also dismissed Geoff Twentyman, the club's chief scout for nineteen years. An unprecedented and inimitable system of progression had been fatally sabotaged. Herein lies the root of Liverpool's more recent problems. Though schooled in Anfield folklore, Dalglish was very different from the club's former managers and its back-room staff. Paisley, Fagan, Evans and Lawler, never fully in the spotlight as players, were peas from the same pod. Dalglish had been integrated into the pass-and-move tradition, but he remained a star in his own right, doubtlessly because his name stayed on the team sheet, and his celestial status followed him into management. The impact of Hillsborough upon his decision to stand down cannot be underestimated (significantly, he was originally appointed in the wake of Heysel), nor can his managerial record of three Championships and a League and FA Cup double. But with his appointment came the first signs of disruption behind the scenes. When he resigned, Evans was overlooked once more, and things lurched from bad to worse. New incumbent Graeme Souness, whose personality cast a shadow arguably greater than that of his predecessor, soon sacked Phil Thompson, another former defender who had replaced Lawler as first-team trainer.

Consistently, remorselessly, we were taught that Liverpool promoted from within because they knew what they were getting – those familiar, inbred values of honesty, pride, industry and unquestioning loyalty, all of which were reciprocated. When summoned to follow Shankly's act, Paisley was comforted by the fact that 'the overall pattern would remain the same'. Similar rhetoric appeared in Dalglish's first autobiography: 'The back-room staff look on Liverpool as their family . . . they all have their jobs and they do them the way the players are asked to do theirs – with 100 per cent effort for the club.' The dedication and selflessness of a coaching team that constantly undervalued its own contribution in public could not fail to be noticed and imitated by the players. Before Dalglish, no member of the back-room staff had been sacked. Shankly made a point of guaranteeing Paisley, Moran and Reuben Bennett, the club's original chief coach, their jobs when he arrived in 1959. He applied the same rules to the players that he retained in a system of man management that he likened to a confessional. 'I would always remind the players not to argue with the referee,' he recalled, 'and I would try to put them at ease a little by saying things like, "don't think any individual is expected to win the game by himself. Don't worry that we are depending on you too much. Share out the worries. We want all of you to do something . . . play together and keep going." '

These are sentiments echoed by Evans today: 'Our team talk, week in, week out, is "it's great that you've got a talent, but the most important thing is how the team plays and how you play for the team. You'll always get a chance to use those individual talents, but if you want to stand out, the way to do it is to play for the team." I like the players to enjoy training and certainly enjoy the games. It's not always possible, and there's got to be serious moments when the manager has to blast away, but it's a game that you should enjoy.'

If the board of directors were not desperate when they appointed Evans, they were certainly concerned. They had tampered with the hereditary line, and Evans, hastily promoted to assistant manager twelve months before Souness admitted defeat, had to repair it. Bereft of a groomed successor, he approached Tottenham's Doug Livermore and made him his first-team trainer, an appointment that echoed down the years. Paisley had known what he was getting with Lawler. Evans knew what he was getting with Livermore: 'a guy who was Liverpool-minded . . . it was never going to be a problem, how he was going to fit in'. Livermore was an old teammate from the reserve days, steady and reliable; in short, a budding Boot Room acolyte. He had left Anfield to coach Norwich and Spurs, as well as work with the Welsh national side. But his thoughts on coaching had a familiar ring: 'Keep it simple, it's always been that way. It's a simple, simple way.' Lawler's old post of reserve-team trainer was filled by Sammy Lee, home-grown, hard-working. Football is a simple game. Why complicate it?

With one or two new additions, notably full-time physio Mark Leather and goalkeeping coach Joe Corrigan, it remained a back-room staff built along classic Boot Room lines: like-minded, low-risk men working towards a common goal codified by the manager: 'We try to keep the whole thing bubbling. The final say is mine, and that's how it should be, but we all get stuck in and do our bit. On a day-to-day basis we're just trying to improve on the basics of passing, control and movement, and our training sessions are geared to that.' Six words: get it, give it and move. The Shankly coaching motto, easy to digest and easy to remember. 'If you have a good team,' he declared, 'a tactical talk at the start of the season is enough – unless your players have bad memories ... football matches are played on football pitches and not in exercise books.' The message to the players may have been simple, but it was founded on scrupulous detail. Daily training observations were recorded by Ronnie Moran, who still takes notes to this day. Evans calls them 'our little scribbles'.

Liverpool had to have the right kind of players to make this pre-programmed pinball machine work; players who were equally proficient in control, touch, movement and work-rate. To this end, and bearing in mind that expensive new signings were still a thing of the future, the available squad was split into groups of six in training, each concentrating on its own weaknesses. A little psychology never went amiss. Ray Clemence, for example, was a nervous goal-kicker. As well as encouraging him to work on his technique in training, Shankly took the added precaution of removing the flags from the top of the Kemlyn Road Stand. If they weren't there to snap and flutter, Clemence wouldn't worry about kicking into the wind. 'I made it my business to know all about my players,' said Shankly. 'I even knew the colour of their eyes.' Paisley was more intuitive. Ex-players talk of his perspicacity, his ability to sum up a player's strengths and weaknesses. Former skipper Phil Thompson likened the coaching staff to agony aunts. Kenny Dalglish talked of their 'deep and thorough knowledge of the players ... they would know if there was anything wrong with any player, whether he had something on his mind. They are so finely tuned to each individual player, they know straight off and ask him when he's leaving the ground.'

This intimate knowledge included an appreciation of each player's physical limitations. In their respective progressions from reserve-team trainer to first-team trainer to manager, Evans, Paisley and Fagan all worked as running-repair physiotherapists on the pitch. Accordingly, training was geared less to slavish contests of strength and more to building stamina and preventing injury – getting players fit and keeping them that way. Pre-season began with light exercises, gradually building up to more strenuous workouts. Shankly always maintained that he had the fittest side in the First Division: 'Some people might think we are lazy, but that's fine. What's the point of tearing players to pieces in the first few days? We never bothered with sand dunes and hills and roads; we trained on grass where football is played.' The players were ferried to and from Melwood by bus. The journey back to Anfield gave them time to cool down and loosen up before bathing and changing. It also familiarised them with a stadium that habitually intimidated its visitors.

Fitness also bred familiarity in the dressing room. It was a system that worked, time and time again. In season 1965/66, Liverpool used fourteen players to win the Championship, and one of those, Bobby Graham, played only once. In season 1978/79, they romped to the title with fifteen players, one of whom, Sammy Lee, played just twice. Three consecutive Championships between 1982 and 1984 were achieved with 21 players.

In 1993/94, Graeme Souness employed 26 players, the most the club had ever used in a single season. Liverpool finished eighth, their lowest position since their return to the top flight in 1963. As the club plummeted from its silver stratosphere to a soundtrack of gnashing teeth and brow-smoting, the alarming increase in player turnover was blamed on an injury epidemic. This in turn reflected a new, punishing training schedule under assistant manager Phil Boersma (midfielder Michael Thomas, who spent months on the sidelines, remembers how teammates would playfully warn him to steer clear of the new right-hand man), and the abandonment of the bus service between Anfield and Melwood. At the same time, with heathen impudence, the Boot Room was bulldozed into history.

Souness heralded his arrival with ominous talk of the 'massive task' facing him. Like Toshack at Swansea, he came not to carry on the Boot Room tradition but to emulate Shankly, to impress a giant personality on Anfield. He fought against the myth and lost. On the whole, he signed players of apparent quality, and there were occasional glimpses of the old class. But the team played like strangers. In Liverpool's hour of need, Evans knew he had to reinstate the old training methods, trim the squad, reacquaint the remaining players with each other and educate any new signings and unlicked cubs in the art of patient possession football. He succeeded, to the extent that, less than twelve months after signing for the club he had supported all his life, Jason McAteer could claim, 'a lot of things have been coached out of me since I left Bolton.'

This ability to harness and refine raw talent is the Boot Room's *raison d'être*. At the beginning of 1997, the back-room staff consisted of Ronnie Moran (chief coach), Doug Livermore (first-team trainer, traditionally heir apparent), Mark Leather (physio), Joe Corrigan (goalkeeping coach), Sammy Lee (reserve-team trainer), Steve Heighway (youth development officer) and Ron Yeats (chief scout). It was the biggest coaching team yet, but there were no sinecures nor room for egos, a point emphasised by the manager. 'Twenty guys, all with big personalities, need a reasonable amount of attention, physically, mentally and certainly in their preparation. There's a fair job to be done, and that's why we have a fair amount of staff. A good team can do fantastic things on its own because the talent is there, but it is important that the management team organises that talent and keeps them on the straight and narrow. There's never been a great manager without great players. But there's got to be someone who can work with them, who can make sure that they apply themselves in the right way. It is a simple game. But it's very difficult to keep it simple.' The result, theoretically, is a team of talented individuals playing measured, deliberate football as a unit, the Liverpool Way. Shankly: 'You can't score until you've got the ball, so when you've got it you must keep it. That might mean playing cat and mouse for a long time, switching the ball around and apparently not getting very far; but then, suddenly, an opening will appear.' Evans: 'You haven't got to create a goal with every pass. It may take ten passes, but if at the end you've created the opening then you've achieved.'

There are other ways. AC Milan, the world's greatest football-ing empire of modern times, abandoned the possession play favoured by Liverpool and Italian football in general for a more aggressive, harrying style, combining their native finesse with a steely British resolve to press their opponents and exploit their mistakes. There are similarities with Manchester United, where Alex Ferguson had his own formidable myth, that of the Busby

Babes, to confront. There have been great players at Old Trafford before, but none who worked so hard as a team as those under Ferguson, especially in the early 1990s. But neither United nor Milan placed as much importance on teamwork as Liverpool.

It worked best with minimum fuss, and minimum changes to personnel on both the playing and coaching sides. This wasn't a system geared to winning the Championship once, it was designed to win it again and again and again. The consistency it encouraged is breathtaking. Liverpool were never out of the top five for 26 consecutive seasons from 1965/66 to 1990/91, finishing first twelve times.

There is myth, and there is momentum. Other Championship-winners, notably Howard Kendall at Everton, George Graham at Arsenal and Howard Wilkinson at Leeds, talked of the paradigm that Liverpool provided, not just on the pitch but off it, and found their own spirit willing but their foundations weak. From stability comes success, and in this Liverpool are unique. Morever, their calculated reputation began to precede them. Confronted by the legend, and daunted by a thousand mawkish eulogies in the press, opposing teams were defeated before they had run on the pitch or even started the season. This is Anfield, home of hokum.

'Back room' is defined in the dictionary as 'a place where secret work is done'. The secret work at Anfield was to create a working myth. We stared at the pictures of those old, modest Methuselahs and bought into the sanctity, the simplicity and the tradition. But we were not alone. 'A manager has got to identify himself with the people,' wrote Shankly. Like us, Liverpool believed, and continue to believe, their own deliberately underplayed propaganda. If the club crest had a motto, it should be, 'Do good by stealth and blush to find it fame'.

Ultimately, Liverpool brought about their own reckoning. The Boot Room was buried, not physically when Graeme Souness called in the demolition men, but when Kenny Dalglish, the superstar, was appointed player/manager in the summer of 1985. The unbreakable chain had been broken. When Dalglish walked away, the pain of managing the club – what Shankly called 'a lifetime of dedication' which 'follows you home, follows you everywhere, and eats into your family life' – finally became public. Behind the blue eyes and inculcated diffidence of Roy Evans, the man chosen by Paisley to perpetuate the myth, perhaps lurks the paranoia and insecurity of his predecessors. 'You never switch off,' he admits. 'I can go home and do other things for a while, but it's always there. You never get it out the back of your mind.' These are changing and challenging times, and Liverpool are not immune. Superstars used to play for other clubs. QPR fans had posters of Gerry Francis on their bedroom walls. Manchester City supporters gazed adoringly at Rodney Marsh before the lights went out. We had the whole team: eighteen or so grinning players interspersed with the obligatory wizened Boot Room face. Rangers and City both ran Liverpool close, in the 1976 and 1977 title races respectively, and both failed to maintain the charge in subsequent years. They were one-season wonders, shackled by a flawed star system which brought with it a contentious wage structure and the all-too human traits of envy and discontent within the team. Prima donnas were not allowed at Liverpool, and all that possession football never slouched into arrogance. Leeds United's exhibition passing against Southampton, caught on camera for posterity in the 1970s, was matched by Liverpool on countless occasions, but the Boot Room made sure the 'Big Heads' never executed it with such sadistic delight. While other teams who had beaten them celebrated as if they'd won the Championship, Liverpool never crowed after a victory. Trophies would come and go, but they were 'always looking to improve', accordingly adding one or two new faces to the squad before the start of each new season to keep the heat on the established players and maintain the team's relentless standards of effort and commitment. No one in the Boot Room would – or could – get carried away. Nurtured to dismiss success with a shrug, their humility was designed to rub off on the side.

This is past-tense nostalgia from a world without agents – creatures from whom Paisley, and even Shankly, would have shrunk – or the baying demands of an increasingly intrusive media, and seemingly at odds with the homespun, humdrum philosophy of Evans. 'Things haven't changed for the worst, they've just changed,' he claims, a little unconvincingly. 'I try to be straightforward with the press because if you want to be clever with them, they can be twice as clever with you, they've got a platform every day. Shanks wouldn't have liked agents, and sometimes none of us like them. But there are good ones and bad ones. Our approach is to stay totally honest, say what we think and be up-front. It saves a lot of problems at the end of the day.' Nonetheless, a stratum has appeared at Anfield, as elsewhere, between stars and superstars, and with it an incorrigibleness and insolence among the playing staff, borne of vast transfers fees and valuations and self-regard which not even the old, sacred values of the Boot Room can dispel. This is the future, for Liverpool and for everybody else. When Evans was appointed manager, his chairman called him 'the last of the Boot Room boys'. Whatever his achievements, the myth will die with him. His successors may discover that, without it, the world will be a mighty stranger.

3 The Scots Clan

By John Colquhoun

At that dinner party you didn't want to attend in the first place, when the conversation turns to the predictable boring crap that only serves to reinforce your belief that your reluctance to attend was entirely appropriate, for us Scots the only game we cannot wait for is the 'what have you ever done for us?' challenge.

Everyone can stand back and have a chuckle at their Belgian guests as they put forward their contributions – Jean-Claude Van Damme, Eddie Merckx and Marc Dutroux – but for anyone of Scottish origin, this is where we are able to claim that for a nation whose population has never exceeded five million we are probably the world's greatest over-achievers in almost every field.

Sir Matt Busby, John Logie Baird, Bill Shankly, Alexander Fleming, Jock Stein, Alexander Graham Bell, Kenny Dalglish, James Watt, Alex Ferguson, Sir James Dewar and George Graham – the list seems almost endless.

Now you may not have recognised all the above names but they will certainly have made a difference to your life. From televisions to Thermos flasks, Scotland has benefited the world in almost every way.

Not everyone reading this far may have recognised the name of the man who invented the steam engine, but all will, undoubtedly, have recognised that of the man who first brought the European Cup to British shores, which if you don't mind me suggesting so probably says more about the reader than it does about the achievement of James Watt.

Spanning two generations, the achievements of these six Scottish managers is unparalleled by any comparable country or even *region* of a country in modern sport.

The question is why are we so good at producing managers?

The social and economic climates in which the managers built successful teams must play some part. For Busby, Stein and Shankly postwar Britain was a very different place to the supposedly borderless European nation in which the modern-day football gaffer works.

When researching for this chapter I pondered whether or not to chronicle the successes of the main characters. It was suggested to me that, although today's supporters know that the three older men were great managers, it isn't until the facts are down in black and white that the almost unbelievable extent of their achievements becomes apparent.

Sir Matt Busby was born in Lanarkshire, on 26 May 1909, to a hard-working poverty-stricken family. His father was killed in the First World War. Like so many other young men of the time, he was forced to find work in the mines. Grafting away in the earth's bowel was not a happy time for Busby. Whilst plying his trade he also played for a junior side (semi-professional) for half a dozen matches before being invited to sign for the team that were to become his city rivals, two decades later. Eventually settling into the team as a right half, Busby brought to the Manchester City team of the time a thoughtful passing game, which helped City to two FA Cup finals in the early thirties. The second of these, the 1934 final against Portsmouth, was to prove the only time Busby was to enter the winner's circle as a player.

Winning a Scottish cap in 1936 against Wales, in the same year he was to move to Liverpool for the not inconsiderable sum of £8,000. This was in the days before you had to pay two million for a Premiership reserve centre-half who couldn't pass the Prime Minister's house if you sent him up Downing Street.

Just after the Second World War Busby brought the curtain down on a proud playing career. Offers to remain in the game were quickly relayed to him, including the opportunity to coach Liverpool and manage Manchester United, which shows there must have been some directors with a modicum of game knowledge back then.

He chose to take his chances at a bomb-damaged Old Trafford, long before it was one of the finest stadiums in England. If the city centre can be rebuilt to the same degree, after the IRA bomb attack of 1996, then the citizens of Manchester can look forward to the millennium with great hope. Mind, they will need to wait fifty years and endure some barren times along the way to finance it.

Busby realised that a superior scouting system was imperative to the fulfilment of his dream. Setting up a network of scouts, he was successful in persuading the cream of England's young talent to sign for United, who at that time weren't the biggest name in the country; this was Wolverhampton Wanderers.

Winning the Championship with a side whose average age was 22 in 1956, retaining it the following year, Busby, possibly aware of the dominance his young side would have in England over the next few years, understood that to test themselves they needed to look further afield. Against the wishes of the English football authorities, a good enough reason for doing so in itself, Manchester United were the first English club to enter the European club competitions, reaching the semifinals before being defeated by the all-conquering Real Madrid side which included Puskas, Di Stéfano, *et al*.

Disaster then struck when, on a fateful, snowy night in Germany, the plane carrying United from a game in Belgrade crashed at Munich airport. Eight of the team known as the Busby Babes perished and two never played the game they loved again. Busby himself was seriously hurt and his physical injuries took a long time to heal. The mental wounds never would.

Showing an incredible inner strength, Busby returned to the task he set out to do, and rebuilt the club through the development of youngsters. He reached the pinnacle of his management career at Wembley in 1968 when Bobby Charlton was presented with the European Cup. They were the first English club to win it and the last United team to do so, much to Alex Ferguson's chagrin.

Busby retired in 1969. The club was to wait until 1992 to win the League Championship again under the stewardship of someone else.

Receiving a thoroughly deserved knighthood, if there is such a thing, for services to football, Sir Matt was president of the club from 1980 until his death in 1995.

When you are at school or a member of the armed forces, to call you by your surname is an authoritarian method of keeping you in your place, to ensure that you know who is in charge. In adulthood it is more a measure of your achievements. Shankly, like Peel or Lennon and McCartney, needs no Christian name. The uniqueness and fame of these people are enough, but it is more than that – it is a measure of the affection in which they are held.

Shankly was born in a mining village called Glenbuck in Ayrshire in 1913. The ninth of ten children, and the youngest of the five boys, Bill started his working life down the mines, his escape being the chance to play football for the famous junior side with the mouth-wateringly delicious name of the Glenbuck Cherrypickers. So close-knit were the community and so large was his family that most of his teammates were related to him.

Desperate to escape from the work, or lack of it – the Depression was already settling over the country – Shankly was delighted to sign for Carlisle United in 1932. After only a few appearances he was transferred to Preston North End, helping his new team to promotion and eventually to Wembley for consecutive Cup Finals, resulting in a winners' medal in 1938. As with so many players of that generation the war curtailed his career – a smaller price, however, than many young men of the time paid.

Retiring from the playing side of football, with an injury, four years after the end of hostilities, Shankly was to state later that he felt robbed of some of the best times of his life. Following a gradual managerial learning curve, which involved stops at Carlisle United, Grimsby Town, Workington and Huddersfield, where he introduced Denis Law into the English game, and with as yet no tangible signs of the management style that was to become so apparent, destiny then delivered him to Anfield, home of Liverpool, a club that had secured five titles in its history but a mid-table Second Division side going nowhere at the time.

The foresight of the chairman at the time was of biblical proportions, bringing in the man who was to become a saviour to the supporters of the famous Reds. Shankly brought with him a professionalism, a desire to succeed and a very personal vision of how he thought the game should be played. These skills were to turn Liverpool into the most successful English club ever. It has been suggested by far more politically aware people than I that although football and the city of Liverpool, in particular, were to benefit, had Shankly's talents not flourished in football then he should have taken his charisma and vision into the political arena. It is hard to imagine a young Bill Shankly, disgusted by the conditions forced upon him down the mine-shaft, then watching whilst his community was ripped apart as the industry was run down, taking no part in a political solution if football had not totally consumed him. Socialism's loss was Liverpool Football

Club's gain. Anyway, it is difficult to picture him suffering the fools of Westminister gladly. If televised politics are ever to become compulsive viewing in this country then we must all live in hope that we are one day given a choice between a student of Churchill and one of Shankly. There probably wouldn't be any more decent legislation, but the one-liners between the two would make Prime Minister's Question Time a must-see.

Shankly built two great sides who, between them, won one Second and two First Division Championships, as well as twice triumphing in the FA Cup and once in the UEFA Cup. His legend still reverberates not just around the club but the city to this day. Despite his undoubted professionalism, Shankly always maintained an aura of unpredictability and he surprised everyone when he retired suddenly in the summer of 1974 (a decision he almost immediately regretted). He left the foundation on which a mountain of success was built. Sadly he died in his adopted city in 1981.

If the one word every commentator seemed to use to describe Shankly is gregarious then his great friend Jock Stein was most often called taciturn. If that is a true description then my Concise Oxford English Dictionary is lying. *Taciturn*: habitually silent, not apt to speak or talk. When reprinted that esteemed publication should carry the true meaning of the word, because it must surely signal footballing genius.

Having been brought up a Celtic supporter, I am perhaps a little biased on this one. The man born in Burnbank, Lanarkshire, naturally went down the mines upon reaching working age ... fourteen was in those days considered old enough. Even Forrest Gump might detect a pattern here. There may have been time in the earth's inner sanctum for these three men to work out some grand plan of how they were going to leave their footprints on the world. As they chipped away at the black rock there was no other escape route for these well-brought-up young men. As young black men in the tough districts of America's inner cities see their only way out of the ghetto being through professional sport, so the young Scots saw football as the only ticket to breathing fresh air during their working hours.

Stein was to struggle to join the full-time ranks of professional football, leaving a Scottish semi-pro team, Albion Rovers, at the age of 27 for the not at all glamorous non-League Welsh club

Llanelli, who were to tempt him away from his home town. Retiring early through injury, Stein was to arrive at Celtic Park via Dunfermline Athletic and a short spell at Hibernian to awaken the Glasgow club from its slumbers. So violently did he shake the club that it was to be sixteen years before it would take a nap and endure a trophyless season. Ten Championships, nine Scottish Cups and six League Cups were enjoyed by the club during his tenure.

Stein is best known for moulding a group of mostly local lads together to become European champions on an unforgettable night in Lisbon in 1967. It is impossible, in these days of cosmopolitan teams, to comprehend that a team of men born within 27 miles of the club could prove themselves to be the best team in Europe. Any conversation with players who played under Stein leaves you in no doubt that his style of management combined tactical knowledge with a consummate ability to handle men. Players who needed an arm around them, to coax a good performance from them, found a favourite uncle; men who needed a kick up the arse found the school captain demanding they play well. They were all to be rewarded by becoming part of the first British team to win the European Cup, beating the mighty Inter Milan, treating the depressing style of defensive football dubbed *catenaccio* with the contempt it deserved, sweeping it away under a tidal wave of aggressive, attacking football. As Jock Stein said at the time, 'We don't just want to win this Cup. We want to win it playing good football, to make neutrals glad we've won it, to remember how we did it.' His wish has been fulfilled!

Stein left Celtic in 1978 to manage Leeds United for just 44 days before becoming Scotland team boss, taking his country to the 1982 World Cup finals in Spain. Tragically he died of a heart attack at the end of a crucial qualifier for the next World Cup. Our nation mourned regardless of club allegiance. Jock Stein was bigger than that.

The three modern-day managers, George Graham, Alex Ferguson and Kenny Dalglish, need less introduction, not because their achievements eclipse those of the oldsters, but because in our society of sporting media saturation, if there is anyone out there who is unaware of who they are then English is obviously not their first language.

All were born into working-class families. Ferguson was raised in Govan, within shouting distance of Ibrox, home of Glasgow Rangers. Despite reaching the heights of European football he has never forgotten where he has come from. The local boys' clubs still receive all the help Ferguson can give them in terms of raising funds and giving his time generously and freely, traits not often found in the multi-million-pound business that football has become. A decent club player, his true calling was as a manager. He served a thorough apprenticeship with several Scottish clubs before turning a provincial club, Aberdeen, into the dominant force in Scottish football, ending the nine-in-a-row march of Stein's Celtic, without the financial muscle and fan support that the Old Firm enjoyed. Honing the psychology that he uses to great effect now, he exploited the fact that there was 'a west coast bias' against his team, in the same way as he revels in the 'we all hate Manchester United' syndrome today. His teams are among the toughest mentally that Britain produces.

Aberdeen scaled unexpected heights when they defeated the mighty Real Madrid to win the European Cup-Winners' Cup in 1983.

Manchester United persuaded him to try his hand down south in November 1986. After three trophyless years, the tide was to turn dramatically for Ferguson and United in an FA Cup final replay against Crystal Palace, a game that emphatically demonstrated the big man's will to win. After a first match that United failed to win through what he thought was questionable goal-keeping from his long-time number one, Jim Leighton, the decision to drop him from the replay must have involved a lot of soul-searching. By all accounts the one thing Ferguson can do is separate his personal feelings for men he has known and counted on for years from what he considers is best for his club. The 1990 Cup victory was the springboard to major success – winning the Cup-Winners' Cup again, then clinching the elusive title that United had been chasing since Busby's team had won it in 1967. Since then, of course, they have invented the double-Double.

Not without trouble along the way. Controlling his influential striker Eric Cantona after the Frenchman attacked a spectator during a match has been one of the biggest tests of his managerial career. Like all great managers he has now set his sights on a new challenge, following in Busby's footsteps once again and reclaiming the European Cup for his club.

George Graham, also born on the outskirts of Scotland's most passionate football city, in 1944, differs from the other recent managers in that he was to play and coach all his football in England. He is the only one to have won all three English trophies as both player and manager.

He started his managerial career in one of the hardest learning places in the country. It is said about New York 'if you can make it there you can make it anywhere'; well, the song was surely first sung down at the Den, home of Millwall Football Club, before some opportunistic Yank claimed it for the Big Apple. The fact that he lasted four years is testament to the progress he made with the club. I played for Millwall, so I know what I'm talking about. For the record I lasted ten months. He is managing Leeds United and I am writing this chapter and struggling to get a game for Hearts, so my theory on longevity at Millwall being a yardstick for future employment within the game seems to be holding up.

Taking the job at Arsenal in 1986, he led them to two Championships, League and FA Cup glory, and also a Cup-Winners' Cup win.

He was to exit Arsenal in a blaze of bad publicity when he was accused of financial irregularities involving a Norwegian agent, Rune Hauge. Subsequently he was found guilty and given a worldwide football ban for a year.

Now back in the game with Leeds United, he is following the pattern of his previous successes, attempting to build the foundations for another club with good coaching and shrewd dips into the transfer market.

Although I can appreciate the merits of Elvis Presley, there is only one man who is worthy of being called The King – Kenny Dalglish, my boyhood hero.

The media perception of a humourless, dour Scotsman is the one he wishes them to hold. Having met him on several occasions, I found him extremely amiable and genuinely interested in others.

The first occasion was the most memorable for me . . . for all the wrong reasons. Sitting at breakfast during my spell playing for Celtic, I was sharing the table with Scotland's greatest full-back,

Danny McGrain. This was before I had learnt the footballers' game of being blasé about absolutely everything. I was still looking around, hoping everyone would notice I was with McGrain, when who did I spot walking across the room but Dalglish! Now anyone who is familiar with Harry Enfield's teenage character who only communicates in words that all have three letters made up in the order of 'huh!' will find it easy to imagine how intelligent I must have sounded when Danny introduced me to Kenny. Even writing that sentence reminds me of how much in awe I was of these two men.

Anyway, I was involved in a conversation about the upcoming game Celtic were about to play against Rapid Vienna in the Cup-Winners' Cup. Far from being monosyllabic, Dalglish spoke eloquently and concisely about football, discussing how Celtic had been playing and how Liverpool would approach the game differently from Celtic. It was a fascinating part of my education.

Chronicling the career of Dalglish would be far too time-consuming, winning as he did everything the domestic game could offer on both sides of the border, in the process scoring a hundred goals in each League, winning European Cups, beating the Scottish record for international caps – and that is just as a player! Becoming player/manager of Liverpool, he led them to glory again, but just as importantly he helped them deal with two tragedies, Heysel and Hillsborough, where Liverpool supporters lost their lives. In his recently published eponymously titled autobiography he says, 'All that mattered to me was to support the people of Liverpool because they had always supported me.' Dalglish will always be remembered by the city not only for his football but also for his compassion.

Citing stress, he unexpectedly retired in 1991, saying he needed a complete break from the game. Revitalised, eight months later he returned to manage Blackburn Rovers. Jack Walker provided the funds, Dalglish the football expertise to catapult the Lancashire club from First Division also-rans to Premiership champions in 1995, the trophy clinched ironically at Anfield. Now he is back in the game at Newcastle and aiming for an unprecedented Championship with a third club.

Explaining exactly why we Scots have been able to produce the quality of managers we have is probably a task more suited to a modern-day Freud than to an ageing footballer. Peering deep into the Scottish psyche is not the most inviting of tasks. We seem to be far happier being a satellite state of our neighbours from the South than going to the trouble of actually governing ourselves, preferring to annoy from within the status quo rather than smashing it, secure in the knowledge that the safety net of the Union is in place. Which means that our sense of national identity needs to manifest itself in ways other than the political, or perhaps we expend too much energy looking for sporting victories to worry about the bigger picture. Well, so what if our favoured political party isn't returned to power? The important question for us is can we qualify for the next football World Cup. This is how much football means to the majority of Scots. No wonder we supply great managers.

The usual glib theory is that it is to do with the mines or the Protestant work ethic Scots of all religions are born with. Undoubtedly, we are the hardest-working region of the British Isles, but it is more than that. Mining is definitely a factor producing a special breed – of men, women and children, because they were all in it together. More than any other community they were bound by fear of death, and any way out was a blessing. An escape that promised a life earning money by playing football must have been akin to walking from the pit cage to board a bus which had Utopia as its only destination.

For the three men who were to start life down the pit and end up bringing sporting joy to whole cities, the lessons of their early lives must have determined not only that they succeed but that they do it with style.

It was about learning to work for your team as well as yourself, knowing that your life was dependent on the whole team rather than any individual within it. All their sides bore the hallmarks of the areas they were bred in, fostering a great team spirit that a city could latch on to.

Deep under the soil there could not have been a great deal to talk about. In small communities where nothing much would happen worth discussing in the eerie underbelly of Scotland, nothing except the football, so the game would be dissected, whether it be a local game or the last professional match the men had watched.

Another theory (mine, I must confess) concerns our version of

The Cult of the Manager

Egyptian artwork – paintings on the walls of pyramids featuring humans in profile with their arms in an S shape in front of them and one eye enlarged and enhanced. In the seams of the Scottish coalfields our men were shown how to rule the football fields of Europe through messages etched into the black rock, passed down by ancient Scottish gods so that we could be held in awe by virtue of our knowledge of the world's most popular game. Evidence? There was loads of it, but sadly it went up in smoke. So, we will have to settle for the hard-working explanation, I suppose.

For the three modern-day managers there was a precedent already set for them. In the same way as Bjorn Borg spawned a generation of world-class Swedish tennis players, it could not have discouraged any gifted Scottish football coach to look to the top of their profession and see their countrymen reigning supreme. By the time these men were striving for immortality, the excellence of Scottish managers was evident in the history books and the trophy rooms.

In some respects it made their jobs easier. There was less need to contend with the common English view that Scottish football and everything it touches is 'Mickey Mouse'. The pressure to succeed was even greater, however. The shadows of Stein, Busby and Shankly will never be completely shaken off. There will always be some triumph that is now arguably more difficult to achieve, be it on the field or on the terraces. Never again will football be as close to the working-class, thick-and-thin supporters, as it was in the sixties.

Every one of these managers had their individual idiosyncrasies that transformed them into truly great managers of teams. To achieve this, though, they all had one quality above others – they were great managers of players. All knew when to put their arms around a vulnerable player and when to throw a teacup around the dressing room. None were scared of making the decision that would upset a player as long as the club would benefit. Dalglish is the only one who couldn't be described as prudent in the transfer market, although he was not profligate. In the modern game building a team in the marketplace is a much-sought-after skill. Moulding them into a Championship-winning team presents as many difficulties as rearing your own talent then supplementing it through big-money buys, if not more.

The accusation that all these men were control freaks is probably justified. Footballers are strange creatures; very few want the licence to perform a totally free role. Most are at their best when given a specific job to do. We are not trusted with our own passports on foreign trips, for God's sake. If we believe in a manager and his methods then we will do almost anything he wants. Players under these legendary managers believe absolutely.

When these men step down, can we expect another generation to step in? Sadly not. Very few pits are left, and it is impossible for the transient industries of today to foster the spirit that formed the basis of a team as a mini-community.

Today's game demands different, fresh, ever-changing ideas. Nutrition, flexibility and a healthy lifestyle are as essential as tactical awareness. For a nation with the highest percentage of heart disease, caused basically by our love of red meat, asking a Scottish manager for dietary advice would be a bit like asking Nick Leeson to look after your financial portfolio. With the arrival of Arsène Wenger and Sven Goran Eriksson, the next region to dominate English football is a wee bit bigger than our beautiful country – Europe.

Fear, prudence, tactical genius, discipline, pride, knowledge, hard work and respect are all reasons why they succeeded.

And we are not finished yet!

4 In Defence of the Realm

Is managing England really an impossible job?
By John Kelly

This royal throne of kings, this scept'red isle,
This earth of majesty, this seat of Mars
This other Eden, demi-paradise,
This fortress built by Nature for herself
Against infection and the hand of war,
This happy breed of men, this little world,
This precious stone set in the silver sea,
Which serves it in the office of a wall,
Or as a moat defensive to a house,
Against the envy of less happier lands.
This blessed plot, this earth, this realm, this England . . .

William Shakespeare

It was the best of times, it was the worst of times. Saturday, 30 July 1966. It is a date forever etched in the memory of everyone old enough to remember Beatlemania, the Great Train Robbers and pounds, shillings and pence. I wasn't even a twinkle in my father's eye on *that* day, when England registered a 4–2 extra-time victory over West Germany in the World Cup final, but I know the exact date it all happened. I also know that Argentina won the 1978 World Cup, at home, even who scored the goals. But I have no idea as to the actual date of the match. And yet I know exactly when England, Alf Ramsey's England, won the Jules Rimet Trophy.

Since then, I have watched and waited. Waited along with the rest of the nation for England to bring the World Cup back home once again. To bring any trophy home for that matter. But it hasn't just happened, has it?

Perhaps if we were honest, really honest about it, we might be tempted to think that England will never win the World Cup again. And perhaps if we were really, really honest, we might even be tempted to think that winning it in 1966 was the worst thing that could have happened in over a century of Association Football.

Such a thought, at first, seems too awful to even contemplate for a nation that swells with pride at reading the words of Richard II at the beginning of this chapter. England is a proud nation, and it desperately wants to be proud of its football team. For one glorious afternoon, Alf Ramsey and his Wingless Wonders truly did the nation proud. But the legacy of 1966 *and all that* has had far-reaching effects that would wipe the toothless grin off Nobby Stiles' face. The problem is one of expectation. Since that day, over 30 years ago now, England's fans have been burdened with expectation, rather than heartened with hope. We are driven crazy by a media-led conspiracy that still wants us to believe that England really are in with a chance, still able to do the business when it matters.

The words and images of that sunny day in 1966 have become woven into the fabric of our culture. 'Some people are on the pitch, they think it's all over ... it is now!' is arguably the most famous single sentence in the entire history of British television (it even has a TV show named after it, for heaven's sake). Mention the name Geoff Hurst in any pub in the land and somebody will start a debate with you about *that* goal. You see, you knew immediately which of Hurst's three goals I was referring to, didn't you?

Every aspect of England's World Cup win is looked back on through rose-coloured glasses that Dame Edna Everage would simply die for. And now, worst of all, our whole view of England's place in the world of football is distorted by the fact that we think we *should* win the World Cup, that we *deserve* to win it. A throwback to the days of empire when we were on top of the world in every sense. But if you ask a Spaniard about 1966, you are unlikely to hear much about Nobby's jig of delight, or Hurst's third goal. You are more likely to hear about biased referees, dodgy linesmen, large lumps of luck and a draw fixed to suit the hosts.

The bottom line is this: we have no right to expect England to win the World Cup. And yet we do. We fall for it every four years, if things go well in the qualifiers. We can't help it. But for every day we go on expecting England to win, we go on fooling ourselves. It also makes it harder for the England manager, because as the burden of expectation grows, so does the pressure on the man entrusted with the nation's prime directive – returning the World Cup to where it rightfully belongs, 'back home' in England. Right now, 30 years on from that glorious July afternoon, most England fans would give their granny's right arm for another taste of the ultimate football high.

Had England failed in 1966, things might be very different now. England were expected to win the World Cup in the 1950s, but didn't. In many ways, 1966 represented a last chance to confirm that England were still masters of their own game. The victory gave substance to the myth that England were still a power in the world game, a myth perpetuated to this day by the media, the fans, and a nation growing ever fonder of nostalgia. Had Ramsey's side lost in 1966, England might still be waiting for a first World Cup victory. They certainly couldn't cope with the Brazilians in 1970, they failed to qualify in 1974 and 1978, the 1982 campaign fizzled out, Diego Maradona single-handedly sunk England in 1986, the 'lucky' Germans did for them again in 1990, and 1994 was a non-starter.

Knowing all this, it is a wonder anybody can be persuaded to take on the job of England manager, and yet it is still regarded as the pinnacle of the managerial game. It doesn't even pay that well these days – Glenn Hoddle is reputed to be earning £250,000 a year as England coach, while Sven Goran Eriksson will get £1.1 million for managing Blackburn Rovers – yet it is still considered to be an honour even to be mentioned in connection with the job. Obviously, there are perks. The hours are good, plenty of foreign travel, and if you get it right, you become a legend. Success brings the adoration of an entire nation . . . Alf Ramsey didn't get a knighthood for his charm, did he? But failure brings contempt in equal measure, and there is nothing in between. Since Ramsey led the Boys of '66 to victory, every succeeding England manager has been swimming against the tide. The football public demand too much from the outset, they demand that England be the best in the world when the statistics show that they are only ninth best (see table opposite). Ninth, that is, on average in every World Cup England has entered. Ninth may be nowhere near good enough to satisfy the average supporter, but there it is, ninth, take it or leave it.

FINISHING POSITIONS IN THE WORLD CUP

Year:	30	34	38	50	54	58	62	66	70	74	78	82	86	90	94	Ave
Finalists:	(13)	(16)	(16)	(13)	(16)	(16)	(16)	(16)	(16)	(16)	(16)	(24)	(24)	(24)	(24)	
Germany	D	3	9=	D	1	4	5=	2	3	1	5	2	2	1	5=	3.3
Brazil	5=	9=	3	2	5=	1	1	9=	1	4	3	5=	5=	9=	1	4.2
Italy	D	1	1	5=	9=	D	9=	9=	2	9=	4	1	9=	2	2	4.8
Argentina	2	9=	D	D	D	9=	9=	5=	17=	5=	1	8=	1	2	9=	6.4
England	D	D	D	9=	5=	9=	5=	1	17=	5=	17=	5=	5=	4	25=	9.1
Uruguay	1	D	D	1	4	9=	9=	5=	4	9=	17=	25=	9=	9=	25=	9.8
Spain	D	5=	D	3=	17=	17=	9=	9=	17=	9=	9=	8=	5=	9=	5=	10.0
Sweden	D	5=	4	3	17=	2	17=	17=	9=	5=	9=	25=	25=	17=	3	11.3
France	9=	9=	5=	14=	9=	3	17=	9=	17=	17=	9=	4	3	25=	25=	11.6
Holland	D	9=	9=	D	D	17=	17=	17=	17=	2	2	25=	25=	9=	5=	13.3

Ave = average finishing position in World Cups entered.
D = did not enter.

Note: in instances where a country failed to qualify, they are considered equal to the number of finalists, plus one. For instance, there were 24 finalists in 1994. England did not qualify, therefore their finishing position for 1994 was equal 25th. Ignoring countries which entered the World Cup competition, but failed to qualify for the final stages, would put them on a par with countries which had not entered. Further, it would distort any comparison between countries because of the fact that different numbers of countries have been allowed into the final stages as the competition has developed. Ignoring non-qualifiers would mean countries failing to qualify for a 16-nation finals would be considered on a par with those which failed to qualify for a 24-nation finals.

In reality, ninth out of the entire world is really not that bad; it's actually quite good. We'd settle for ninth on the Olympic medals table, wouldn't we? But when it comes to football, and England, ninth is simply not acceptable. However, when you compare that to Spain and France, two countries with roughly similar aspirations and football infrastructures, England fare pretty well. The same statistics show that the Spanish finish tenth, on average, and the French eleventh in the World Cup (neither country has ever won, but both won the European Championship on home soil). The Germans, *naturlich*, are the best with an average finishing position of third (blast them), with Brazil and Italy both ending an average World Cup campaign in fourth place. Beyond that, the Argentinians usually finish sixth, the Uruguayans ninth, the Swedes eleventh and the Dutch thirteenth.

The Uruguayans, the dominant force in the early days of the World Cup, have more or less accepted their current situation, and stopped tormenting themselves about becoming world champions once again. They concentrate on more attainable goals these days, such as the Copa America, and often send an entirely different team to the World Cup, when they qualify. I'm not suggesting for one minute that England shouldn't even try to win the World Cup. And I am not trying to argue that winning it in 1966 was a *bad* thing, far from it. In playing devil's advocate, all I am saying is that we shouldn't expect too much, that's all.

Because it's not just the Germans, Brazilians, Italians and Argentinians, who usually finish higher than England, that we have to worry about. Every World Cup seems to herald the arrival of a new force on the world scene, a one-off generation of talented players who take their country to new heights, if only for a brief time. In the 1950s it was the Hungarians, in the 1960s the Czechs, Holland's Total Football dominated the 1970s, while Poland's footballers finished third in 1974 and 1982. Denmark emerged in the late 1980s and early 1990s, and now it could be Croatia, or Colombia, or Nigeria, or the United States. Thus, in any World Cup, there will always be half a dozen or so countries who are better than England, or at least finish higher than England.

The last two countries, Nigeria and the US, are particularly frightening because they, along with Asia, represent the new world of football, one that will be dominated by Sony, General Motors, and the spirit of Africa. Sir Walter Winterbottom, England's first manager, once claimed that an African nation would win the World Cup by the end of the millennium. That does not look like happening, but it won't be too far into the next one. Nigeria, remember, are the current Olympic champions (having beaten Argentina in the final, Brazil in the semis). The Nigerians are not even African champions – that title belongs to South Africa, another major threat to the established order in world football. While much of African football is crippled by disorganisation and an acute shortage of cash, the South Africans have both the resources and the set-up to make them serious contenders and they will, almost certainly, become the first African nation to host the World Cup.

In Asia, Japan and South Korea have already won the right to stage the World Cup, in 2002, and both countries are improving all the time, thriving on healthy domestic leagues created specifically to benefit the national team. These countries cannot simply be dismissed as cannon fodder for the group stages any more, and with the benefit of home advantage ...

And then there's the Americans. Their new Major League Soccer enjoyed a quietly successful debut season, indeed it went better than they'd dared hope, and we are constantly being told that 'soccer' is the fastest-growing game with the kids in America today. How long do you think it will be before the power of the dollar and the abundance of raw talent collide in one unstoppable team? It is almost inevitable. The only thing that can stop it is America itself, with the same introverted, snobby attitude that makes British fans so reluctant even to attempt to understand baseball. But if the MLS keeps on growing, and if only half of one per cent of the American kids who are supposed to be playing the game turn out to be any good, then heaven help us all.

Of course, an exceptionally talented generation of English footballers *might* emerge. Glenn Hoddle's Continental touch *might* deliver the goods, and England *might* well win the World Cup again in the future. It would be foolhardy to discount them completely. England will nearly always be there or thereabouts when the World Cup comes around, but there will always be other teams equally capable. The difference between them is often no more than the width of a post, or the arc of a ball as it deflects off a defender's boot. Realistically, England's chances of winning the World Cup should be rated as possible rather than probable. If the reverse were true, why have none of England's managers – bar Ramsey – said so publicly?

Accepting, then, that England's place in the order of things is more like ninth, rather than first, makes it far easier to assess the nine brave men who have held the nation's every dream, hope and desire in their hands. If ninth is England's average position in the World Cup, then by qualifying for the finals England would have done as well as they could expect to. Reaching the quarterfinals, where the competition is pared down to eight teams, would effectively be better than expected. Armed with that knowledge, we have at least some hope of giving each man a fair trial.

Winterbottom: the Scholar

Walter Winterbottom became England's first manager, a job he combined with the post of director of coaching at the FA, in 1946. Before the war, the England management had been shared by members of the FA Council, and despite Winterbottom's appointment, they still selected the players. Under such circumstances, which seem impossible to modern football-watchers, Winterbottom set about his business.

England refused to enter the first World Cups in 1930 and 1934, again through sheer bloody-mindedness, the 'it's our ball and we're not playing any more' mentality strongly to the fore. Many feel that England, then a genuine force in the game, would have won the World Cup in its early days, though that was always fiercely contested by Vittorio Pozzo, the legendary Italian manager who led the Azzurri to victory in 1934 and 1938. England decided to enter in 1950, by which time Winterbottom had had four years to prepare his men.

Winterbottom, tall and bespectacled, had a scholarly air about him, although this never alienated him from his players. England won the first game of the new era, 7–2 against Northern Ireland, and with Billy Wright, Alf Ramsey, Stan Mortensen, Stanley Matthews, Jackie Milburn and Tom Finney all selected in those early Winterbottom years, England travelled to Brazil for the 1950 World Cup in high spirits. Many back home genuinely believed England would waltz off with the trophy, but a Haitian-born American called Larry Gaetjens made certain they didn't.

England's 2–0 win against Chile and 2–0 defeat by Spain are

rarely recalled, but mention the 1950 World Cup and everybody knows about Larry Gaetjens. Or at least they know about the goal he scored in Belo Horizonte, a goal that proved enough for the amateur Yanks to knock England out of the World Cup (the fact that England beat the US 6–3 and 8–1 later in Winterbottom's reign is also largely overlooked). Back in England, there was disbelief. One newspaper, refusing to accept the 1–0 scoreline it received by wire from Brazil, printed the result as a glorious 10–1 victory for England! Others simply placed a black border around the report to signify the blackest day in England's international history.

Three years later, the dark clouds gathered over English football once more, as the dazzling Hungarians tore England to shreds, winning 6–3 at Wembley (and 7–1 in the Budapest return six months later). Overnight, the aura of English invincibility – which had survived Belo Horizonte on the grounds that it was a freak one-off result – was smashed. Now it would be even harder to win the World Cup.

England reached the quarterfinals in 1954, thanks to a draw with Belgium and a 2–0 win against Switzerland, but any illusions of a return to greatness were shattered by the Uruguayans, who won 4–2. Winterbottom's side had flopped once more, and he realised he would need to spend more time with his players before international matches to get the best out of them, something the League clubs had always resisted. In this respect, he was ahead of his time, and the seeds sown then are being harvested now in terms of blank FA Premiership weekends before England's current World Cup matches.

Whether Winterbottom thought he would need new faces for 1958 is open to debate, but the decision was made for him anyway, not at Lancaster Gate but in Munich. Four England players died in the Munich air crash of February 1958, the emerging Bobby Charlton was seriously injured and Eddie Colman, another hoping to make the trip to Sweden, also perished. Just 48 hours later, England learned that they would face the Soviet Union, Brazil and Austria in Sweden. England, the least-experienced team in the finals, drew their three group matches and had to play the Soviets once again in a play-off. England hit the post twice, the Soviets hit the post once, the ball went in and England went home. Home to a public that was now beginning to wonder if England were ever going to win the World Cup, and to media that were preparing the first broadside in a war of words that continues to this day. The first serious criticism of Winterbottom emerged because he had left Charlton and Brian Clough out of the team. Charlton did travel to Sweden, but was replaced by Bobby Robson, while Clough – 40 goals for Middlesbrough that season – was left at home.

Winterbottom survived, though, perhaps partly riding the residue of sympathy still surrounding the Munich disaster which had robbed him of half his team. He led England to the finals again in 1962, in Chile, but England fell at the quarterfinal stage, losing 3–1 to the Brazilians. Chile was Winterbottom's swansong. His critics argue that he was too much of a thinker and that he lacked the steel necessary to make England world-beaters. But Winterbottom should be rated a success, certainly for his two World Cup quarterfinal appearances, but also for his diligent work under immensely difficult circumstances. He won 78 of his 137 England matches, and although he never won the World Cup when England might legitimately have been expected to, he laid the groundwork for others to follow. Coaching was virtually unheard of before Walter Winterbottom, but his legacy touched every club in the country, changing the way the game was conducted, and paving the way for Alf's Wingless Wonders.

Ramsey: the Maverick

Alf Ramsey, it seems, was always destined for greatness. Certainly his staring eyes and clipped tone suggested a man with a mission, a man who knew exactly where he was going. He enjoyed a fine career as a player with Tottenham (as part of Arthur Rowe's 'push and run' side) and Southampton, winning 32 caps for England, before starting his managerial career with Ipswich. In just six seasons, he steered the country hicks from the back of beyond out of the old Third Division and all the way to the top, pipping Tottenham's 1961 double-winning side to the 1962 Championship. Even this astonishing success did not guarantee Ramsey the England job. Winterbottom, before bowing out, had suggested Jimmy Adamson as his replacement, but the Burnley manager decided not to get involved. The FA then bravely chose to ignore the obvious, successful candidates – Bill Nicholson of Tottenham and Stan Cullis of Wolves – and gambled instead on Ramsey's maverick talent. It turned out to be the best decision the FA ever made.

Ramsey had an automatic advantage over his predecessor: he picked the team. And while that meant assuming greater responsibility and taking more flak when things went wrong, Ramsey was quite prepared to put up with it if it meant he could have complete control of his players.

England lost their first game under Ramsey, 5–2 to the French, and were then beaten at home by the Scots, whom Ramsey hated only marginally more than he did the French. But, a month later, came what might loosely be termed a turning point. England held an admittedly weakened Brazil to a 1–1 draw at Wembley, and Ramsey was on the way to fulfilling his footballing destiny.

Ramsey, a taciturn, bad-tempered man who disliked talking to the press and despised the creeping commercialism already evident within the game even in the early 1960s, seemed to hate almost everything and everyone at times, except the eleven players he put out on the pitch ... his boys. He demanded 100 per cent respect and commitment from them, and offered the same in return. He was stern when he needed to be, but always defended his players when they were being criticised, and he expected them to show him the same degree of loyalty. Ramsey always had an unshakable belief in his own ability, and he wasted no time in getting this across to his players. Long before their hour of destiny in July 1966, Ramsey said at a press conference that England could and *would* win the World Cup. Like no other England manager before or since, he placed his cards on the table and was prepared to stick his neck out. It proved to be a masterstroke, endearing him to the players, who gradually began to feel that it was not just an idle boast, and that the boss meant business.

Ramsey also had the good fortune of having three genuinely world-class players in his side – Gordon Banks, Bobby Moore and Bobby Charlton. He added to these players he knew could do the jobs he wanted done. They were not always necessarily the best in the country, but Ramsey perhaps placed reliability above all else. That's not to say he was over-sentimentally loyal to his players, as Jimmy Greaves found out. Greaves, then the hottest English striker in the game, was by no means a grafter, and when push came to shove, Ramsey dropped him in favour of the more workmanlike Geoff Hurst.

There's no real need to detail what happened during the 1966 World Cup: everybody knows that England won 4–2. Everybody knows that Hurst scored the first and so far only hat trick in a

World Cup final. Everybody knows that England had the match won, only to concede a late equaliser which meant they had to win it all over again in extra time. Everybody knows that 'it's only twelve inches high, it's solid gold and it means England are the world champions . . .'

But what if Hurst's second goal hadn't been given? The debate on that will probably rage on forever, but the most obvious conclusion is that the ball never did fully cross the line. Ramsey's entire life's work came down to the decision of a Soviet linesman with grey hair and baggy shorts. It's all too easy to forget that referees and linesmen are human beings, with human emotions, and that factor may have been crucial in deciding England's fate. As the Swiss referee, Mr Dienst, walked over to consult Tofik Bakhramov (actually an Azerbaijani, not a Russian), what must have been going through his mind? With no clear view of the 'goal' he had to act on gut feeling alone. Such split-second decisions are outside the sphere of a manager's influence, but where Ramsey came into his own was in motivating his players.

At the end of 90 gruelling minutes, and having let victory slip from their grasp, England seemed drained and doomed. But Ramsey urged his men to one more colossal effort, simply by telling them that they had beaten the Germans once, and they could do it again. It was a simple enough plea, but one that would have failed but for the tremendously close bond between Ramsey and his players. This, crucially, was Ramsey's greatest ability, and it carried him and his team through to the ultimate triumph. Ramsey had honoured his word, fulfilling the ambitions of the nation that gave the game to the world in the process. Ramsey's 1966 World Cup winners may not have been the most entertaining team in the world – in fairness to the Germans, they may not even have been the best team in the world – but they had kept their word and delivered salvation . . . what more could we ask for?

It has been argued that Ramsey's 1970 team was better than the one that triumphed four years earlier, but any advantage was surely negated by the fact that the finals were played in stifling heat, at altitude in Mexico. Despite disruptions caused by noisy late-night hotel visitors, dicky tummies and allegations that skipper Moore had stolen a bracelet from a hotel shop in Bogota *en route* to Mexico (Ramsey naturally backed Moore to the hilt), England again reached the quarterfinals, where they faced the

Germans in a classic rematch. Leading 2–0 with only 22 minutes to play, England conceded a goal to the West Germans and then disintegrated before the disbelieving eyes of a massive audience back home, watching a live colour transmission for the first time. At this point, Ramsey made one of the most controversial moves of his career, one for which some sections of the English football public never forgave him. Leading 2–1 still, Ramsey decided to make two substitutions, taking off attackers Charlton and Martin Peters for workhorse Colin Bell and Norman 'bites yer legs' Norman Hunter. The Germans, perhaps sensing a lack of conviction on the England bench, went for the jugular and secured another equaliser, just as they did at Wembley four years earlier. This time round, though, extra time produced a different ending as Gerd Muller shot Germany into the semifinals.

The Germans also knocked England out of the 1972 European Championship at the quarterfinal stage, giving more ammunition to the growing band of Ramsey's critics, which included Brian Clough and Malcolm Allison, who had been so quick to leap on his substitution blunder in Mexico. And when Poland and their goalkeeper Jan Tomaceswki – dubbed a 'clown' by Clough – knocked England out of the World Cup in 1973 with a 1–1 draw at Wembley, Ramsey's time was at an end. In April 1974 he was given the sack, but not before leaving another important legacy to the English game. Before he left Lancaster Gate, Ramsey presented the FA with a dossier of ideas designed to help the national team. Chief among them was the recommendation that England players should have a week together before World Cup and European Championship matches. Thank you, Sir Alf, and so long.

Revie: the Paranoid

'Uncle' Joe Mercer actually followed Ramsey into the England hot seat, but only on a temporary basis until the FA could find the right successor. Mercer was only in charge for six months and seven games, so it would be unfair to assess his time in office. The record will show, however, that Mercer's England won three, drew three and lost one of those seven games, and all agreed he had done a good job keeping things ticking over while the FA looked for Ramsey's replacement.

Initially, the FA sized up Gordon Milne, Jimmy Bloomfield and

The Cult of the Manager

Gordon Jago, choosing to ignore the growing clamour for Brian Clough – 'the people's choice' – to become manager. But as soon as Don Revie showed an interest, the FA had to look no further and, it's worth noting, most of the country backed their decision. Revie had played in the top flight, for Manchester City, Sunderland and Leeds United, he had played for England, and as manager at Elland Road, he had transformed Leeds from second-rate also-rans to winners at home and abroad.

Revie, from a poor working-class home in Middlesbrough, was a strange character, seemingly at odds with himself most of the time. He was deeply suspicious, highly superstitious (remember his lucky blue suit?) and had two great loves in life: football and financial security. The former provided him with the latter, although in the end, his craving for cash led to his ignominious end. At Leeds he had fashioned a truly magnificent team which sadly never enjoyed the blessing of the Fleet Street press corps. Leeds were dismissed as too negative . . . too nasty . . . too northern. His side, gifted with great talent, did have a ruthless streak a mile wide, and it is safe to say that Revie's Leeds were never that popular with the rest of the country, despite the two League titles, two Fairs Cups, the FA Cup and the League Cup won during his reign. Without the press firmly behind him, Revie was always going to be fighting an uphill battle, every setback magnified by journalists just waiting for him to trip up.

Revie's main priority was to ensure that England qualified for the 1978 World Cup finals, but things went wrong almost from the start, despite opening win against Czechoslovakia. Revie's constantly changing team selections upset many established internationals, and as the results began to slip, he desperately tried to motivate his team. At Leeds it had been easy, but the difference in managing an international side, where you have the players only for a few days every month or so, proved a real stumbling block. Revie was never able to develop that 'it's us against all them' mentality which had served him so well at Leeds. He persuaded the FA to set up a lucrative new bonus scheme for the players, only for the press to dismiss the idea as a distraction. Failure to qualify for the 1976 European Championships raised further questions about where England were heading, and when the Scots took the home international series as well, the knives were well and truly out for Revie, whose huge dossiers on opposing teams and attempts to turn the England squad into one big, happy family suddenly became standing jokes.

Still, the World Cup was all that mattered, but here again the gods conspired against Revie by placing England in a winner-takes-all qualifying group with Italy. A 2–0 defeat in Rome was a huge setback, meaning England would have to win the home leg and record a higher score against Luxembourg to progress to the finals.

In the summer of 1977, quite out of the blue, news leaked out that England no longer had a manager. Revie, unwilling to put up with all the aggravation any longer, had done the unthinkable. He broke his contract with England and took up a post with the United Arab Emirates, a move that led to him being banned from the game in England for ten years, though this was later quashed in the civil courts.

Whatever the merits of Revie's decision to jump ship, it was certainly a brave one. He had a couple of years left on his contract, and when he mentioned his intentions to his bosses, the FA backed him with a full vote of confidence. It was too late, though; the news had been leaked to the press who rightly had a field day. Allegations of bribery were dredged up and vigorously denied, and he was condemned as a grasping, selfish man who presented 'a notorious example of disloyalty, breach of duty, discourtesy and selfishness', according to the judge who over-turned the ten-year ban.

Revie, ultimately, paid the price for putting his family before his job. He genuinely believed he was doing the right thing in going, he just went about it all the wrong way. Unquestionably, Revie must be judged a failure in terms of his England career, yet the blame for England failing to make the 1978 World Cup was not his alone. The players he had available were, quite simply, not good enough, and that, as much as anything, proved his undoing. To the bitter end his old Leeds players refused to hear a word said against him, but the rest of the country never forgave him for walking out on them.

Greenwood: the Conservative

Ron Greenwood was a disciple of Walter Winterbottom, a tacti-cian and thinker who liked his sides to play attractive as well as effective football. At West Ham, Greenwood reigned for thirteen years, presiding over the East London club's 'school of soccer science' – a grandiose term for a decent football team. He had also coached England at youth and Under-23 level, and was a technical adviser to FIFA for the 1966 and 1970 World Cups.

After the débâcle of Revie's sorry exit, the FA needed stability at the top, and Greenwood fitted the bill perfectly. His coaching credentials were impeccable, and equally important, he was the kind of conservative, almost bland figure needed to steady a rocky ship. The fact that Greenwood, who was by then general manager at West Ham, was available was another important bonus for the FA. The 1977/78 season was already under way when Greenwood took up his post, so persuading any other clubs to release their manager would have been difficult and costly.

Initially, Greenwood was appointed only for three games, but a vainglorious win over Italy in the World Cup return at Wembley partly helped him hang on to the job for another four and a half years. After the three-match probationary period, the FA had five names on their list of suitable candidates: Brian Clough, Bobby Robson, Lawrie McMenemy, Allen Wade (FA director of coaching) and Greenwood. The caretaker boss won the vote, and then began setting up his back-room staff. In a bid to foster continuity, Greenwood employed Clough (briefly), Robson, Don Howe, Dave Sexton, Terry Venables and Howard Wilkinson within the England set-up, grooming the England managers of the future.

Liverpool provided the backbone of Greenwood's team, an understandable move given that the Anfield Reds were busy sweeping all before them at the time. Led by Kevin Keegan, England qualified for the 1980 European Championship in Italy with relative ease, but failed to make a major impact in the finals. A win, a draw and a defeat were not enough to progress beyond the first round, although the rioting England fans in Turin, who were tear-gassed by Italian police, made as many headlines back in England (the game, against Belgium, had to be stopped at one point because goalkeeper Ray Clemence was temporarily blinded by the gas). Had Trevor Francis been fit, Greenwood's team might have had the fire-power to mount a serious challenge in what was a pretty poor tournament, but untimely injuries were to be the bane of Greenwood's England career.

The qualifying group for the 1982 World Cup began well with a 4–0 win over Norway at Wembley, but things took a turn for the worse after that. England won only once in their next eight matches, the worst run in the team's history, and Greenwood was suddenly a target for the tabloid hounds. A violence-marred defeat in Switzerland left qualification hanging by a thread, and Greenwood cracked under the pressure. In private, he advised his FA bosses that he would quit after the tie against Hungary in Budapest, a game England had to win.

England did win, 3–1, to keep the World Cup flame flickering, and as the plane headed back to blighty, Greenwood informed the players of his intentions. They were amazed at first, and then tried to persuade him to change his mind. Dick Wragg, chairman of the FA's international committee, had one last go as the England party headed through the arrival lounge. Greenwood, swayed by the loyalty of those around him, changed his mind and decided to stay. Amazingly, the press never got a whiff of the story. England, with games against Norway and Hungary to come, still had a chance of reaching the finals, but the events in Oslo three months later must have made Greenwood question his decision to stay on.

Norway's 2–1 victory, their first ever against England, sent England's hopes crashing and launched one local commentator into a vitriolic A–Z of famous English names, from Lord Beaverbrook to Maggie Thatcher, whose boys took one hell of a beating that night. The beating continued for days afterwards in the papers. Shock was soon replaced by dismay, and Greenwood had to endure the worst abuse of his career. Then luck suddenly turned England's way. The other teams in the group conspired to beat each other, so that when the Hungarians, who had already qualified, came to Wembley, England needed only a draw to join them in the finals. A scrappy goal by Paul Mariner secured a victory, and England were off to Spain.

The early signs were encouraging, as Bryan Robson scored after 27 seconds against France in a 3–1 win. The Czechs were beaten 2–0, Kuwait 1–0, but the diminishing goal tally told another story. England were playing without the injured Keegan and Trevor Brooking, and without decent supply from midfield the stream of goals was being choked to a trickle. In the second round, England failed to score against West Germany or Spain, and were eliminated despite remaining unbeaten. Keegan and Brooking returned for the final match; both missed chances to win the game and Greenwood's reign was over.

The Cult of the Manager

Had Keegan and Brooking been available throughout the final tournament, Greenwood's side would probably have progressed to the semifinals at Spain's expense. From there, who knows? Injuries, one of the many things beyond a manager's control, had proved Greenwood's nemesis. All those days of hard work on the training pitch, all those hours invested in meticulous planning, undone by injuries to a couple of key players.

Greenwood was able to retire with dignity and the thanks of the FA after the finals, and they were probably well merited. The second round of the 1982 World Cup, with eight teams, was effectively the quarterfinals, so in this sense Greenwood did as well as could be expected. While the England team had not really progressed very far under his guidance, it had not gone backwards either. That, as far as the FA seemed to be concerned, was good enough under the circumstances.

Robson: the Defiant One

After the disappointment of the 1982 World Cup fade-out, Bobby Robson emerged as the unanimous choice to succeed Greenwood as England manager. Robson, a native of the north-east heartland which has produced so many of our great football talents, had been a top-flight pro with Fulham and West Brom, and won twenty caps for England.

His managerial career has taken him from Fulham to East Anglia, to the England job, on to Holland, Portugal and currently Spain, where he is managing FC Barcelona, a job it seems he was destined to have one day. Yet it all began in Canada, where Robson accepted a post with the Vancouver Royals. The move was a fiasco. A new owner took over, installed another coach and then bounced all the cheques. He returned to England, older and wiser, and took a big pay cut to take over at Fulham, his former club. Robson lasted just nine months back at Craven Cottage, once again forced out by a new owner with his own agenda.

Robson applied for the vacant Ipswich job in the winter of 1969 more or less on a whim. Billy Bingham and Frank O'Farrell were the clear favourites for the job, but Robson got it, and a verbal promise of at least two years to make a go of it. He stayed for thirteen years, and revived a club that had fallen into disrepair following Ramsey's departure for the England job in 1963. Under

Robson, Ipswich won the FA Cup and the UEFA Cup, twice finished second in the League and were regulars in Europe. In 1981, when they narrowly missed an exotic treble, Ipswich were voted Europe's Team of the Year by the Continent's sports press. Along with the success, Ipswich developed a reputation as a good footballing side. Robson liked the ball played to feet by players who were comfortable with the ball. He built three fine sides at Ipswich, with the last arguably the finest. It contained ten internationals (only the goalkeeper Paul Cooper was not capped) but had cost less than £1 million to assemble in the days when Manchester City were regularly throwing that sort of money away on the likes of Kevin Reeves.

During his time at Ipswich, Robson turned down offers from Everton, Manchester United, Sunderland, Derby, Leeds, Newcastle, Barcelona and Athletic Bilbao. He turned them all down because of his loyalty to the club, and to his chairman Patrick Cobbold in particular. But when he got the call to manage his country, Robson felt he could not refuse. Ipswich reluctantly agreed to let him go, almost twenty years after they had let Alf Ramsey make the same trip.

Robson's England reign was a real rollercoaster ride from the opening match, a 2–2 draw with Denmark in a European Championship qualifier. The Danes won the return 1–0 at Wembley, England's only defeat in the qualifiers, but one that cost them a place in the finals. Already the knives were out. Indeed, they had been drawn from the start after Robson dropped Keegan from the squad. Later, Robson would admit that those early years in charge were the hardest of his career. The sniping got worse later on, but this was probably one of Robson's lowest points.

Nine months later, England pulled off a memorable 2–0 victory in Brazil, with John Barnes scoring the best goal of his career. Suddenly there was renewed optimism in the England camp. Robson's side qualified for the 1986 World Cup with four wins and four draws, and they stretched their unbeaten run to eleven games in the friendlies that followed qualification. A 1–0 defeat to Portugal, followed by a 0–0 draw with Morocco (in which Ray Wilkins was sent off and Bryan Robson carried off with a busted shoulder), left England needing to beat the Poles to go through to the second round. Robson switched to a 4-4-2 formation, with Peter Beardsley partnering Gary Lineker in the attack, and the new line-up clicked. The Everton trio of Gary Stevens, Peter Reid and Trevor Steven combined to set their team mate Lineker up for a hat trick, with Beardsley playing a starring role in support. Paraguay were no obstacle at all in the second round as England strode confidently on to face Argentina in the quarterfinals, three years on from the end of the Falklands War.

The match, which was the subject of some tension on both sides of the Atlantic, became a World Cup classic. Diego Maradona scored two outrageous goals, the first with his fist, the second with nothing but sheer genius, while Lineker's late reply was not enough to salvage the game for an England side who had given their all. It was a truly glorious defeat, and but for Maradona's sleight of hand, England might have triumphed in the most difficult circumstances. As it was, the team returned home bloodied but unbowed, proud to have reached the quarterfinals and confidently looking forward to the new season. The press, under the circumstances, had to go easy on Robson. Maradona, Robson's destroyer, also proved his saviour in a perverse sort of way because he diverted the press away from the manager and any awkward questions about England's shortcomings.

After the high times at high altitude in Mexico, England came back down to earth with a thud two years later, in the European Championship finals in West Germany. England went to the tournament as second-favourites with the bookies, after conceding just one goal in six qualifiers, and that came in a 4–1 demolition of Yugoslavia in Belgrade. But the finals were a nightmare. England lost all three matches, conceding three goals in the game against Holland, and another three against the Soviet Union. The final match, against the Soviet Union, was the biggest disappointment because the team 'capitulated', as Robson put it afterwards. This time the media pack closed in, demanding Robson's resignation for what had been a truly miserable show in Germany.

It was another low point for Robson, but things got even worse when England drew 1–1 with Saudi Arabia in Riyadh. 'Go, for the love of Allah,' was one of the more memorable tabloid headlines of the time. The media onslaught was so fierce that it had the opposite effect, and actually rallied the ordinary fan to Robson's colours. More importantly, Robson had the personal backing of FA chairman Sir Bert Millichip, guaranteeing he could continue until the World Cup in 1990.

England qualified for Italia 90 without conceding a goal in their qualifying group, but a month before the tournament began, Robson announced that he would be quitting after the finals. He had intended to wait until afterwards, but a trashy front-page exclusive in a tabloid newspaper brought matters to a head. When the FA made it clear that his contract would not be renewed, Robson took up a job offer from Holland's PSV Eindhoven.

Robson headed for Cagliari knowing Italia 90 would be his swansong, unless England actually won the trophy. A month later, they were a penalty kick away from a place in the final, which would have been a rematch against an Argentinian team nowhere near as good as the 1986 vintage. Despite Gazza's tears, Lineker's goals and Robson's greying hair, England fell in the semifinal, beaten on penalties by the Germans. For once there was no attack by the press; even Robson's sternest critics realised that he had almost pulled off the biggie. The semifinal, at least, represented the best performance by England since 1966, and this was away from home.

Robson worked hard during his eight years as England manager; he took every shot the papers fired at him and still came out on top. That alone makes him a successful England manager, and does not even begin to take into account the difficulties of being the national team's coach during a period that included both Heysel and Hillsborough.

Taylor: the Tinkerer

Graham Taylor became England's seventh manager when his two main rivals for the job, Howard Kendall and Joe Royle, pulled out. His track record appeared impressive; he had taken Watford from the Fourth Division into Europe, and he had turned Aston Villa into serious contenders for the League Championship. But from the very start, Graham Taylor's England reign was going to be a difficult one.

He had enjoyed a professional career as a player, but he had never played in the top flight or internationally. There's no direct evidence as to whether this affected his relationship with his England players, but it became a real talking point which diverted concern away from the serious problems at the heart of the England team.

Like it or not, Taylor was a disciple of the long-ball game, as preached by Charles Hughes, the FA's director of coaching. Using the quickest route possible to deliver the ball into the opponent's box, Taylor had taken Watford all the way to Wembley in the FA Cup, and Villa to runners-up spot in the League, just before he left for the England job. The long-ball game provides instant success but ultimate failure, a quick fix for the short-sighted. There is a fatal flaw in the whole doctrine: it will not work at the highest level, because international defenders are too skilful these days to be continually caught out by aerial bombardment. Like a tiny defect in an aeroplane's superstructure, which goes unseen until it is too late, the seeds of Taylor's destruction had been sown long before England fell apart on the road to USA 94.

Taylor also had to cope with a hostile press from the outset. There were many loud dissenters when he was appointed, and a large section of the sports media seemed to have accepted him on approval only, like an item from a catalogue.

Things actually started well, with England unbeaten in their first twelve games under Taylor. They qualified for the 1992 European finals, in Sweden, but there Taylor's nightmare began. Up until then, the press had given him a fair crack, but as England crashed out with just one goal in three games, the press turned on him with a savagery never seen before in this country. England had lost 2–1 to Sweden in the last match, prompting one tabloid to run the headline 'Swedes 2, Turnips 1' across its front page, with Taylor's head depicted as a turnip below. Worse still, he had substituted Lineker in his final match, when he was still one goal shy of Bobby Charlton's record of 49. The debate about not being able to handle star players surfaced again, and many simply felt he had an unnecessary and tactless way of doing things. Taylor later admitted 'from that moment on, I was the villain'.

The 1994 World Cup campaign got off to a worrying start when Norway rescued a point at Wembley. The Dutch followed suit, and when Taylor's ever-changing side drew in Poland a month later it was the beginning of England's summer of discontent. Four days later, a bewildered England side lost 2–0 to Norway in Oslo. Seven days after that, the United States beat England 2–0 in Boston. The summer tour ended with a draw against Brazil, and another defeat, against Germany. Worse still, the whole shambles had been filmed by Channel 4 for the documentary series *Cutting Edge*. What had been intended to be a record of England's triumphant march to the USA ended up being a tragicomic B-movie, showing the tensions and confusion within the England camp with alarming regularity.

Taylor and his cohorts effed and blinded their way through an hour of TV hell, while the bemused players sat around numb with tactical reshuffles and ever-changing game plans. In one scene, Taylor spends five minutes briefing substitute Nigel Clough on his duties. When he finishes speaking, Clough points to entirely the wrong area of the pitch, and asks, 'You mean over there, boss?' It was cringe-worthy, gut-wrenching stuff, like watching a man drown in quicksand.

A 2–0 defeat in Rotterdam in October left England needing mathematical miracles to qualify for USA 94, and when San Marino took the lead after thirteen seconds of England's final match, it seemed somehow a fittingly depressing end to Taylor's England career. His side bounced back to win 7–1 that night, but it was all too late to save the manager. As England's hopes of qualifying grew slimmer, so the attacks on Taylor grew stronger – a candidate representing the Sack Graham Taylor Party even stood in a local by-election! With things going so awry on the pitch, and the constant hassle off it, nobody was too surprised when Taylor announced his resignation after the San Marino game.

Obviously, Taylor is ranked as a failure in terms of the England job, but he suffered from the same problem Revie did: a lack of quality players. Alan Shearer played in only three of the ten qualifiers, and in Rotterdam England twice hit the woodwork and were denied a possible penalty when Ronald Koeman hauled down David Platt. Koeman should, at least, have been dismissed, but he stayed on the pitch and later scored the opening goal with a twice-taken free kick, the first a pile-driver, the second a delicately floated chip. If it wasn't for bad luck, Graham Taylor would have had no luck at all as far as the England job goes. His own constant tinkerings, with the team and the tactics, certainly did not help matters, but once again, if luck had been a little kinder, Taylor might still be manager today.

Venables: the Media Man

Terry Venables was the unanimous choice to succeed Taylor, and yet it was a brave move by the FA to appoint him. Nine months earlier, Venables had had his contract as chief executive at Tottenham terminated by his fellow directors. It was the start of a long and at times bitter feud with Tottenham supremo Alan Sugar, which led to Venables being dragged through the courts and for a while banned from White Hart Lane. In the same month he was appointed, January 1994, *The Financial Times* printed new allegations about his business dealings, following up an earlier *Panorama* programme on the BBC. Serious stuff.

But Venables was appointed with all due pomp and ceremony, and given the task of making sure England were ready when football came home in the summer of 1996.

Venables had many things going for him. He was popular with the fans, especially in London, where he played for four of the capital's clubs, returning later to manage three of them. He had always been a 'player's gaffer' and the accepted wisdom was that he would not have the same problems dealing with England's finest the way Taylor did. His track record as a manager wasn't bad either, although one FA Cup and the Spanish title was not exactly outstanding either. But he was a highly respected coach, schooled in the new philosophies of modern football and seen as the ideal cure for the tactical malady Taylor had left behind. Above all else though, Venables enjoyed the backing of the media, and he knew how to get the best out of the relationship from the start.

Venables has always been high profile, whether he was managing FC Barcelona or his wine bar in Kensington. He co-wrote the Hazell detective books back in the 1970s (later turned into a successful TV series), appeared in TV commercials, has written several football books and has attracted more publicity in the 1990s than any other British football figure. Some of it hasn't been exactly complimentary, but then there's no such thing as bad publicity in football these days, is there? Only publicity itself is important. Venables is what the *NME* might impolitely term 'a media slag'. That is not as derogatory as it sounds: slag implies someone who knows the system and uses it to their advantage, as well as the obvious meaning.

From the start, Venables was hampered by the fact that England would have no competitive matches for the first two years of his time in office because Euro 96 was being staged at home. And while the inevitable comparisons with 1966 boosted the 'feel-good factor' among the general public, a succession of Wembley friendlies against mostly nondescript opponents was hardly the right preparation for his players. When England did venture overseas, the 'friendly' in Dublin was abandoned after 27 minutes following disorder among a section of the England supporters, who, were it not for the dead-giveaway shaven heads and Doc Martens, might well have been trying to stop the match because England were a goal down and looking like getting a good beating by Jack Charlton's Irish side.

The Venables era kicked off with a quietly satisfactory 1–0 win against Denmark. Those first games were pretty dull, as Venables tried to sort the players into his 'Christmas tree' formation, but the press and the public were prepared to give him time to sort things out. They were even prepared to hold their fire when England struggled in the Umbro Cup against Japan, Sweden and Brazil in the summer of 1995. There were encouraging signs, but not enough to substantiate the belief that England could win the European Championship. All the while, Venables was battling to clear his name in the courts. He was also seeking reassurances about his England future, but the FA, seemingly faced with an endless stream of new legal wrangles, were keeping their options open. Venables wanted an extension to his contract before the finals started, something the FA had never agreed to, and under such uncertain circumstances they were not likely to change their minds.

A week short of his second anniversary in the job, Venables announced that he would resign after Euro 96, worried that he might spend more time in the witness box than in the dugout during the qualifiers for the 1998 World Cup. His game of brinkmanship with the FA's International Committee had failed. Now for the 'other' battle, the one played on grass.

A pre-finals trip to the Far East a month before Euro 96 proved more eventful than the itinerary looked: a spot of sight-seeing on the Great Wall and a friendly against China in Beijing, followed by an 'exhibition' against a scratch side in Hong Kong. The Chinese leg went well enough, but when England only managed to beat the Hong Kong team 1–0, the press back home went into a last-minute panic about England's chances. Stories of players out drinking in a Hong Kong nightclub did nothing to improve the mood in England, and when 'unnamed' members of the squad damaged TV screens on the Cathay Pacific flight back home (celebrating Paul Gascoigne's 29th birthday), there was indignation.

Venables, true to form, sided with his players and defended them. The squad, in turn recognising that their manager was sticking his neck out for them, closed ranks and erected a wall of silence around the whole affair. Fortuitously, a chance incident 30,000 feet above the Indian Ocean had unified the team's spirit and strengthened their faith in each other . . . just in time for the finals. Statistical football books will show that England lost in the semifinals of the 1996 European Championship, on penalties to the Germans once again. *En route* to the last four, they had drawn with Switzerland, beaten Scotland 2–0 and Holland 4–1 in the group stage, before squeezing past Spain on penalties in the quarterfinals. Those same books will probably not mention just what an extraordinary month June 1996 was.

England started slowly, won the 'important' game against the Auld Enemy, and then destroyed the Dutch with a performance which literally drew gasps as the goals flew in. The nation was suddenly right behind Venables and his boys, and suddenly it was like 1966 all over again. As the going got tougher, the press got nastier, though it was all directed against England's opponents, notably the Spanish and the Germans. 'Three Lions' became the national anthem for a month, the company which made England flags couldn't keep up with demand, mothers were naming their offspring after the team, grown men were wearing plastic 'cross of St George' hats in the pub . . . and nobody gave a monkey's. England were in with a serious chance of winning the trophy, and that was all that mattered.

Football did come home in the summer of 1996; it reminded us all why we love it so much, and then it eloped with the Germans again. Another heartbreaking penalty shoot-out had denied England a place in the final, against an eminently beatable Czech Republic side. Darren Anderton hit the post in sudden-death extra time, Gascoigne was a stud's length from reaching a cross two yards in front of goal, but Germany went through and ultimately took the trophy home with them. England had played their hearts out during the tournament and had given the entire country something to cheer about, but in the end all those hopes and dreams were shattered by the methodical, relentless Germans.

Later, as the afterglow of such a close brush with success

receded, critics asked why Venables hadn't made any substitutions, especially in extra time. Fresh legs at that stage could have shifted the balance England's way, especially as the Germans had made all their allowed changes. Venables may well have become a victim of his own relationship with his players, remaining steadfastly loyal to the men who had brought him this far when all conventional wisdom demanded that the substitutes should have gone on. Despite this, Venables was certainly a success as an England manager. He had almost won the trophy, but perhaps more importantly than that, he made the football public believe in England once again.

Hoddle: the Enigma

Following Venables was always going to be a difficult balancing act. On the one hand, England now had a respected team that was expected to carry on the good work started by Venables. On the other, the first game after Euro 96 would be an awkward World Cup tie in Moldova, which left little room for experiment. Increasingly, too, the press were starting to be seen as a major problem. While Venables' England record was beyond anything more than minor quibbles about unused substitutes, certain papers made the most of his personal and financial problems, to the point where there appeared to be a vendetta in operation.

One by one, the main candidates for the vacancy – Bryan Robson, Gerry Francis, Kevin Keegan and Ray Wilkins – withdrew from the running to concentrate on their club careers. Hoddle, meanwhile, was growing increasingly frustrated at Chelsea's haggling over his new contract, and so decided to accept the FA's invitation. A month before Euro 96 kicked off, he was announced as England's new coach.

It is far too early to venture an opinion on Hoddle's career as England manager, but he has made a fine start. England have won their three opening World Cup qualifiers (for the first time in 50 years under a new boss), and the team – largely the same as Venables' – looks as though it is becoming a settled and happy unit. All a far cry from Hoddle's England career as a player, when he was reckoned to be a fantastic talent never given the chance to show it at international level. Hoddle won 53 England caps, but was rarely given the free creative role in central midfield he coveted. At times, he even suffered the ignominy of being banished to the flanks. Other nations would have built their side around him, but England only used him in bit parts. Now Hoddle has the chance to do things *his* way.

Clearly, managing England, the football team, is not an impossible job. Alf Ramsey proved that when he steered his team to ultimate success in 1966. But managing to fulfil the nation's expectations and keep an ever-more-intrusive media happy, at the same time as producing results on the pitch, is another matter entirely. The pressure to succeed is now enormous. England simply cannot afford not to qualify for the 1998 World Cup, with all the attendant loss of revenue that would entail. Financial pressures alone make the job one of the hardest in football, but not an impossible one. Only two of England's nine managers can be classed as outright failures, and yet England have only won the World Cup once. Success can be measured in many ways, but ultimately, in England's case, it has been an elusive quarry down the years.

At the time of writing, England have just moved up to twelfth place in the official FIFA World Rankings. These rankings, while interesting and amusing, are basically meaningless because it is the World Cup which really counts. As we have already discovered, England on average finish ninth in the most important competition of them all. Doing better than that is going to get a lot harder in the future as the millennium heralds a new world order of football, a world less suited to the Europeans and South Americans.

England invented the game. England carried it to all points of the globe and then 'rightfully' reclaimed it as their own in 1966. England, as a nation, expects to have a good football team to represent it. The man who takes on the responsibility of managing that team must be prepared to shoulder the burden of his own fears, the media's suspicions and a nation's hopes as part of the job. Archbishops are about the only people trained for *that* sort of thing.

Glenn Hoddle should not have 'England Manager' stamped in his passport. Instead, it should simply read 'Defender of the Faith'.

5 The Manager as Surrogate Mother

By Eleanor Levy

'That's right – just be a baby till you pack in football'

**Gazza (from the *Cutting Edge* documentary,
'A Year in the Life of Paul Gascoigne')**

Let's face it, footballers are weird.

As the career of Paul Gascoigne has illustrated only too well, the life of a pro is perceived to be as much about refusing to grow up as it is about living in hotels, strapping on sponsored shin guards and, if they're really lucky, winning the odd match. After all, where else would a man of 30 still be referred to as a 'lad' by his boss?

So it's no wonder that some of the most successful managers of all time are remembered not so much as great leaders or tacticians, but as father figures. Bill Shankly, Jock Stein, Matt Busby, right up to the most successful British manager of this generation, Alex Ferguson – all are revered not just as makers of teams but as 'makers of men'. How often do you see a player interviewed about the influence their manager has had on their career who acknowledges 'he's been like a father to me'? It's not surprising. From as young as thirteen, a player is plucked from the bosom of his family to be moulded into the next Alan Shearer. Along with the expansion of his pecs and removal of his personality, he is often expected to move away from home and friends and fend for himself just at the age when he is emotionally most vulnerable. His new employers become his stand-in family: providing for him, guiding him, educating him in the ways of the footballers' world.

Sometimes, having looked after the player as part of their extended football family, they'll discard him – offloading him to someone else because they just don't want him any more. In other words, telling him he's not good enough for them. Is it any wonder, then, that so many products of this sort of insecure upbringing end up as drunks, thugs, womanisers and wife-beaters? And who do you blame when kids go off the rails? Why, the parents, of course.

OK, that's the sociological claptrap out of the way. Let's return to planet Earth.

It's easy to get lost in theory about how footballers are made. What relevance does that have to a book about managers? An awful lot, considering that part of the role of the manager is to produce the next generation of players. If you like, it is their responsibility to go forth and multiply, ensuring the survival of the footballing human race. With very few exceptions, all professional managers were once professional players. It is a dictate, written in stone along with 'Thou shalt not kill' and 'Thou shalt not laugh at an episode of *Oh Dr Beeching* on the television'.

And if you're looking at managers who are around today, you're talking about men who were players before recent attempts by the Professional Footballers Association and some of the clubs to educate these impressionable youngsters, not into how to kick a football, but into the art of living in the real world. These current gaffers didn't have the players' union or any fancy youth liaison officers to help them cope. But if they were lucky, they had a manager who looked out for them.

Anyone who thinks being a football manager is primarily about signing players, fitting them into a tactical system and being made to wear comedy headphones in post-match Sky TV interviews is obviously a few buttons short of a bench-coat themselves. As with any boss in any business, it's mainly about managing your resources. And for most clubs, the main resource has to be its players. The problem is, football is a team game. It's not about one or two stars. It's about the eleven people on the pitch representing your club. How often do you hear players being criticised for being too individualistic? It's the same in the armed forces, where effective, disciplined units are what's needed, not renegade glory-seekers shooting off like a loose cannon. As Mr Spock once almost said: the needs of the many outweigh the needs of the few.

Which is why players are actively discouraged from thinking for themselves. Which is why players are kept deliberately dependent on the manager and the club to look after them at an age when most normal human beings are desperate to strike out on their own. Which is why football is such a strange and old-fashioned world. So, the football manager is like a surrogate father to the players he is put in charge of. Nothing particularly radical about that, is there? Terms like 'The Busby Babes' and 'Fergie's Fledglings' have acknowledged this football parenting metaphor before. Former Manchester United winger Steve Coppell remembers the late Sir Matt Busby from his days as a player at Old Trafford in the 1970s.

'I saw him as a great uncle who showed tremendous fondness to all the players who passed through the club,' Coppell recalls. This is not the whole story, though. For not only does a manager have to be like a father to his young players when called on – but more importantly, the really successful ones are just as likely to be their stand-in mother too.

Now, before we start getting carried away with images of Ron Atkinson in stockings or Brian Clough hosting a Tupperware party, let's examine the evidence.

Traditionally, football is seen as the epitome of masculinity. How many articles do you read in the so-called quality press – particularly in these post-*Fever Pitch* days – extolling its male bonding properties for players and supporters alike? A recent rant in the *Evening Standard* by Sally Feldman, the editor of Radio 4's *Woman's Hour*, was a perfect example of this lazy thinking. The writer dismissed football as nothing more than a boys' club that actively alienates women and all they stand for in some blind, Neanderthal celebration of testosterone.

Well, yes, OK. It's a man's game, Brian. It is also undoubtedly true that the violence that's been related to football since the mid-1970s has been very much a male thing. A police officer working with the National Criminal Intelligence Unit, which monitors and controls organised football violence in the UK, once told me that out of 6,000 names on their hooligan register, only two were female – and they had been fighting each other.

Yet nobody ever seems to point out that football – whether playing or spectating – is one of the few areas in life where men can display stereotypically female traits. Where else can a grown man profess undying love in public without being thought 'soft'? Yet 20,000 of them can shout 'We love you Arsenal' without fear of being ridiculed. Well, almost.

Where else can a man snog another man in public without people thinking they're gay? When Middlesbrough striker Jan Aage Fjortoft kissed Blackburn keeper Tim Flowers on the lips in the middle of *Match of the Day* it was seen as one of those amusing football moments destined to end up on dodgy 'it's a funny old game' videos fronted by overweight 'new lad' comedians. No one questioned the players' sexuality. Yet imagine if the same two men had done it in the middle of a pub or walking down the street.

Where else can a man cry in public without appearing weak, immature or both? Paul Gascoigne has fashioned a legend out of it.

While you'd have to be particularly stupid to argue that football is a feminist issue (although you'd probably earn a fortune if you wrote a book with that title), it's true that football – playing and watching – is one of the few areas where men can openly display emotions that in the rest of their lives would be seen as weak or effeminate. Likewise the person around whom a football club revolves – the gaffer. He is there to nurture the young talent under his care, bringing his charges through to maturity. In short, he's there to be their mum. Aah.

Which brings us back to the Gazza quote at the beginning of this chapter. Professional footballers in this country are deliberately kept from growing up. And it's the managers that do it. Terry Venables is seen very much as Gascoigne's mentor. The former Tottenham boss is almost as well known for his karaoke singing at his Scribes West club as he is for getting England to the semifinal of Euro 96. Yet even he has that traditional surrogate-parent air about him. He may bang out a cracking version of 'Bye Bye Blackbird' and be known to enjoy a good night out, but when it comes to his management style Terry Venables has far more in common with *EastEnders* former landlady Pat Butcher than he does with former ICI chairman Sir John Harvey Jones. This is nothing to do with a London accent or a liking for American Tan tights, but everything to do with what we shall call 'The Mother Hen' approach to football management. To qualify as a Mother Hen you must fulfil the following criteria: (1) talk about your players as if they are your own sons; (2) refuse to recognise that they are adults; (3) act as protector against the evils of the outside world, defending them against attack at all costs.

Let's go back to point (1). Witness Venables when manager of Tottenham. The club's successful youth policy had spawned a clutch of up-and-coming talent shining in the England youth and Under-21 teams. Three of them, Darren Caskey, Sol Campbell and Nick Barmby, were due to travel to Australia to play in the World Under-18 Tournament. Barmby had at that time broken into the Tottenham first team on a regular basis and Spurs were beginning to get things together in the League as well as embarking upon an impressive FA Cup run that would eventually finish in defeat to arch-rivals Arsenal in a Wembley semifinal. Barmby was an important part of that success and the last thing Venables wanted was to lose him for a month for a tournament that had traditionally meant very little to domestic audiences. Despite the authorities – in the shape of the FA – throwing their weight around, Venables was determined not to lose his young midfielder in a vital part of the season. It was only after the death of England's 1966 World Cup-winning captain Bobby Moore that Venables relented, feeling that it was not the time to indulge in a personal crusade against the people representing the shirt that 'Mooro' had worn so proudly. His short statement conceding defeat spoke volumes: 'The boy goes.' Venables would have done Albert Square proud. He'd done his duty and looked out for his 'son'. At that time there had been a lot in the press about the danger of shin splints in young pros who had been playing too much football. Indeed, as it turned out, Barmby suffered lengthy injury problems at the end of that exhausting season. Venables was also seen to be looking after the interests of his 'family'. Tottenham needed Barmby and we all know that whatever anyone says, both managers and fans would rather have a successful club than a successful national side.

The second criterion for the Mother Hen manager is a complete inability to acknowledge that your players are men who have long since grown out of short trousers. Maybe this is because most of the time they *are* still wearing short trousers. Now, Nicky Barmby may have looked like he'd have trouble getting into a film with a PG certificate but he was nineteen years old – old enough to vote, sit on a jury, get married and have children. In fact, he was well past the age when in the real world people would object most vehemently to being called a boy. But he was a footballer – and it was par for the course.

Alex Ferguson is a strong believer in not rushing his players into the pressures and responsibility of manhood. He argues the case with an evangelical fervour – and not unconvincingly – stating that players should be allowed to grow up in their own time.

'Why should they be bothered with interviews at eighteen years of age?' he said in the *Independent* in 1992. 'Ask any parent if they would be happy having their boy the focus of newspaper and magazine articles and personal appearances to open shops. They don't want all that.'

And again in the *Sunday Mirror*. 'A father wants to make sure his son does well. He's in control of his kids and he wants the best for them. I'm a father so I know what it's like and it's only natural that you care.'

So much so that when his most celebrated protectee, Ryan Giggs, was photographed on a beach in Antigua with his topless girlfriend, Fergie leapt into action. 'I'm just fed up to the teeth with it,' he raged. 'Well, we're going to stop all that carry-on.' Yes, Mother.

Fergie, if you like, is the embodiment of the manager as Mother Hen – and not just because he looks like he's perpetually trying to pass something large and uncomfortable from his nether regions. He has turned the manager-as-surrogate parent role into an art form – and a highly successful one at that. He will remember only too well the accusations that when the much-protected Ryan Giggs was 'let off the leash' to throw himself into a succession of high-profile endorsements – and Dani Behr's arms – people were quick to point the finger when the player's form began to dip. You get the feeling that the Old Trafford boss won't let that happen twice.

Fergie openly acknowledges his role as a surrogate parent to his younger players. Speaking in the *Independent* in 1994 he said: 'To build a football club you have to build a good, loyal base. The best is with the young kids you have brought in at thirteen years of age and you have said to their parents "do you trust me to look after your boy" and they have given that trust.'

Of course, young kids sometimes need discipline to mould them into fine human beings, and Fatherly Fergie knows just how to administer it.

According to Gordon Strachan, who played under Ferguson at both Aberdeen and Manchester United, 'he used fear as a motivator'. One celebrated incident while he was in charge at Pittodrie illustrates his managerial style perfectly. 'He once had four Aberdeen players publicly reciting a string of nursery rhymes – "Baa-baa Black Sheep", "Little Miss Muffet", "Humpty Dumpty" - after a landlady had reported them for damaging her airing cupboard during some high jinks,' reported Frank Keating in the *Guardian*. 'If they act like children,' explained Fergie, 'I treat them like children.'

The phrase 'Fergie's Fledglings' was coined to describe the first crop of young players he brought forward on joining Manchester United from Aberdeen. It conjures up images of a caring, nurturing figure, feeding those open-mouthed and open-minded youngsters with knowledge and experience until they are big and strong enough to fly the nest.

While we can safely say it is highly unlikely that Fergie ever actually put Ryan Giggs or David Beckham to the breast, metaphorically, at any rate, this is exactly what he has been doing. The warmth and pride in his words when describing the emergence of Beckham at Manchester United illustrates perfectly that there is more to the manager–player relationship in a successful football team than between worker and boss in most 'normal' walks of life.

'[When he was twelve] I said to his mother, don't worry, he'll grow,' he told Julie Welch in the *Sunday Telegraph*. 'And at fifteen he just shot up. Six foot one and gangling. They're like new-born foals those ones.'

So is it any wonder that, like real parents, managers often find it hard to realise when to let go and acknowledge that their players have grown up? They will often do everything for players: ferrying them from A to B, teaching them which knife to use at dinner, even telling them what to wear. (How many managers stamp their authority on a club when taking over by insisting on implementing a dress code for match days?) Some managers even organise courses designed to teach their players how to deal with the media. In other words, they're even telling them what to say as well!

The final, and possibly most telling, criterion that helps you identify the Mother Hen manager is the need to defend your charges in public at all cost. You might bawl players out in private but must never, ever let the outside world see you siding against them. This may leave you open to gossip and disapproval from outsiders, but it lets the player know that you're on their side. Alex Ferguson is a master at this, refusing to criticise any of his players in public even to the point of being accused of defending the indefensible. 'If anyone ever tried to criticise them in my presence they would get both barrels,' he has admitted.

As the ageing TV pundit Jimmy Hill discovered when Ferguson called him 'a prat' after the large-chinned one attacked Eric Cantona for a stamp on the Swindon Town player John Moncur. Apart from being the single most popular thing Alex Ferguson has ever done as a manager, it was a perfect example of the Mother Hen throwing a metaphorical protective wing over her chick and squawking loudly at an unwelcome outsider.

Everyone knew it was a diabolical action from Cantona – and at that time not an isolated one. Fergie probably thought so too, but there was no way he was going to take anyone's side against his prize 'garçon'. Instead the United boss, as so often before and since, used the criticism to help maintain the siege mentality he has established so successfully at Old Trafford.

'There were times when we deserved a kick up the backside,' remembers United striker Brian McClair. 'But he never publicly criticised us.'

Terry Venables is another manager to employ this tactic effectively. The best example occurred prior to Euro 96 amid the media outcry over the infamous Cathay Pacific flight home from the team's pre-tournament trip to the Far East. Whatever did or didn't happen to what may or may not have been overhead lockers and TV screens on that journey, the then England boss was resolute in his determination to support his team in public. By refusing to name the 'guilty' men or confirm the facts of what actually happened, he became the team's champion and protector as well as their coach. It was a master stroke. From being a 'good bloke' as well as a tactician the players respected for his past record, he suddenly became the 'responsible adult' who was shielding them from the condemnation and anger of the outside world – taking all the flak for what his charges had done and refusing point blank to blame them. Instead, he turned his righteous indignation and anger on the press corps baying for 'justice' and successfully managed to end up presenting the journalists as the guilty ones in many people's minds. How much effect this had on the England team's subsequent strength of spirit is hard to say, but it's unlikely to have done them any harm.

This is a favourite tactic among many managers, although it's not always so admirable. Often it will leave outsiders scratching their heads at the apparent inconsistency of it all. Some managers will turn a blind eye to their little darlings screwing around or beating up the wife but will fine them a week's wages for saying 'bollocks' in public. It never fails to amaze me that the most complaints we've had from managers about anything we've written in *90 Minutes* has been if we've quoted them or their players swearing. One manager rang up genuinely upset because we'd quoted him using a rude word. His complaint wasn't that he hadn't said it – he admitted he had – but that his children or his players might see it. How could he command their respect if they were to read something like that, he asked? The fact that he linked the two in his mind was telling.

One problem that every parent encounters when providing a home environment which encourages your charges to remain adolescents is that you can't be with them 24 hours a day. And when adolescents are let off the leash they tend to run a bit wild. The most celebrated example of this in the football world was, of course, George Best. Under the tender loving care of his first, inspirational manager, Matt Busby, he became one of the most exciting players of all time. But once Busby gave up the manager's chair at Old Trafford and a succession of new figureheads took over, none of whom matched the man who had taken Best under his wing or could command the respect that Sir Matt did, the player's form dipped until he became more famous for his off-pitch activities than for what he did on the park. The spectre of Best still haunts football – he is held up as a constant reminder to managers of what can happen if you don't control your players. His is seen as a wasted talent – and Alex Ferguson has admitted that it's had an effect on the way he nurtures youngsters coming through at Manchester United now.

'We are trying to do better for our young players now,' admitted Ferguson to the *Independent* in 1992. 'To let them grow up in their own time.' Bestie had talent, of course, but one thing he didn't have was a wife. Not to love, cherish and obey him but to do the manager's job at home when he wasn't around.

'Generally, I like family men,' former Bolton boss Bruce Rioch told *90 Minutes* on taking over at Arsenal in the summer of 1995. 'The only single man I bought at Bolton was Alan Thompson and he was nineteen at the time. We put him into digs and worked on finding him a girlfriend – which we did.' As if a reasonably good-looking nineteen-year-old footballer would have had any difficulty finding one on his own? As if it was really any of Rioch's business?

So what is it that possesses a football manager to think that, just because he represents the people paying a player's wages, that gives him the right to make personal decisions for him? Probably the fact that managers are rarely trained in the actual management of people. As with bringing up children, there are no courses in rearing players – it's all learned experience from the people who nurtured them in the football world.

Here, Rioch is the epitome of the over-protective mother. He feels the need to guide his charges – men who, in other walks of life, would be encouraged, indeed expected, to fend for themselves. Witness Phil Babb's recollection of an incident when he played under Rioch at Millwall.

'Bruce allowed us to go out as long as we were back by 11 p.m. Once I got back about 12.30 a.m. and Bruce was sitting by the front door. I was fined a week's wages and put on the transfer list.'

In an article in the *Sunday Mirror* in 1984, Alex Ferguson revealed a similar need to see his charges settled down. 'I have to admit I quite like my players to be married,' he said. 'They're young and good-looking and you hope they are going to meet a nice girl and settle down. A father wants to make sure his son does well. He's in control of his kids and he wants the best for them . . . it's only natural that you care.'

Fergie may think he's being a father figure but he's displaying classic Mother Hen characteristics here.

Of course, this is not just a parent's wish to see their little darling settled down and happy. There are very sound, practical reasons for this kind of approach to 'man-child management'. For if you find your players a good woman to settle down with, you are effectively providing them with a surrogate mother to take care of them in your absence. Your job of primary nurturer is done.

Shelley Webb, the wife of former England midfielder Neil, once recalled that when the couple went on a family holiday her husband – generally thought of as one of the more articulate and intelligent players – didn't even know what to do with his passport. Despite having travelled the world through his work, he'd always had someone else to make sure he got where he was going – to do his thinking for him. The common stereotype of the footballer's wife is of a big-haired, big-chested blonde, picked up in Stringfellow's, who'll put up with her man-child's tantrums and prolonged absences when playing away from home (in all its meanings) for a stone-clad mock-Tudor Barrett home and occasional breast augmentation operation to say sorry for any indiscretions that may have come her way. Like getting caught. Yet it's surely no coincidence that in real life the footballer's wife is usually an eminently capable, sensible woman.

Alex Ferguson is one manager who recognises the importance of this often-overlooked member of the squad. 'This is the man who gave the Aberdeen players' wives a tough team talk before the 1983 Cup-Winners' Cup final against Real Madrid,' recalled Sue Mott in the *Sunday Times* in 1991. Trying to find them a good woman – at least one that hasn't been picked up in a hotel bar on a pre-season tour – is only the half of it, of course.

Traditionally in this country, the manager's role has been a complex one. Not just a case of choosing and coaching the players, but negotiating their wages, conducting transfers, talking to parents of potential schoolboy and apprentice signings and – in David Pleat's case during a recent interview with *90 Minutes* – answering the phones as well. It's a role that in some clubs is changing with the introduction of this year's current craze: the Technical Director, following on from previous 'must have' football accessories like training tops with the manager's initials on and, er, wing-backs. At most clubs, though, the manager is still the public and private face of the club – and most of them like it that way.

'I think managers take on too much,' says Luton Town chairman David Kohler. 'They build their own little empire around them. They're the father figure, which is OK, but at the end of the day, if it's not going right, they have to accept the blame.'

One thing managers are increasingly doing is getting involved in the commercial side of football by advising their players on the sponsorship and promotion deals they are offered. It's not something they have to do – and you could argue that very few of them would have the necessary experience to be able to advise with any

real insight into the subject. But the Mother Hen manager sees it
as another area where their sons need a protective hand guiding
their every move to stop them being exploited.

Often a young player will be unable to sign a deal without
getting the all-clear from his manager, who may have to oversee
individual contracts for wearing boots, shin guards, gloves and
leisure wear. For the overworked gaffer, it's a question of weigh-
ing up the financial benefits such things can bring an emerging star
against the dangers of the footballing side of their profession being
submerged under a sea of contractual obligations.

Kevin Keegan, one of the few managers who experienced the
promotional and endorsement merry-go-round as a player, appeared to be one of the most relaxed about dealing with this
aspect of the game. Maybe it's because he knows it is possible to
come through that whole media circus and keep not only your
sanity but the dosh you earned from it as well. Or maybe because,
unlike Alex Ferguson, he didn't try to be his players' parent.
'Football is having a boom time, everyone's talking about it,' he
told Michael Hodges in *Goal* magazine shortly before his resignation. 'But you can't say, "I want a private life, I want to be away
from it." You can't have your cake and eat it. That's the way it is
and we accept that.' Or not, as seems to be Keegan's case.

A Mother Hen manager would never appear on nationwide TV
offering to bow down and worship one of his own players, as
Kevin Keegan did to Newcastle midfielder Rob Lee during the
1995/96 season. It would – pardon the pun – upset the pecking
order; an unthinkable challenge to the traditional player/manager
role.

Keegan was content to let high-profile players like David Ginola
and Les Ferdinand go off on their own to indulge in the odd spot
of modelling or single-handed promotion of the English raspberry
jelly industry. Publicly anyway, he treated them like adults. Kevin
Keegan represents the new breed of manager in this country: the
young, independently wealthy men who made a fortune out of the
game as players and travelled abroad to widen their knowledge of
the game – and life. People who have grown up within the new,
more money-obsessed football world. People who don't have to
do the job for the money. People who can walk away.

Though a manager of the new breed may lose his rag with
members of the media and wield power in his own domain with

just as much ruthlessness and determination as a Ferguson or Brian Clough, he knows how to play the game on and off the pitch, as competent commercially as he is tactically.

Alex Ferguson is very much of the old school. Anyone who is not part of his Manchester United empire is automatically treated with mistrust. What do they want out of us? How do I protect my family from this outside threat? How can I make their lives as difficult as possible and the lives of my players free from pressure and untainted by the evils of commercialism?

Who's to say he's wrong? His record speaks for itself. It's often been pointed out that of the talented youngsters at Aberdeen like Eric Black and John Hewitt whom Ferguson brought on during his successful managerial spell at Pittodrie, few went on to fulfil their enormous potential as players. This is no doubt a major clue as to why Ferguson has developed his fiercely protective managerial style, in which he is openly antagonistic to anyone from outside the safe confines of Old Trafford. Quite simply, he sees them as a threat to his players' current and future chances of success. Ultimately, it's a wish to prolong childhood; to keep the pressures and troubles of the real, adult world away from his virginal, unblemished footballing innocents. Yes, even Roy Keane.

6 The Rise and Fall of Arrigo Sacchi

Is a manager's playing background little more than an anecdote?

By Gavin Hamilton

Arrigo Sacchi slipped almost unnoticed into Milanello, Milan's palatial training complex, during the summer of 1987. The Dutch internationals Ruud Gullit and Marco Van Basten, new signings from PSV Eindhoven and Ajax Amsterdam respectively, and two of the most exciting footballers anywhere in the world, attracted all the attention. Sacchi, in contrast, was a little man from a little town, Fusignano, a few kilometres from the Adriatic coast. He had never coached a First Division team, and yet he was to be the making of the modern Milan, guiding them to the Italian Championship, two European Cups and two World Club Cups in four trail-blazing years at San Siro.

Football is full of success stories. It is the nature of the game. But what was most remarkable about Sacchi was that he never played professional football. He was not even a decent amateur. The Arrigo Sacchi story is not the tale of the journeyman footballer who became the all-conquering manager. Sacchi never made the journey in the first place.

Italy, of course, under Sacchi's management and with more than a little help from Roberto Baggio, reached the 1994 World Cup final. The coach of the Brazil side that won that dour match on penalties at the Pasadena Rose Bowl was Carlos Alberto Parreira, another ugly duckling who, like Sacchi, never kicked a ball in professional anger. Sacchi and Parreira are living proof of what many had suspected all along: that you do not need to have been a successful player to be a successful manager. Or, as Sacchi has put it, 'you don't have to have been a horse to be a jockey'. You don't have to have been a player to know how to organise them. The best managers are those who understand their players and have a playing system the players understand. Period. But is that all there is to it? Is a manager's playing background little more than an anecdote, a mere footnote on his CV? What are the factors that guarantee success in modern football management? And do Sacchi's subsequent experiences with Italy at Euro 96 suggest that international management is a complex business for which no mere mortal can be properly prepared?

Silvio Berlusconi, the media mogul whose millions were the initial catalyst for the rise in Milan's fortunes in the 1980s, took a huge gamble when he plucked Arrigo Sacchi from obscurity at Second-Division Parma. Sacchi had taken the Serie B side to the brink of the Italian First Division since his appointment in the summer of 1985, when Parma were down in the dumps after relegation to the Third Division. In April 1987, the day after Milan sacked Swedish coach Nils Liedholm, they crashed out of the Italian Cup at Parma. A few weeks later, Sacchi got the call from Berlusconi.

Sacchi had begun his career with home-town team Fusignano, a modest amateur side but nothing more. As a player he had not been good enough to grace even their ranks and was advised to switch his interests to coaching, initially with the youth team. As he looked for his break, the young Sacchi spent his days working as a salesman for his father's shoe company. References to Sacchi's former career as a shoemaker fall wide of the mark. Cobblers, you might say. Anyway, he soon left it all behind to pursue his coaching ambitions on a full-time basis.

From Fusignano, Sacchi moved to another amateur side, Bellaria, before achieving success with the Cesena youth team. He moved on to Rimini in 1982, before moving to Parma three years later. There, he began his technical and tactical revolution, introducing a zonal defensive system and developing the pressing game that was to prove so successful at Milan.

Sacchi arrived at Milan as the club were emerging from one of the darkest periods in its history. The 1978/79 League title, Milan's tenth, had been followed within a year by a match-rigging scandal which resulted in punishment by relegation to Serie B. By the time Berlusconi took control of the club in 1986, Milan had won promotion back to the top division, been relegated again, this time purely as a result of events on the pitch, and returned to Serie A with a gutsy promotion challenge, only for the then club president Farina to run off to Africa, leaving the club with large debts.

Just as Berlusconi was to revolutionise the club off the pitch, with his (pipe)dream of a European Superleague, Sacchi was to have a dramatic impact on team affairs. The Englishmen Ray Wilkins and Mark Hateley had been released by the club that summer to make way for Gullit and Van Basten. Frank Rijkaard arrived a year later. The Dutch trio, under Sacchi's tutelage, helped Milan become one of the greatest club sides of all time.

The biggest change was not *what* Gullit, Van Basten and Rijkaard did; it was *how* they were allowed to do it. Sacchi developed a playing system that gave freedom of expression to the Dutchmen's imaginative and skilful soccer. The tired old *catenaccio* approach – literally, the padlock: a sweeper, strict man-to-man marking and reliance on the cautious counter-attack – was replaced by zonal marking and a chasing and harrying game. It was an exciting approach which lent itself to attacking soccer, and it changed the face of Italian club football.

Gullit was impressed with Sacchi: 'He's a good coach who appears to know what he's doing,' he said. '[Giovanni] Trapattoni at Inter believes that good habits start with getting the defence right. Sacchi places more emphasis on going forward.'

At Sacchi's Milan, the philosophy was simple: get them before they get you. Previously, players had been motivated by fear. 'Twenty years ago, all our football was based on fear of the opposition and how to stop them,' Sacchi told *World Soccer* in 1992. 'Some teams still play that way, but now we have teams who want to entertain the supporters by winning with skilful, attacking play.'

Milan won the *Scudetto* in Sacchi's first season. In a dramatic North v. South title decider in Naples, they beat Maradona's Napoli 3–2 at the San Paulo stadium. Van Basten, who had missed much of the season through injury, scored the winning goal. The gateway to Europe, and Berlusconi's dreams, had been opened.

In Sacchi's second season, an injury-hit Milan stuttered their way into the new year in mid-table, a poor run of results capped by defeat against Inter in the derby. Sacchi was under pressure to deliver because Berlusconi wanted a return for his money. Milan responded with a spectacular 5–0 defeat of Real Madrid in the Champions Cup semifinal second leg, followed by a 4–0 rout of Steaua Bucharest in the final. Milan, and the three Dutchmen in particular, were in earth-shattering form that balmy night in Barcelona.

Milan went on to win the World Club Cup in Toyko that December, with a 1–0 defeat of Atlético Nacional of Colombia. That was followed by another Champions Cup (1–0 over Benfica in Vienna) and the World Club Cup again, this time against Paraguay's Olimpia. It was the first time in 25 years that a European side had retained the intercontinental prize.

Under Sacchi, Milan took their tally of international trophies to eleven, more than any other club in the world. Crucial to the success was the form of the three Dutchmen. The other team players, Italian to a man, responded to the Dutchmen's brilliance, argued Sacchi, by raising their own game. 'My dream, and the dream of Milan, was to have a side totally comprised of Italian players. That is difficult in Italy because you have six or seven clubs who will not sell their players to anyone. So you are forced to enter the foreign market. These imports have been extremely useful because their experience, knowledge, skill and resilience are a source of great information. They produce different ways of playing, and the Italian players improve because they have to make an effort to match that level of excellence.'

Sacchi, the mould-breaker, revelled in the praise. At Milan he was the Great Innovator, the man who came from nowhere to release *calcio* from the shackles of *catenaccio*. The Italian players provided the technique and discipline, the Dutch offered the fantasy and invention, and Sacchi took the credit. Here was a man who may not have played professionally, but he knew what was needed to win, and with style, too.

While Sacchi's Milan were easily the best club side in the world, Italia '90 came and went. The national side, coached by the amiable Azeglio Vicini, 'failed'. Defeat by Argentina on penalties in the semifinal hurt, not least because expectations, as always, were so high.

The position of Italian team manager carries the weight of expectations of a whole nation. And few nations expect as much as Italy, especially as Vittorio Pozzo set such a high standard by winning the World Cup in 1934 and 1938. Since then, with the notable and worthy exception of Enzo Bearzot's victorious 1982 side, the expectations have proved too much.

Vicini was an honest, hard-working coach who had never played international football, nor been a club manager, though he was a useful outside right with Sampdoria. He was groomed through the Federation coaching system, the loyal assistant whose chance came after achieving success with the Italian Under-21 side. At the 1990 World Cup, Vicini conducted himself with great dignity, but that was not enough. He paid the price for not winning the tournament on home soil. Critics saw him as *un uomo del Palazzo*, a Federation yes-man who did his job diligently and obediently, but not outstandingly. Vicini's Italy were not winners.

Under Vicini, Italy were still playing *catenaccio*. They cracked under pressure. They lacked ruthlessness, a killer touch. They never won the games that mattered. What was needed, said Federation president Antonio Materrese, was someone with a winning record as a club coach. 'The team cannot invent a coach, but has to go for a coach who has had international success at club level and who is available.' Never mind that he never played the game professionally. Arrigo Sacchi, come on down.

It had long been hinted that Sacchi would take over as national team coach. Milan were playing the sort of football that, if transferred to the international arena, would blow all the opposition away. 'Milan are light years ahead of all 24 teams at the World Cup,' boasted Berlusconi at Italia '90. 'Thank goodness Milan cannot play in the World Cup,' exclaimed Brazil manager Sebastião Lazaroni. 'No one else would stand a chance!'

Sacchi formally resigned from Milan on 31 May 1991, officially because of stress. Despite his phenomenal success, his departure was not greatly mourned at San Siro. Berlusconi had had his fair share of disagreements with his coach over transfers and wanted someone who was more receptive to his 'expert' opinions (a big *ciao!* to Fabio Capello). Meanwhile, some of the players, notably Van Basten, were fed up with Sacchi's sergeant-major approach.

Sacchi's appointment to the national team post raised the stakes significantly. He had arrived at Milan with nothing to lose, an average amateur footballer with no reputation to protect. He was now Sacchi the Great Innovator. A nation licked its lips in anticipation of an Italy side playing the sort of football that won Milan worldwide respect and a record number of trophies. With Sacchi now under the spotlight, the more sceptical could now ask the Big Question: namely, how much of Milan's success was down to Sacchi, and how much to the Dutch trio of Gullit, Van Basten and Rijkaard?

Sacchi's Italy switched to a zonal defence after years of man-to-man marking. He brought the rump of his Milan side into the national set-up – Donadoni, Evani, Baresi, Maldini, Costacurta, even the ageing Ancelotti. Italy qualified for the World Cup finals in the USA, but not with any of the great panache that had been hoped for. Sacchi demanded a national team that worked hard, ran hard and played hard – but it soon became clear that not all the players were responding to his approach. At one training session, an exasperated Sacchi was heard screaming at his charges: 'There are people here who are not helping me. I need people to help me!'

The Great Innovator had difficulty forcing his requirements on players who were used to club managers who advocated a more cautious approach. Sacchi demanded a work-rate from players that inevitably stifled their creative talent. His approach had worked with Milan. And there was the rub. It was a whole new ball game, and Sacchi found he could not adapt. He wanted his Italy to 'do a Milan'. But the *Azzurris*' performances under Sacchi were not the convincing, winning displays from which Milan drew their enormous self-confidence. And when their confidence began to drain away, the players reverted to their more defensive club game. When the star men, the Baggios and Signoris, played within themselves or were excluded, the lesser players had no way of raising their game.

When players would not respond to his methods, Sacchi refused to accept that he was wrong. The stubbornness that had been apparent in disputes with Berlusconi over players appeared again. (Sacchi had stood his ground over the arrival of Frank Rijkaard in 1988; Berlusconi had wanted the Argentinian Claudio Borghi as Milan's third foreigner.) Sacchi's response was to bring in new faces – all the time. There was almost constant turnover. He shuffled his pack according to the needs and form of the moment.

In his first eighteen months, Sacchi called up 55 players, By the time Italy left for the USA finals, 68 players had received the call. And yet, in America, Italy reached the final. Sacchi, some argued, had finally worked his magic because he had the players together for an extended period of time. Others thought, and suggested, differently. Vicini did not criticise his successor directly but said: 'Second place in the World Cup finals was a great result, all right. But fans know how to tell one thing from another. Italy got into the second round as the sixteenth of sixteen. And then in subsequent games, particularly against Nigeria, the side was within inches of elimination. The team survived on the last-minute improvised brilliance of one or two individuals rather than on any established team pattern.'

Someone at the Italian Federation agreed. Details of Sacchi's enormous pay deal (£5 million over four years) were leaked. The news put Sacchi under enormous pressure, which became almost unbearable when, in November 1994, Italy lost in Palermo to Croatia. The 2–1 scoreline concealed the extent of Italy's humiliation. They had scored in injury time, little consolation for a performance in which they were utterly outclassed. 'SHAME ON YOU!' thundered the *Corriere dello Sport*. A telephone poll revealed that more than 70 per cent of fans wanted Sacchi to resign immediately.

There appeared to be no way back. Sacchi retreated to his bunker, refusing to relent on the stubborn approach that had made him so many enemies. He could find no place in his squad, let alone his team, for Roberto Baggio, Giuseppe Signori or Gianluca Vialli. Although qualification for the 1996 European Championship was achieved, ensuring that Sacchi's job was safe for the tournament, humiliation followed. Italy, one of the pre-tournament favourites, crashed out in the first round.

Yet Sacchi came out fighting. He was castigated for playing the clearly weary Alessandro del Piero. For starting with Casiraghi, in preference to Ravanelli, against Germany when the striker had been so ineffectual as a sub against the Czechs. Above all, for dropping five players for the Czech game (lost 2–1). He fired back: 'My biggest mistake was not to pick up on the drop in athletic tension after the opening game against Russia. Our concentration wasn't quite right and I did nothing to correct this . . . Our soccer was second to none, yet as far as our mental attitude goes, we were inferior.' He went on to call his critics mere 'word traders' and said that he had no intention of changing his tactics.

That was too much for the *Corriere dello Sport*. 'But This Sacchi, He's Learned Nothing,' bellowed its front-page headline. On the same page, an angry leader proclaimed: 'Sacchi continues to behave as if the Italian team were his own toy. That's not the case. Among the many, too many things that Sacchi has failed to understand, there is the consideration that the Italian team belongs to us all. But he, however, has nothing to share with the world, except a limitless arrogance that is daily more insufferable.'

That Sacchi lasted as long as he did owed a great deal to the failure to elect a successor to Federation president Materrese, who carried the can for the failure in England. The offer to return to Milan in December 1996 gave Sacchi the chance to jump before he was pushed. Milan, it has since emerged, approached former coach Capello a matter of months after he had been replaced by the hapless Uruguayan Oscar Washington Tabarez. But Capello declined to break the contract signed that summer with Real Madrid. So Sacchi it was.

That Sacchi should return to Milan, the scene of his greatest triumphs, after his failure with Italy is poignant. He said in early 1994 that 'My Italy will be a great team only when it seems to have lots of time on the ball and, in contrast, is quick to win back possession.' In other words, when it is Milan Mark II. Yet Italy, as Sacchi never realised, or was never prepared to accept, could never be a club side. He wanted Italy to adopt Milan's *panchina lunga*, the 'long bench' system where you effectively have two teams to choose from. In five years he called no fewer than 93 players to squad sessions, using 77 in 53 games. Fifty-five received their first caps and one, 32-year-old Mauro Tassotti, entered the record books as the oldest debutant in Italian history.

Sacchi's experiences with Milan and Italy expose some crucial differences between club and international football. With Milan, he cracked it because he changed players and tactics but had time to explain those changes to the players. With Italy he never had that luxury. Bobby Robson has said that club football is nothing like the international game. It takes time to adapt, he says. 'When you manage a club and you get beat it's only a couple of days to the next match and you can turn everything around. With England, if you lose, you carry the weight of that for a month, sometimes two months or three. It's a different kind of pressure and nothing in the club game can prepare you for it.'

Sacchi never escaped the jibe that his Milan side owed a great deal to the three Dutchmen. The then Soviet manager Anatoly Bishovets summed up many people's feelings when he said: 'Milan's success was based on three players on whom Sacchi cannot call for Italy.' Giovanni Trapattoni, rumoured to be the Federation's first choice ahead of Sacchi in 1991, has said: 'Sacchi's Milan won one out of four championships, but its style of play was glorified by an effective propaganda machine. I'd like to have seen that Milan without the three Dutchmen and all those Italian internationals. You can try explaining the same tactical dispositions to eleven ordinary players and they'll still be eleven duffers.'

The most damning evidence for the prosecution was the record of Fabio Capello, Sacchi's successor at San Siro. Capello, a former Italian international and loyal assistant to Sacchi, won four League titles in five seasons. His Milan side played a more cautious game, not least because he did not have the three Dutchmen to provide the flair. Rijkaard was back in Holland, Gullit had decamped to Sampdoria, and Van Basten was battling with the ankle injury that was to force his early retirement from football.

Because Sacchi never answered the Big Question about the three Dutchmen, his lack of playing experience was never used as a stick to beat him; his critics never needed it. Ultimately, Sacchi failed with Italy because he was out of his depth. He survived on a wing and a prayer, hiding behind tactical schemes and systems. In the end, Sacchi the amateur could not stand shoulder to shoulder with his star players and look them in the eye. His past caught up with him.

Compare and contrast Sacchi's Italy with Carlos Alberto Parreira's Brazil. For Parreira, it was all about preparation – 'approach is everything,' he said – and Brazil won the 1994 World Cup because they were the best-prepared team. Parreira may have not played the game professionally, but he was no World Cup virgin. His first experience of the World Cup had been in 1970, as physical trainer to Mario Zagallo's winners. He had also been in charge of Kuwait in 1982 and the United Arab Emirates in 1990. Zagallo was Parreira's assistant in America, and between them they had experience of seven World Cups. Parreira is one of only two men, the other is Bora Milutinovic, who has been in charge of three different countries' World Cup finals campaigns.

Parreira knew what to expect of his players and, in turn, he knew what the players expected of him. 'I didn't have to teach our players how to play football,' he said, 'but I did have to teach them how to play as a unit, which is very difficult for Brazilian players because they are all such individuals.' With shades of Sacchi, he added, 'my prime concern was for my players to concentrate on playing without the ball. In the past World Cups we had been good only when we were on the ball.'

Brazil's 1994 vintage may not have been one to savour, but Parreira had learned the lessons of history. 'My learning began in 1970. That's where I saw what was necessary to be a World Cup winner. In 1970 and 1974, I learned what mistakes *not* to make.' The side he put out was more traditional than Lazaroni's work-manlike 1990 side, but more modern than Tele Santana's 1982 crowd-pleasers. He also made sure that off the pitch the players bonded. At the training camp, newspapers were banned, as were wives and girlfriends. Nothing would drive his players to distraction.

Unlike Sacchi, Parreira stayed loyal to his players and was not afraid to consult them. Romario was able to declare before the tournament: 'The players are a lot more important than the coach. I'm important. All I have to do is put my shirt on and score goals.' The captain, Dunga, said after the finals: 'I have played under many coaches but Carlos Alberto was exceptional. He gave us the freedom to discuss things and speak our mind, but he was always in charge. He wasn't afraid to consult us and act on what we told him. He gave us what you might call a winning mentality.'

Parreira also quit while he was ahead, moving to a club position in Spain after the 1994 finals. His first spell in charge of the national side had ended after Brazil lost to Uruguay in the 1983 South American championships. 'There's no fun in being Brazil's national coach because the responsibility is so vast,' he said. 'There was pressure all the way, partly because it was such a long time since Brazil last won the World Cup. Maybe at the next World Cup the pressure will not be the same again. Either way, I decided I was not interested in finding out. Three years in the job is more than enough for any normal human being.'

Parreira had been a successful club coach – he won the Rio championship with Fluminense and the Brazilian national title twice, with Fluminense and Bragantino – but it was experience of international football, with Brazil and others, that was important. Parreira proved that the only way to gain experience of international management is on the job. Experience of club management is of little use.

The Italians, in replacing Sacchi with Under-21 coach Cesare Maldini, went for an in-house appointment, just as they had done

The Cult of the Manager

with Azeglio Vicini. Maldini may revert to a *catenaccio* style, but he has a proven track record at international level, winning three European titles with Italy's Under-21s.

The Italians no doubt cast a jealous glance in the direction of Germany, the most successful country of the modern era. Helmut Schön became number two to Sepp Herberger's West German side in 1955, becoming national manager in 1964. In doing so he set a pattern of succession that has been broken only once, when Beckenbauer, one of Schön's protégés, was appointed in 1984. Current manager Berti Vogts went straight from playing to the DFB coaching staff in 1979, first taking charge of the youth side, then the Under-21s, before becoming the Kaiser's assistant in 1986. At Euro 96, he did an admirable job making a silk purse from a sow's ear.

That neither Sacchi nor Parreira had a playing career to speak of proved little more than a footnote. Sacchi's 'failure' with Italy had nothing to do with his lack of playing experience. At Milan, the players responded to Sacchi's ideas. With Italy, they did not. Sacchi, more than anyone else, proved that a manager can be successful irrespective of his playing background if he brings a set of ideas to a team which the players respond to.

Roy Hodgson, Sven Goran Eriksson, David Pleat, Lawrie McMenemy, Javier Clemente, Richard Moller Nielsen, Leo Been-hakker, Valeri Lobanovsky, Sebastião Lazaroni, Craig Brown, Andy Roxburgh. I could go on. All successful modern managers who either couldn't cut it as professional players, or whose playing careers were cut short through injury. The ugly duckings who turned the tables. Arsène Wenger's immediate success with Arsenal is a case in point. Eyebrows were raised when the London club, who had enough alcoholics, gamblers and drug addicts on their books for Highbury to pass for an annexe of nearby Holloway prison, sacked the disciplinarian Bruce Rioch and brought in the cerebral Frenchman. Swift exits were predicted for such ageing and cumbersome players as Steve Bould, as Wenger cleared the decks for a new Continental class. Yet, the new manager made few personnel changes and quickly fostered a team spirit and sense of belonging among the players that took Arsenal to the top of the Premiership.

Wenger never achieved a great deal as a player; the highest level he reached was the French Second Division with Strasbourg. Yet his ideas and his knowledge of the Continental transfer market reaped early rewards for Arsenal. No other Premiership manager would have had the nous to sign Patrick Vieira, the thinking man's Carlton Palmer.

Compare Wenger's Arsenal with Bryan Robson's Middlesbrough. Much was made of Robson's reputation as a player attracting quality foreign players to Teesside. But where has it got Boro? Robson was an aggressive but inspiring character as a player. As a manager, where a more thoughtful approach is needed, his judgement has often been found wanting.

Player/managers have never been a great success in England. The most successful, Kenny Dalglish, did the double with a Liverpool team that was built by someone else, Joe Fagan, and quit when the players got too old and the pressure got too much. Player/managers are a rare breed on the Continent, where often you have to gain a certificate before you can coach, not necessarily a good idea, but something players tend to do when they have retired.

If a manager's playing career is of such importance, why have so many of the world's great players failed to make great managers? Johan Cruyff and Franz Beckenbauer are the exceptions that prove the rule. Even then, there are many in Barcelona who do not worship at the altar of Cruyff, the coaching genius. Beckenbauer has gone on record as saying how frustrating and unrewarding he found management. As coach of West Germany, he discovered that it's impossible to teach 'ordinary' players the skills that came naturally to him.

Diego Maradona's brief spell in management proved disastrous. Michel Platini took over the French national side and led them on a record unbeaten run, but the team caved in without a fight at the 1992 European Championship in Sweden, the sort of stage on which Platini would have excelled as a player. Alfredo Di Stéfano and Ferenc Puskas took Valencia and Panathinaikos respectively to European finals, but those successes were mere trifles when compared to their playing careers.

Of the sixteen coaches in charge of teams competing in the 1996/97 UEFA Champions League, only four ever played international football, three if you discount Oscar Tabarez, replaced at Milan by Sacchi ... For the modern manager, blood and thunder are not enough. He must understand his players and have their respect, but most of all, he must have a set of technical and tactical ideas which the players can understand at the training ground and implement on the pitch.

Arrigo Sacchi brought a set of ideas to Milan which turned out to be revolutionary. His ideas worked because the players knew they had a system to play to, and with teammates of the quality of Gullit, Van Basten and Rijkaard, the players' confidence was raised. The same ideas failed with Italy because Sacchi failed to recognise the different game he was playing.

It's no coincidence that Sacchi returned to Milan a few months after the journeyman's journeyman, Graham Taylor, was welcomed back at Watford. Taylor, like Sacchi, was found to be out of his depth at international level. He refused to accept that the basic methods that had worked so well at Watford would not take England to the World Cup finals. Perhaps we all find our rightful level in the end.

7 The Life of Brian

By Ian Edwards

John Robertson hovered, smirking in the background, as Brian Clough administered one of his sternest rebukes, his right index finger jabbing at an unsuspecting journalist who had shown the temerity to suggest in print that a victory the previous night had been 'flattering'. Clough's attention swiftly turned to Robertson and he barked: 'Robbo, put that bloody fag out now.' Quick as a flash the cigarette was under the left foot that helped win the 1979 European Cup and extinguished in the same emphatic manner as the Scottish winger disposed of his opponents.

Before the smell of burning carpet had dissipated, Clough was on his way across the car park, heading for his office, bouncing a tennis ball. Robertson sat disconsolate, head in hands, and admitted: 'I'm 37, married with children and I'm still frightened to death of the bloke.'

Robertson's fear was an emotion Clough could inspire in the strongest of men. His lionheart captain, Stuart Pearce, whose courage knew no bounds, let slip that even he had been scared on one or two occasions, but common theories about Clough's managerial style, which dismiss him as a sort of Fidel Castro of football, are misguided and woefully inadequate.

Brian Howard Clough was much more than a dictator in a green sweatshirt. No one could have dominated football in word and deed for almost three decades on such a flimsy ticket. Even the most uncontrollable megalomaniacs are eventually overturned by rebellious uprisings. If all Clough possessed in his make-up was the ability to frighten the wits out of people, his players would not have been able or willing to perform for him, he would never have won a trophy, and he certainly wouldn't have lasted 28 years in an industry with a casualty rate slightly lower than that of an abattoir.

The fact that his name is etched in the record books as a two-time winner of the League Championship, with two such unfashionable clubs as Derby County and Nottingham Forest, who he also guided to successive European Cup victories, could never have been achieved simply by taking a stick to his players. The Derby side, which he assembled from scratch with his partner Peter Taylor, certainly wouldn't have displayed such loyalty as to place themselves perilously close to breach of contract with the Football League by threatening not to play a match in a bid to get Clough reinstated after he and Taylor resigned in 1974.

Clough's legacy is far more complex and extraordinary, so much so that in his autobiography he writes: 'They tell me that people have always wondered how I did it. That fellow professionals and public alike have been fascinated and puzzled and intrigued by the Clough managerial methods and technique and would love to know my secret. I've got news for them – so would I.'

If Clough could have sat down and written the definitive blueprint for successful management it would have debunked virtually all the dogma and theory that cluttered up the desks of all his contemporaries. He was the first to realise that two men could manage better than one. He despised the coaching manuals, especially if they came from Lancaster Gate. He was innovative in his handling of his players, making sure they were relieved of the tedium of routine, and for that he received what every manager needs to be a success: respect. That is the key when it comes to analysing the brilliant, brash, eccentric and unconventional approach that made him unique. Quite simply, Clough redefined the art of management with a heady cocktail of ingredients which took him to the pinnacle of his profession and made him, by public consent, the best manager England never had.

Clough could be an awkward cuss, unforgiving, bombastic and downright rude, yet in the next breath he could be charming, compassionate and generous. He was once described by club secretary Ken Smales as 'a wolf in sheep's clothing. Sometimes a sheep in wolf's clothing. But mostly he is just himself.'

When he became the youngest ever to pass his FA coaching badge at the age of 29, after his career as a goalscorer was cut short by a cruciate ligament injury, even he, with his unbridled confidence, didn't know whether he had what it takes to manage.

It's one thing having a badge with the FA's three lions on it. How, or whether, you can use it is another. Management, as Clough went on to prove unquestionably, is more than just rigid following of dogma. If it were as simple as following coaching routines, why aren't all managers on the same level?

Clough first cut his managerial teeth as a youth team coach at Sunderland, where he quickly discovered that young players preferred to play the game, rather than performing endless laps of the training ground. It was a method that served him well. Coaching, tactics and training as organised by others can complicate and confuse players. Clough sought to eradicate any such problems by simplifying *everything*.

For all the explanations given, pointing to his unorthodox ways, many miss the point entirely. When boiled down, his views and methods were based around a commonsense approach designed to get the very best out of each and every one of his players.

As his attitude to training perfectly indicates. Forest's training was known throughout the League as the least strenuous. Some even tried to blame their relegation in 1993 on a lack of physical jerks, although that was due to other reasons which we'll come to later. Clough's training methods for the previous 27 years as a manager had never been questioned, and how could they when his results were so startlingly successful? He could never see the point of spending hours slogging his athletes and leaving nothing in their legs for matches, and there is nothing strange or complex in that. Players like to play football, not run as if training for a marathon, and Clough recognised that, preferring a stroll down the banks of the Trent, a five-a-side and a stroll back for a hot bath.

He argued that playing the game was practising what was expected of his men when they were playing League and Cup matches. He was never fond of athletes. Robertson is a perfect example of that. He couldn't run and was one of the worst trainers at the club, but give him a yard of grass with the ball at his feet and he performed magic.

Coaching was equally simple. There were four basic principles according to Clough: defenders headed the ball or tackled, wingers crossed it or had pace, strikers scored goals or made them, and midfielders had to have the basic ability to pass.

There were no blackboards or chalk. No huge dossiers on opponents. Clough operated on the 'bollocks to 'em' theory of football management. He never worried about the other side, only about what his own team was going to do, and the one thing he insisted on above all else was a simple approach to playing the game.

He would accept nothing less than seeing his players pass the ball so that it brushed the grass. Kick-and-rush, route-one football was anathema to him, and players have been substituted by him for attempting something too complicated when a simpler option was available.

Often he would not be seen until ten minutes before kick-off. He would walk into the dressing room, place a towel on the floor, put a ball on it and say: 'That's what we play with. Go and win it.' Why do people argue that such actions are those of an eccentric? What was more unusual was the idea of him forcing all his players to drink ten bottles of champagne between them on the eve of a Wembley final, which they happened to win 3–2 against Southampton the following day.

Such actions would be severely frowned upon now in the days of 48-hour curfews and high-carbohydrate diets, but all Clough wanted was to make sure his players were relaxed. That to him was the key to virtually everything.

What's more, he and Taylor had it down to a fine art. If the dressing room was particularly tense, Taylor would crack a one-liner and the players would fall about laughing in an instant. Simple. Clough, unlike many, recognised that for people in any walk of life – not just professional football – to perform at their very best, they have to be calm and at ease with themselves. He made that crucial discovery when he made his debut for Middlesbrough. His manager, Bob Dennison, sent him on to the field as a nineteen-year-old with the words 'It's up to you now, son' ringing in his ears.

Clough remembers one thing about the game: he failed to score. It was one of the few blank days in a professional career that brought him an amazing 251 goals in 274 matches. 'He sent me out on a downer. He put fear in my heart when he should have put me at ease. It was a mistake I never made in 28 years as a manager,' Clough said in later years.

Psychology, man management, motivation, call it what you will, it was one of his strongest points. If a player was having a hard time on the pitch, or was taking unreasonable flak in the papers, Clough would come into his own. He would make sure he said the right things in public and in private, make sure his wards were protected. He knew when he had to leap to a player's defence, and if they merited it, sometimes even if they didn't, he would give them his seal of approval which was worth ten times that of any other manager.

Clough was an intensely loyal man. If players reciprocated he would go out of his way to defend them. John McGovern, who followed him from Derby to Leeds and on to Forest, suffered terribly at the hands of the Forest supporters, but Clough never deserted him. In such circumstances it would have been easy for a player to seek a way out, to bow to the criticism and leave. Managers, though few would ever admit to the negative influence of those who walk through the turnstiles, have made decisions to protect players, but Clough would go the other way and shame the supporters into appreciating a player's qualities if he was certain of them.

Such a show of solidarity made players want to play for him. Virtually every player that signed for Nottingham Forest did so because of him. A glance through all their cuttings files will show how desperate they were to play for the man. He attracted players as a magnet does iron filings, and those that came saw their stature grow throughout the game. When you have players queueing up, ready to give everything they have and more, then success is never too far away. Players looked at Clough's League record and instinctively knew he was talking sense. They looked at his managerial statistics, which reeked of success.

Players are not stupid. When someone who has only played non-League football tells them to do something and it fails, they naturally question the grounds on which this order was made. They could never do that with Clough, and he knew it.

Once, he had his men running through nettles, as Forest trained behind the Iron Curtain before a European Cup tie in vests and shorts in freezing temperatures, while he stood watching in a fur coat. But the very fact that players were prepared to go through such rituals, without moaning directly to him, was his way of ensuring they were with him.

If anyone ever became too big-headed they were always the first to be dealt with. Clough instinctively knew when to come down hard to avoid a particular individual getting out of hand. He had this uncanny knack of humiliating people in front of their peers. Pearce, his captain and England international at Forest, was often made an example for everyone else. Trevor Francis, the man Clough made the first million-pound player, made his debut for the A team and then spent his first few senior games making tea at half-time! In Clough's domain, no one individual was bigger than the collective, not even Francis, who went on to win him a European Cup.

I was present on the team coach when Clough informed Nigel Jemson, who had gone off the rails, that he had a hamstring injury and could not report for duty for the England Under-21s when he was in line for his first cap. The night England played, Jemson was at Molineux playing for Forest reserves. Just one example of the kind of rough justice Clough could dish out, but ... Jemson eventually ended up scoring a goal that won Forest the Rumbelows League Cup.

In the same way that 'Big-Time Charlies' were squashed, any dissenters were similarly viewed as bad for morale. Clough would not have the team's morale threatened, because he knew in turn it would threaten him. Troublemakers were weeded out and dealt with clinically. He once said that you have to be a dictator in 'this game' or you haven't got a chance. He was capable of making those painful decisions, and they were made swiftly and with little fuss. Clough was always at pains to ensure that he carried the team with him. Without their respect he could do nothing. He knew he couldn't train, laugh, or most importantly, win matches. Much of his success was down to Taylor, his right-hand man for many years, who was supremely shrewd in the transfer market. It is in this arena that the most astute inevitably rise to the top, and Taylor had a remarkable talent for spotting players. He found them and Clough did the negotiating.

In Clough's time at Derby and at Forest he never had the millions to throw around that Dalglish had at Liverpool and Blackburn, or the kind of money other managers enjoyed but could still not use to buy success. He had to rely on a well-organised scouting and youth system and the eye for a bargain, unless he sold big to buy big.

The reason Clough and Taylor worked so well here was that they both knew exactly what was required. When building teams from scratch at the Baseball Ground and the City Ground, they had one theme that was a constant: the need for a spine through the team. A strong backbone was always the starting point, which is why Clough signed Peter Shilton at Forest. A good goalkeeper could be worth 15 to 20 points a season, and Shilton was worth that and more.

If that was a routine purchase, then there were more inspired ones. Like the day Taylor urged Clough to sign Dave Mackay from Tottenham. Clough never thought he had a chance, but he still went to White Hart Lane on the spur of the moment and persuaded Mackay to sign. The sight of such an experienced, intelligent, brave and gifted man was the influence the rest of his team needed. Mackay's actions, just like those of most of Clough's captains, inspired everyone else.

Clough was prepared to take gambles as well. He signed Larry Lloyd from Coventry, knowing that he could be trouble. He had Kenny Burns followed around the dog tracks and clubs of Birmingham before he arrived at the City Ground and was transformed from long-haired yob to Footballer of the Year. Clough also took Frank Clark on a free transfer from Newcastle when he was over the age of 30, and the man who eventually replaced Clough as Forest manager also ended up with a European Cup winner's medal. Gary Birtles was another inspired signing. He was carpet-fitting in Nottingham and playing non-League football for Long Eaton United when Clough and Taylor called. He eventually cost Manchester United £1 million.

Taking rough talent, wayward talent or genuine talent and giving it the chance to express itself was Clough's forte. He knew just where every cog would fit into the machine, how they would improve his own unit, what their capabilities were, before he signed them. In much the same way as he tended his roses to coax them into bloom, he lavished time on his players to bring out their best. He was constantly pointing out tiny things that happened in a match and that would have been forgotten by virtually everyone else. He had the memory of an elephant, and continually sought to make his players better.

He and Taylor had an almost telepathic relationship, and the latter's influence on Clough's marvellous career should never be understated. Neither should Clough's loyalty to Taylor, a huge indicator of how much he valued his advice, which was always on tap. Clough was so loyal he walked out of Derby County after a director questioned Taylor's role at the club. It was a mistake he still regrets, but an indication of his impetuosity and proof that he was human after all.

Any suggestion that Clough was unable to manage alone is refuted by the fact that his record at Forest after Taylor quit included two League Cup successes, two other Wembley finals, two FA Cup semifinals and a place in the last four of the UEFA Cup. It was only when Taylor left that Clough had to stand alone when it came to mistakes. Previously, any bad buys were down to his partner and the good ones to him. Between them they made some errors in the transfer market, and where he failed most was ironically when it came to buying strikers and spending large sums of money. Justin Fashanu was an unmitigated disaster after signing for £1 million on the strength of a much-publicised goal for Norwich which was featured on *Match of the Day*. Peter Ward from Brighton fared little better, and there were others like Gary Megson and John Sheridan, neither of whom played more than a single game for Forest. But the one thing that can be said of Clough, despite his vanity and unbridled arrogance, was that he swiftly admitted his mistakes and rectified them by shipping players out at the first opportunity. Those who should have arrived but didn't were also down to him. It was his fault that Gary McAllister failed to sign from Leicester City when everything was in place. Clough asked him if he was related to John Wayne, because he was wearing cowboy boots at their meeting. McAllister was unimpressed, and signed for Leeds instead. He went on to captain Leeds to the title and skippered Scotland at Euro 96. His influence at Forest would have been immense, but Clough betrayed his own theory of making sure the spine of his team was its strongest component.

Clough committed the cardinal sin in his final season with Forest of allowing a player to leave without replacing him. In the Clough tradition of not retaining a player who was unhappy in his work, Teddy Sheringham, was sold to Spurs just over a season after joining Forest, but no replacement was drafted in. To compound the error, Clough backtracked on possible deals to sign Andy Cole and Stan Collymore. Cole instead went to Newcastle, where he broke all scoring records, and Collymore arrived at Forest a season later to score 50 goals in two years under Clark. The goals they both would have undoubtedly provided could have saved Clough from the indignity of relegation.

It was a mistake born out of stubbornness. Clough never acknowledged that he could be relegated. His faith in his own ability led to the one major failing of his 28-year career, but even then his charisma and glorious record saved him from the kind of acrimony others in a similar position could expect.

Clough, like all others, had to rely on fortune. Roy Keane, a £25,000 unknown from Ireland's Cobh Ramblers, had displayed his talents only for 45 minutes of a reserve team game before he was given an unexpected debut as an eighteen-year-old at Anfield. Keane's ability would not have been in doubt, but not even Clough could have predicted with any degree of certainty the way he blossomed into a player who would later become the country's most expensive footballer, generating a £3.7 million profit for Forest in the process.

Clough must take some of the credit for recognising Keane's precocious talent, but there are other factors outside the manager's influence which must be mentioned, such as talent scouts. They recommend as many players who don't make it as do.

Luck and external influences have to be taken into account, but Clough – from the moment he encountered Alan Brown, a man whom he admitted he was on occasions 'downright scared of,' as his own manager at Sunderland – knew that anyone who wanted to be a success in that position had to take complete control. Brown ran Sunderland from top to bottom, and Clough vowed to imitate him, hence the detestation of shabby clothes and long hair. Clough's teams were immaculately turned out, highly disciplined and never gave any trouble to referees. The personal appearance and the respect for officials were other examples of Clough's complete influence.

It didn't stop there, either. Chairmen, chief executives, youth development officers, FA officials were all treated with equal contempt. Like Brown at Sunderland, Clough was to run Derby and Forest from top to bottom. He was the man in charge and he would sink or swim on the success or failure of his players. He was at all times prepared to back his judgement, knowing that he and not the chairman would pay the ultimate price if things went wrong. Clough always maintained that the best team in the land was always the one that won the Championship. Nobody can argue with statistics, but managers can never be measured in that way. There are far too many outside factors which are not constant. In much the same way the person with the best Formula 1 car wins the World Championship: they have the top mechanics, the best engine, the best technicians. Damon Hill is arguably a lesser talent than Michael Schumacher, but his equipment compensated for that deficiency. Likewise, Clough never had the money that Bill Shankly had or the clout of Liverpool to attract players that Dalglish inherited. He never had the finances enjoyed by managers at bigger clubs. Most of the money he earned from European Cups, and selling players he raised for little cost was spent on redeveloping the ground, not in revamping his team.

Nevertheless, in sixteen seasons at Forest, he only twice failed to finish inside the top ten; seven times his side finished fifth or better. All that on smaller resources, smaller squads and smaller contracts than those boasted by most of the other teams represents a manager who *does* make a difference.

In the same way that his failings in Forest's relegation season meant that it was the manager who was responsible for the club being relegated, it was Clough's ability to spot talent that others overlooked, his unwavering confidence in his judgement and the fearless way he backed it, which was responsible for the trophies and medals his players won.

Players at Forest and Derby would say that they did have a role to play, and that cannot be denied. Forest once went 42 games without defeat, still a record, and that cannot be achieved without consistency. The members of the team rightly claim credit for such a marvellous record, and without them it would have been impossible. But it was Clough who assembled the side. He instinctively knew when people needed a breather, spotted potential, recognised people's short-term or long-term value, and cajoled them into producing a level of performance not seen at other clubs.

Alan Hinton was a prime example at Derby County. He was kicked out by Forest and known throughout the League as 'Gladys' by opposing fans because of his dislike for the physical side of the game. But Clough preferred to concentrate on what he could do, 'deliver a ball as good as any Brazilian'.

John McGovern, in Clough's own words, couldn't run, looked ungainly, but would strive to pass the ball. 'He was the absolute genuine article who made the most of the talent at his disposal. My kind of footballer,' he said. Robertson, according to Clough, was a slob, a late-nighter who used to eat all the wrong things, but Clough persevered with him. How many others would even have spotted his potential? Robertson went on to win trophies galore and 26 international caps for Scotland, including a World Cup finals appearance, but he acknowledged much later, before moving into coaching himself: 'If it hadn't been for Cloughie I could have ended up on the football scrapheap. He saved my career.'

No manager can achieve too much with mediocre players. Clough found that out at Hartlepool and Brighton. In his first season with Derby in Divison Two they finished marginally above the relegation zone, and it took him three seasons to get Forest into the top flight. Similarly, a manager with a proven track record like Clough's cannot win things if his team, no matter how talented, are not behind him. His chastening 44 days at Leeds United offer concrete proof.

The side he inherited from Don Revie possessed household names like Bremner, Giles and Clarke, virtually a whole team of internationals. But Clough was ousted by a chairman using the excuse of player power. For once his arrogance had a detrimental effect. He alienated himself with his open criticism of the club's tough methods. The solidarity in the Elland Road dressing room meant that even Clough could not penetrate the players' world, and the outcome supports the theory that managers do not always control their own destiny, although in Clough's case it was a rare exception to the rule.

On the field he was also bound by the haphazard rules of football fortune. He still argues that Juventus prevented Derby County from winning the European Cup because the referee had been nobbled. He might well have won the FA Cup final that eluded him if Roger Milford had acted properly and sent Paul Gascoigne off when Spurs defeated Forest in 1991. Playing against a team of ten men for around 60 minutes would certainly have improved his chances.

Clough was not averse to playing God either to tip the scales in his favour. He once poured 'half of the river Derwent' onto the Baseball Ground before his team played Benfica to ensure that the surface was less appealing to the silky Portuguese side than it was to his Derby team. Cheating or simply the actions of a good manager? Gamesmanship is probably more accurate, but Clough hated to lose at anything – football, a friendly game of squash, or cards on the team coach going home after a match.

At least his £98,000 pay-off from Leeds allowed him to control his destiny more than most other managers. He was financially secure and could therefore afford to take more risks and lay his judgement on the line more regularly. The extent to which managers control their own destiny is partly indicated by the fact that Clough, the consummate League boss, would probably not have been a success as England manager.

Not that his methods would not have translated from the domestic to the international stage. He would have communicated with and motivated his players in much the same way he did at Forest or Derby, and doubtless he would have assembled a team the nation would have been proud of.

Where he would have encountered problems, though, would have been in the extra-curricular areas, which come as part and parcel of the overall job of England team manager. The speech-making, hand-shaking, and polite necessities of the post. That he would have hated. Clough in a blazer would have been uncomfortable with the frills, and he would have been no ambassador. He would, almost certainly, have ended up on a collision course with Lancaster Gate officialdom – one confrontation even he would have lost.

Trying to manage the FA in the same way he managed his club sides would have left him hopelessly outnumbered, and it is no conincidence that Revie, whose job he wanted, failed, and that Shankly, Dalglish and Busby never moved out of club football. This suggests that club managers play by different rules, and in terms of the domestic scene, Clough must be counted as one of the most influential, innovative and successful managers of all time.

If imitation is the sincerest form of flattery, Clough was paid the highest compliment as a succession of people tried to adopt his quirky, authoritarian style with little obvious success. There are a lot of Hamlets, but only one Shakespeare.

Clough displayed a combination of the qualities he admired respectively in Robertson and McGovern, with talent in abundance and the ability to utilise it to the full.

He was far from perfect, however. The way he sat on the bench beneath the Royal Box at Wembley when his team were in need of some inspiration prior to extra time against Tottenham in the

1991 FA Cup final was a mistake. His argument that they did not need him then does not hold water. Football is mostly played in the mind – ninety per cent inspiration and ten per cent perspiration.

Clough's words might have stirred his team, and even if they didn't, he should at least have tried. Hitting supporters after a 5–1 Cup win over QPR was another occasion when he overstepped the boundaries.

A good manager, as well as knowing all the aspects of the job, should know when to walk away. Clough made a mistake at Derby by resigning prematurely. He made a mistake at Forest by staying too long. He should have retired after that FA Cup final defeat to Des Walker's own goal. It would have been the most opportune moment. Instead he stayed around too long, and must take a large chunk of the blame for Forest's relegation. But to remember him for just that nine-month contribution is grossly unfair. What happened in the preceding 27 years rightly qualifies him for a place among the greats.

He did what many others would have been incapable of. If only it were possible to accurately predict where Forest and Derby would have ended up without him – that would indicate the true value of his role. It is nonetheless fair to assume that their histories would have been less colourful, less interesting and significantly less successful.

With Taylor, Clough created one of the most successful managerial teams the game has ever seen. During his time at Derby and Forest he won fifteen trophies in 26 years. Any manager with an average of more than one piece of silverware every two seasons is rare.

To have gained such success at such modest clubs, with little money and little chance of attracting the very top players, merely underlines the effect he had. Clough never received recognition for his playing expertise at international level, unlike others who went on to become managers. Virtually the whole of the Leeds team that helped push him out tried, and only Jack Charlton made a success of it with the Republic of Ireland. Successful club players don't always make great managers. There is more to it than knowing how to play the game. Motivation, man management, the ability to make decisions, knowing how to spot potential and how to nurture talent, the art of communication, a ruthless streak, and most importantly, the ability to command respect are all part of the job's requirements.

Robertson still remembers the day Clough breezed into the City Ground at the peak of his pomp. Just the way he threw his sweatshirt onto a coat peg commanded respect and indicated that he meant business.

His impact on Robertson, and more widely on Forest for eighteen years, from top to bottom of the club, was devastating. He might have been rude, arrogant, brash, abrasive and bombastic, but Clough also had all the necessary management know-how to back the bravado.

8 El Tel and the Flying Dutchman: Venables and Cruyff at FC Barcelona

By Jeff King

A chirpy Cockney and a dictatorial Dutchman; a journeyman footballer and an all-time great; a coach whose players swear by him and another who inspires fear and loathing. At first glance, Terry Venables and Johan Cruyff are not exactly managerial soulmates. Scratch beneath the surface, however, and they've got plenty in common.

Venables is arguably the most prestigious England coach of his generation. Cruyff is Holland's most successful managerial export ever. Both men took over at high-profile FC Barcelona in difficult circumstances, yet led the Catalan giants to almost immediate glory. In his debut season at Camp Nou, Venables steered Barcelona to their first Championship in more than a decade; Cruyff took slightly longer warming up. In his first two campaigns, Barça *only* managed the European Cup-Winners' Cup and the Spanish Cup, but the next four seasons produced a clean sweep in the League and the club's first ever European Cup.

In the case of both men, though, it all went horribly wrong. By the time Venables was sacked in 1987, morale and crowds at Camp Nou had reached an all-time low. Quite simply, there was not a dissenting voice in the town as the Englishman got his marching orders. Cruyff, the club's most successful coach *ever*, was sacked in 1996 amidst accusations that compromise his reputation, both professionally and personally. Whatever their respective merits, both Venables and Cruyff are striking examples of managers who got it right on the night only to miss their cues in the morning.

At the pressure cooker they call FC Barcelona, a club that boasts 100,000-plus members, 85,000 season ticket holders, and a demanding following of six million 'patriots', there's a particularly thin line between love and hate. It's a line the obsessive attentions of Barcelona's two daily sports papers does nothing to diminish. Both Venables and Cruyff were at first fêted, and subsequently slated. In neither case, however, were things ever so comfortingly black and white.

Venables sowed the seed of his ultimate destruction even *before* winning the League in 1985. To this day, Barcelona's president, Josep Lluís Núñez, insists, 'Whilst Venables was in charge it was my job to defend him. If I'd made public his errors, he'd have been a dead man in two days in Barcelona.' For his part, Cruyff committed a litany of sins even as his celebrated 'Dream Team' swept all before them. In the case of the Dutchman in particular, success was accompanied by an uncommon dose of good fortune. To this day, for every Spanish critic, punter or fellow professional who'll tell you that Barça rewrote the history books *because* of Cruyff, you'll find another who'll claim it was *in spite* of him.

Terry Venables' 1984/85 title-winning season at Barcelona stands as his greatest achievement as a coach. After leading the club to its first championship in eleven years at the first time of asking, the following season he steered Barça to only their second European Cup final. Not surprisingly, when the Catalan club sacked him in September 1987, the response back in England was 'poor ol' Tel, what an injustice'. In Spain, the obituaries were *far* less flattering. Do the Spanish, then, know something we don't, or was it just an Iberian case of kicking a man when he was down?

Barcelona's original choice in 1984 was the England manager Bobby Robson. But more than a decade before finally arriving at Camp Nou, he declined, insisting his goal was 'to lead England to the 1986 World Cup finals'. However, in lengthy conversations with President Núñez and his right-hand man, Joan Gaspart, he had no hesitation in recommending the man who would become 'El Tel'. 'I'm a great fan of the British school of football and I love the kind of quick, penetrating football Liverpool play,' gushed Núñez as his 41-year-old contender signed a two-year contract on 25 May 1984. 'Hopefully Venables can add his own stamp and get our Spanish footballers playing the same way.'

Whatever his subsequent record, it would be churlish to deny Venables credit for Barcelona's outstanding first season under his orders. A 3–0 win against Real Madrid at the Santiago Bernabéu was, quite simply, a dream debut. Crucially, that opening salvo in the arch-enemies' feud established the credibility of the unknown coach and his unfamiliar tactics among his players, described by Venables himself as 'notoriously fickle'.

In the mid-1980s, Spanish sides were schooled to defend deep with the cushion of a sweeper. Venables' decision to introduce an English-style flat back four, and a game-plan based on condensing play and putting pressure on the opposition all over the park, was thus a considerable risk. His other challenge was to curtail the Spanish obsession with indiscriminate playing to the gallery. 'We wanted the players to show off their skills in the right areas and to hunt in packs in parts of the field where they could counter-attack quickly.'

'Terry's secret was to get us playing a rigidly defined *pressing* system and his ability to keep the whole squad motivated,' says ex-Venables charge Angel 'Pichi' Alonso, now a prestigious analyst on Spanish TV. 'He created a genuinely competitive atmosphere where there was no division between first-choice players and substitutes. You knew if you came into the side for a couple of games and did well you'd keep your place. The emphasis on dead-ball strategy was also important. We spent lots of time on free kicks and corners, something that was very unusual in Spain at the time.'

'The outgoing coach, César Luis Menotti, left an excellent squad full of technically gifted players,' says Miguel Rico, editor of the Barcelona-based daily *Sport*. 'Venables' merit was to instil fighting spirit in the players and to introduce English-style tactics that caught opponents off guard.'

The Menotti-built-the-side-Venables-simply-reaped-the-rewards line is a popular if exaggerated one in Spain. After just one full season at Barcelona, the man who had led Argentina to the World Cup in 1978 decided to go back home, claiming to be 'homesick' and 'tired of the violence of Spanish football'. In that 1983/84 campaign, Barça had finished just a point behind kicking-and-brawling champions Athletic Bilbao; if the latter's Andoni 'the Butcher of Bilbao' Goikoetxea hadn't put Diego Maradona out of the game for four months, it's safe to assume Barça would have indeed run out champions. Menotti's attacking philosophy and flip turn of phrase were highly seductive, and the powers that be at Barcelona were genuinely sorry to see him go. 'Núñez begged him to stay,' claims Angel Alonso. Eventually, Menotti was persuaded to accept a retainer and remain 'on standby in case of emergencies', i.e. if 'El Tel' failed!

Venables claims it was his decision to offload Maradona. In reality, the decision to sell the world's best player had already been made. The wayward ace had never settled down at Barcelona (his nocturnal binges are still legend in the city) and he was at war with Núñez, claiming, 'I'll retire rather than play for Barcelona again.' Not surprisingly, when Napoli made their world-record $7.5 million offer, the club decided to cash in their chips. The board did insist on a *de facto* rubber-stamping from Venables, but that was simply to cover their backs in case of disasters.

Given the identity of the man he was nominally replacing, Venables' hand-picked signing from Tottenham, Steve Archibald, represented a considerable risk. Though 'Archigol' soon became a popular figure on the Camp Nou terraces, buying the Scot would prove to be a very, *very* big mistake. Venables blithely admits it was his decision to sign Archibald and reject the man the board had lined up, Atlético Madrid's Hugo Sánchez. In reality, he should dive for cover at the mere mention of Sánchez. Passing on the Mexican was quite simply an error of epic proportions. The following season, Spanish football's most prolific contemporary striker joined Real Madrid, where he swiftly became Barcelona's *bête noire*, piling up a record-breaking 164 League goals in 207 games. In doing so, he led his team to five consecutive Championships. Steve Archibald can hold his head high in most company, but Hugo Sánchez's record puts him on a different planet.

The Scot's fifteen League goals in the 1984/85 Championship-winning season were a reasonable contribution to the cause, but the key figure in Venables' well-marshalled ranks was a restless talent in waiting. Bernd Schuster's decision to turn his back on international football when he was just 21 meant the German midfielder never garnered the wider plaudits his immense talent deserved. Venables, however, describes him as 'the best player I have ever dealt with'.

Schuster's overblown ego had suffered in the shadow of Maradona, and in typically diplomatic fashion he had voiced early doubts about the competence of the new boss. 'He will be some English coach, out in Spain for a holiday, wanting a few beers on the beach.' However, in a canny piece of gamesmanship, the man Schuster dubbed 'the unknown Englishman' handed him both the captaincy and a creative monopoly. For just about the only time in his life, the midfield *übergenius* forwent the off-field tantrums that dogged his career and concentrated on expressing himself on the pitch. The combination of *pressing* and Schuster's inspiration proved irresistible. Barcelona lost just two League games all season and eventually finished 10 points ahead of second-placed Atlético Madrid. The maverick German's contribution was simply mind-boggling. Nonetheless, the Schuster-won-the-League-on-his-own school are being unfair on Venables. If it was so damn easy, why did no one else coax the best out of him?

On paper, Venables' second year was a good one, too. On the domestic front, Barça were runners-up in League and Cup (though, as Venables admits, the latter is 'a very poor relation in Spain') and of course they also reached the European Cup final. 'It's been an extraordinary season, better than last year when we won the League,' was 'El Tel's end-of-term verdict. But from the very beginning, the signs of what would develop into a case of chronic complacency (reflected by that end-of-season quote) were apparent. Worse, the uncommonly generous dose of fortune that helped Barcelona through to the European Cup final went AWOL on the big night, and in Venables' case, never graced his door again.

The only addition to Barça's squad as the 1985/86 season kicked off was the Paraguayan striker Raúl Amarilla – as Venables himself admits, 'an unexpected present from President Núñez for winning the previous League'. The gangly Amarilla made zero impact at Camp Nou, and when the words Archibald and injury-prone began to assume symbiotic status (the Scot managed just thirteen League games between injuries), the lack of cover up front became an insuperable handicap. The 1984/85 Championship season had been kick-started by twelve consecutive wins. A year on, a single victory in half a dozen games saw a resurgent Real Madrid put early and irretrievable distance between the two great rivals. The 'Meringues' eventually ran out champions eleven points ahead of Barcelona, the kind of chasm that would normally mean *adiós* to the man steering the Camp Nou ship, whatever his previous achievements. Luckily for Venables, Barça's run to the European Cup final kept the boardroom vultures at bay.

It really did seem like Barcelona's name was on the European Cup. After making hard work of eliminating Sparta Prague – on away goals after losing at Camp Nou in the second leg – and FC Porto – 'with more than a little help from the referee', according to club historian Antoni Closa – the first big test came against Italian giants Juventus; Platini, Laudrup *et al.* Again, fortune smiled on Venables. An 82nd-minute screamer from the resolutely goal-shy full-back Julio Alberto saw Barça take a 1–0 lead to Turin where Archibald's 'it went in off my ear' goal earned a 1–1 draw and a place in the semifinals.

But Venables' side still insisted on doing things the hard way. A 3–0 collapse against unfancied IFK Gothenburg in Sweden seriously threatened their European dream, especially with the talismanic Archibald injured again for the return. But the Scot's replacement, 'Pichi' Alonso, grabbed his fifteen minutes of fame in memorable fashion, his hat trick prefacing a dramatic penalty shoot-out that took Barcelona through to their first European Cup final since 1961. As things turned out, Terry Venables might have been better off losing the penalty lottery there and then.

FC Barcelona were unquestionably the biggest club never to have been crowned European champions. Fifty thousand Catalans made the pilgrimage to the south of Spain convinced that this eternal blemish on their history was about to be eliminated. 'The 1986 European Cup final against Steaua Bucharest was quite simply the most tragic night in Barcelona's history,' says *Sport's* Miguel Rico. 'They were effectively playing at home [at the Sánchez Pizjuán stadium in Seville] and against less-than-awesome rivals. But after doing the difficult part in getting to the final, Venables' side failed at the crucial moment, when things were easiest.' The coach and his players had made the usual noises about respecting their opponents, but deep down, no one inside the club had contemplated the possibility of defeat. 'Everyone just assumed we'd win,' says Angel Alonso, 'that's why losing was such a massive blow.'

Whatever the whys and wherefores, it was arguably the worst European Cup final ever. The Romanians didn't want to play, Barça simply froze. Archibald limped off a physio's couch in Holland to make the starting line-up; 111 minutes later he hobbled back to the bench having made no significant impact: 'I really needed another week of preparation to be fit,' he now admits. A desperate Venables sealed his date with fate by dragging off Bernd Schuster in the 84th minute. The German may have been out of sorts (though no more so than the rest of the team), but taking off a player who can win matches on a whim was a huge gamble, especially with extra time looming. After 120 minutes of stalemate, the two goalkeepers warmed up before facing their first serious action of the night. Steaua's Duckadam might as well have saved his energy; Barça missed four penalties in a row and handed the trophy to the Romanians on a plate. To this day, Venables admits, 'It was the most depressing defeat of my life.' It was also the beginning of the end for 'El Tel'.

'Venables never overcame the Seville syndrome,' insists Miguel Rico. 'Seville might have marked the beginning of an era; instead it was the end of an all-too brief flirtation with success. Maybe Venables shouldn't have continued. Things could never be the same; an air of sadness took hold of the players, the fans, the whole club.'

'Winning the European Cup was Barça's own personal Holy Grail,' says Angel Alonso, an extra-time substitute against Steaua. 'The team lost its credit that night and the players themselves lost their motivation. The fall-out wasn't immediate, but it would eventually cost Venables his job.' Many of the players had already begun to lose faith in their coach. Marcos, one of the men who missed a penalty that night, insists, 'We may have won less titles, but I honestly believe we had a better squad than Johan Cruyff's so-called "Dream-Team". We had some great players and if we'd had a better, more flexible coach I'm sure we'd have won more. The players deserved to win the European Cup; Venables didn't.'

In reality, Barcelona's stilted performance against Steaua was an accurate reflection of their whole season. 'The team paid for the exertions of Venables' first year,' insists Alonso. '*Pressing* demands an enormous physical effort and it was really difficult to maintain that kind of intensity, week in, week out. It was hard to maintain the same level of motivation after the buzz from initial success. You also got the feeling that Terry had decided on a team of automatic choices and that the rest were just making up the numbers.' The opposition had quickly wised up to Venables' *pressing* game (in many cases, adopting an if-you-can't-beat-'em-join-'em approach) and Schuster was back to his warring ways of old, falling out with both the club (over bonuses) and the boss. 'He told me he was fed up and wanted to leave halfway through the season,' admits Venables. The Barcelona team trudged into the dressing room after the shoot-out in Seville to find that the German had walked off the pitch and out of their lives. After that post-match disappearing act, a furious president Núñez declared, 'Schuster will never play for Barcelona again'.

If the errant playmaker's commitment to the cause had wavered during that 1985/86 season, the same could be said of the man in charge. Venables had actually signed a contract to return to England and take over at Highbury for the 1986/87 campaign. In the end, a mixture of domestic reasons (the end of his marriage) and Arsenal's shoddy treatment of the departing Don Howe convinced him to think again. He had, in fact, already told Barcelona he would be leaving, but with no suitable replacement emerging in the interim, his contract was extended for another year. However, the should-I-go-or-should-I-stay saga raised serious doubts about Venables' priorities.

'By Terry Venables' second season, he'd had time to get to know the city, and the players had had time to get to know him,' says Miguel Rico. 'They realised that he was more interested in other things than football. Barça is a unique club in terms of its high profile and its surrounding pressure-cooker atmosphere. Everybody knows what everyone else is doing in this city and you can only succeed here if you really *live* for the club. Venables' taste for other things led to a lack of personal interest on his part; this in turn bred a general apathy that saw him lose his authority in the dressing room. He might have got away with it if Barça had won in Seville, but the luck that got him there in the first place had run out by the big night.' Venables' extra-curricular activities? Even the man himself admits, 'I did a fair bit of night-clubbing.'

Despite the simmering discontent, the board decided to give Venables both the benefit of the doubt and the money to rebuild. His first recruit was 22-year-old Mark Hughes, a £2.2 million capture from Manchester United. The original idea was to play the strapping youngster alongside the more cerebral Archibald, but when word reached Spain that Everton's Gary Lineker was available, Venables weighed up his options and decided he was a better bet than the injury-prone Scot.

Lineker cost Barcelona £2.7 million from Everton, *before* heading Mexico way for the World Cup. However, when the arrival of the World Cup's top scorer didn't create great expectations in Barcelona, it was clear that the post-Seville syndrome was anything but fleeting. Lineker scored twice against Racing Santander on his debut and swiftly won the hearts and minds of the fans with his goals and man-of-the-people persona. An early hat trick against Real Madrid helped too! However, a half-empty Camp Nou for his debut reflected the reigning pessimism. 'It's very quiet,' was Lineker's stark description of the match-day atmosphere in his first season. 'Camp Nou seems more like a theatre than a football ground. It takes a lot of getting used to. What's strange is that sometimes when you kick off, it's so quiet you think, is that it? Have we started?'

Barcelona's percentage football was enough to earn them another runners-up spot in that 1986/87 season, but it sure wasn't pretty to watch. A far more attractive Real Madrid side were again worthy champions, outscoring their dour rivals by a hefty 21 goals. A double defeat against Dundee United in the UEFA Cup on top of two draws with Flamurtari of Albania, meant there wasn't even the consolation of a decent run in Europe. That unexpected elimination wasn't as disastrous as a 4–1 home defeat against Metz in Venables' first season, but it did reflect an overall record in Europe – P19 W8 D3 L8 – which makes for unimpressive reading.

Venables' rigidly zonal back four and ready-to-rumble midfield might have worked with Schuster orchestrating affairs, but without him the team displayed a pitiful lack of ideas. Spanish international midfielders Victor and Calderé were strong on commitment but sadly lacking in subtlety, whilst Roberto, a close season signing from Valencia and a genuinely dangerous player going forward, spent most of the season sitting in front of the back four in a ludicrously withdrawn role. At 26, Gary Lineker was the jewel in England's crown (he notched seven goals in six internationals that season) and arguably the world's most effective goalscorer, but given the paucity of service, he cut a forlorn figure up front. 'It wasn't unusual to go a whole game without a single half-chance,' he recalls.

In the circumstances, Lineker's 20 goals were a return way beyond the call of duty. The younger, less worldly Hughes wasn't nearly so lucky. 'I was too young and inexperienced to go abroad and my style of play just didn't suit Spanish football,' admits the Welshman with the benefit of hindsight. 'The referees were constantly giving fouls against me but the biggest problem was my lack of goals [just four in 30 League games]. By the end, I was so tense and nervous, I wasn't enjoying my game at all.'

Venables' initial response to criticism of his young charge was to stand firm. 'While I'm coach at Barcelona, I will never drop Hughes,' he asserted. Eventually he backed down amidst rumoured ultimatums from the board, and the man the Catalans had cruelly dubbed 'the Wardrobe' was replaced by Archibald. In reality, dropping the confidence-shorn striker was an act of mercy and Hughes remains a disciple: 'Terry really put himself on the line for me, on and off the pitch. I still regret I couldn't repay his faith in me.' The following season the out-of-sorts youngster was despatched on loan to Bayern Munich, and in June 1988, Alex Ferguson welcomed him back to Old Trafford for a cut-price £1.5 million. The Barcelona board's alleged intervention in the Hughes case was not the only time Venables is said to have bowed to back-room pressure. After his dismissal, *Sport* published rumours about a dressing-room clique of established players who consistently vetoed new signings, a theory that would certainly explain Venables' persistent refusal to reinforce his squad.

In the circumstances, it was a major surprise that Venables started the 1987/88 season still at the helm. He admits in his autobiography that 'both Barcelona and I might have benefited from a change at that stage', but after being beaten to the punch in a QPR take-over by Marler Estates, and with supposed interest from Italian clubs coming to nothing, he took the field for an against-the-odds fourth pre-season press call at Camp Nou. 'Terry's success in his first couple of years, and I include getting to the European Cup final in that equation, gave him a lot of leeway,' claims Angel Alonso. 'Remember, we're talking about a club that was used to winning the odd cup, at best. Núñez had been president since 1978 without winning the League. His decision to extend Venables' contract again may have been a surprise, but it was a personal and political one based on those initial achievements.'

There were no additions to the squad that had stuttered through the previous season, so Venables' pre-season optimism – he claimed 'this team is more complete than the one that won the League' – was to say the least surprising. Admittedly, Schuster was back in the fold after his season in the wilderness (i.e. in court, unsuccessfully suing the club for breach of contract), but he was destined to sleepwalk through his final year at Barça. 'We've broken the ice,' claimed an unusually naïve Venables. 'Last year was difficult for us but it's time we started acting like grown-ups.' The German's idea of more mature behaviour was to sign a mid-season agreement with Real Madrid before crossing lines in the summer. A decade later, Schuster is still unwilling to kiss and make up. 'I was just a pawn in an internal dispute between the president and coach,' he insists. 'Venables wanted to buy more foreign players and Núñez said no. Venables was furious so he took it out on me; he was always looking for a fight and constantly provoking me.'

The side that kicked off the season with a 2–1 win at Las Palmas was essentially the same one that had won the League in 1985, but three years older. Goalkeeper Andoni Zubizarreta, Roberto and Lineker (now the sole forward in the team) were the only players Venables *hadn't* inherited from Menotti in 1984. In reality, the likes of Migueli, Julio Alberto, Victor, Carrasco and Calderé were all past their sell-by date. 'My biggest mistake was that I stuck with the same players too long,' admitted Venables on a recent trip back to Barcelona.

Barça lost 2–1 in their Camp Nou debut against Sevilla, the first time in 43 years that they'd lost their opening fixture at home. Game number three, a derby at traditional whipping-boys Espanyol, produced another defeat, 2–0, and even Venables was forced to admit 'we were poor and deserved to lose'. To aggravate matters, Real Madrid won 7–1 at Zaragoza on the same day. It was a combination that provoked contradictory noises from the Barcelona president. At first, Núñez claimed 'before sacking Terry Venables, I'd go myself'. He then undermined his show of support by claiming the players were 'unmotivated' and dropped broad hints about signing Espanyol boss Javier Clemente.

Next up at Camp Nou were Valencia. Another lacklustre perfomance produced a third consecutive defeat and unprecedented barracking; from the fans that were still bothering to show up, that is. Crowds were now down to an all-time low of 20–25,000, bestowing a desolate appearance on the 120,000-capacity Camp Nou. After the game, enraged fans blocked the exit to the VIP box chanting 'Out! Out! Out!', and a shaken Josep Lluís Núñez – along with Venables, the main focus of the fans' anger – needed the assistance of a police charge to get safely out of the ground.

Venables' post-match response was to claim that Barça had

been 'unlucky' and to promise 'hard work to get us out of this situation'. But in his heart of hearts, he must have known it was all over, especially with the president under siege and his team languishing in the slipstream of the hot-off-the-blocks reigning champions. If you're a Barcelona fan, the *only* rivalry that matters is with Real Madrid – four games into the 1987/88 season the clubs' respective records read: top-of-the-table Madrid – Played 4 Won 4, Goals for 21, Goals against 1; seventeenth-placed Barcelona – Played 4 Won 1 Lost 3, Goals for 3, Goals against 6. Those kick-off statistics reflected an ever-increasing chasm as Madrid embarked on the third season of a record-breaking five consecutive Championship triumphs. To make matters worse, the pivotal role of the home-grown 'Vulture Brigade' – Butragueño, Michel, Martín Vázquez and Manolo Sanchis – threw into stark relief Venables' unwillingness to give youth a fling at a club that for socio-political reasons craves local idols.

On Wednesday, 23 September 1987, three days after the Valencia game, 'El Tel's reign in Spain came to an end. The club couched the blow in terms of a mutual agreement for the benefit of both parties. In fact, new coach Luis Aragonés, had signed a contract the previous day with Venables conveniently back home in London for 'personal motives'. Doubts about whether he was pushed were firmly dispelled when Núñez launched a full-scale attack on the dethroned Englishman the following Monday.

'The players *begged* me to sack Terry Venables,' claimed the Barça president. 'They came to see me and said they just couldn't go on with him, that they were totally unmotivated. They said if I sacked Venables it would be like a breath of fresh air; that they would run more, play better and get the club out of its uncomfortable situation.'

Aragonés steadied the boat temporarily, but just 15 wins in 38 League games reflected a historical low that almost ended Barcelona's unique ever-present record in European competition. Luckily, they caught John Toshack's Real Sociedad side on an off day in the Spanish Cup final, and scraped through to Europe via the Cup-Winners' Cup.

At the time of his dismissal, Venables claimed his sacking was 'premature'. All the available evidence suggests it was long overdue. Where, though, did it all go wrong? The day the new-to-Spain 'El Tel' said no to Hugo Sánchez, the loss of the surprise factor after the first year, Schuster's diminishing contribution, a manifest failure to rebuild an ageing side, the coach's deteriorating relationship with his players in the wake of Seville? Whatever the reasons, it's clear that Venables sowed the seed of his own downfall.

In England, his managerial style has always inspired respect and loyalty amongst his players. By the time he left Barcelona, it inspired anything but. In fact, it was a toss-up whose desire had hit rock bottom first, the 'overburdened and under strain' coach, or his players. 'Terry is a very smart guy,' insists Angel Alonso, 'but keeping the same bunch of players motivated is not easy. When he first arrived, he didn't speak Spanish and his relationship with the players was superficial, basically reduced to giving specific instructions through his interpreters. That was fine at first, but players get used to a manager's way of working, and what works on the first, second and third day doesn't necessarily work on the fourth, fifth and sixth.'

A decade on, Venables is still a popular figure among the non-playing staff at Barcelona. According to one insider, 'He's greeted with open arms every time he comes back.' A case of those in the know understanding that pressure Barcelona-style can get to the best of 'em? Angel Alonso, the ex-player-turned-TV-star, seems to think so. 'As you get to know the city, the peculiarities of the club, and all the hassles of being Barcelona coach, you realise just how important it is, and then the pressure *really* gets to you,' he argues. 'Understanding what the club really means to the Catalans, dealing with all the plotting directors, interest groups and hangers-on, each and every one with their hidden agenda; all these things are a handicap rather than a help the more time you spend at the club.'

The circumstances surrounding his Camp Nou *adiós* may have been unique, but Venables' Jekyll and Hyde turn at Barcelona reflects the law of diminishing returns that has characterised his whole career. His forte has always been swift results and instant payback, followed by a downhill slide and dubious legacies.

In his first managerial job at Crystal Palace, Venables' young side were briefly hailed as the 'Team of the 80s'. In their first season back in the top flight, in 1979/80, there was even loose talk of Championships before a mauling at Liverpool and a tumble back into thirteenth place. The next season, Venables resigned amidst cries of betrayal, leaving Palace rooted to the bottom of the table. The fact that the board were on the point of sacking him may have justified his decision to abandon a sinking ship (Palace were eventually relegated), but it hardly earned him brownie points for outstanding achievement.

Despite Venables' much-vaunted tactical know-how, his Palace team were often accused of gamesmanship; less generous critics dubbed them 'the cheats of the 80s'. His next side, Queens Park Rangers, were another niggly and petulant outfit. The names that spring to mind from that era are the likes of Billy Gilbert, Peter Nicholas and Terry Fenwick. Even the creative players such as John Gregory and Simon Stainrod were abrasive footballers.

In his second year at Loftus Road, Venables led QPR to Wembley and the 1982 FA Cup final against Tottenham, but his side hardly graced the big occasion, drawing 1–1 before losing a dull replay. Steve Perryman, the Spurs captain, suggests that Venables was not in fact unhappy with honourable defeat. 'I don't think Terry fancied getting a very public belting on an occasion like that, which could have happened with a Second Division team against us if they'd tried to take us on . . . I think Terry was happy to lose 1–0 with a lot of credit.'

The following season, Rangers were promoted, and by the time Venables moved on to Spain in 1984 they were established as an average First Division side (with a little help from a plastic travesty they called a pitch). A laudable enough record, but nothing compared to the parallel achievements of Graham Taylor and Dave Bassett in more modest surroundings.

After his unhappy demise at Barcelona, circumstances (David Pleat's) contrived to land Venables another plum job. Once again, he made a bright start, and Tottenham's FA Cup triumph in 1991 looked like the dawn of a promising era. We all know what happened next. Bearing in mind Venables' 'previous' as a player – he left Chelsea after falling out with Tommy Docherty and was hounded out of Spurs by the White Hart Lane boo-boys – the phrase least likely to pass his lips is 'I've started so I'll finish' of *Mastermind* legend.

It would take a revolution called Johan Cruyff to really turn things around at Camp Nou. When the Dutchman returned to the club in May 1988, Barça had added just that solitary 1985 championship to the one he'd inspired as a player back in 1974.

Despite the brief flirtation with success under Venables, FC Barcelona were still a club dogged by scandal and instability; sporting glory was an occasional afterthought. In eight years at the helm, Cruyff would drag the club back onto the sports pages in spectacular fashion.

The Dutchman lost no time in dismantling his predecessor's legacy. No less than thirteen players were given their marching orders before the 1988/89 season kicked off, a purge that reinforces the view that Venables had let the grass grow old under his players' feet. By the time Cruyff led the club to the Championship in 1991, only Zubizarreta was left from the Venables era (Gary Lineker stoically put up with being stuck on the wing for one season before following Venables home to Tottenham in July 1989). Cruyff's first two seasons were spent fine-tuning a revolutionary tactical system, acquiring the players who could implement it, and establishing the authority Venables often lacked. His opening salvo was to ban directors from the dressing room and establish a monopoly on buying and selling, neither a luxury enjoyed by 'El Tel'. The Cup Winners' Cup triumph in 1989, and a sign-of-things-to-come Cup final victory against Real Madrid in 1990, were unexpected bonuses.

The 1990/91 title-winning season was the first of an unprecedented four consecutive Championships. That's four League titles in eight years, compared to the same number in the previous 35. And then, of course, there was the conquest of that aforementioned Holy Grail. Barcelona were the Continent's only major player never to have won the European Cup, a major slight on their history for the proud Catalans and their flagship club. And then came Johan and Wembley '92.

But Cruyff's achievements cannot be measured by titles alone. Arnold Palmer's sporting truism 'Are we playing how, or how many?' is anathema to the style-conscious Dutchman. Yes, he's a natural-born winner, but no, he's *never* been interested in winning at all costs. The most illustrious graduate of the Ajax school of 'Total Football' genuinely believes it's about 'How?' On taking over at Barcelona, he promised, 'I'm going to build a side that gets the fans flocking back to Camp Nou. My team will be committed to attack. I don't see that as taking risks. On the contrary, I believe the side that plays the most daring football will win the most trophies in the long run.' His 'Dream Team' of Laudrup, Stoichkov, Koeman, Begiristain, Bakero and, fleetingly, Romario delivered and then some. Camp Nou attendances quickly rose from the derisory average of Venables' last season to an awesome 85,000.

Despite criticism from the Luddites, notably Spanish boss Javier Clemente, a man who claims that Cruyff is 'just a picker of teams, he's got no idea about tactics or strategy', Barça really did change the face of Spanish football. The days of *la Furia* (the fury), the kicking, cheating, mean-spirited model of old, were banished to the graveyard of killjoys past. Training sessions were dominated by intricate ballwork, the legendary *rondas* (rotations): 'Running is for cowards,' insisted Cruyff. 'The best footballers let the ball do the work.' Flexibility and imagination were the name of the game, versatility the byline of his favourite players; Cruyff, whose Spanish is fluent if decidedly Kafkaesque, even invented a word for them, *peloteros* (roughly translatable as ball players). Whilst the rest of Europe looked to AC Milan and Arrigo Sacchi's supposedly revolutionary 4–4–2, Cruyff was fielding a three-man defence. Even then, two of his nominal defenders were invariably technical midfielders (the likes of Eusebio and Amor) as opposed to more athletic wing-backs. His pivoting catalysts – Ronald Koeman at sweeper, and what simply became known as *el 4*, most often Pep Guardiola – guaranteed intelligent distribution from the back. Meanwhile, Cruyff's forwards would interchange positions so many times in 90 minutes that defenders stumbled back to the dressing room groggy.

But however important the tactics, it was mostly about attitude. 'If the opposition score four goals, we'll score five,' insisted Cruyff. His unflinchingly positive philosophy was epitomised by a game at Rayo Vallecano in December 1992. Down to nine men and 3–1 behind, a flagging Barcelona looked down and out. With ten minutes to go they pulled a goal back, and then with five minutes left scored the equaliser. Any other coach would have been screaming at his men to hoof the ball out of the ground as the seconds ticked away on an against-the-odds comeback. Not Cruyff. No sooner had the game restarted than he was on his feet waving his men forward, anti-football simply not part of his vocabulary.

The Clemente school argue that Cruyff only got away with absurdly suicidal tactics because of the quality of his players. But although the Dutchman inherited a group of Spaniards – Zubizar-reta, Bakero, Begiristain, Eusebio, Goikoetxea and Julio Salinas – who would go the distance, they were strictly supporting players. It was Cruyff's hand-picked foreign trio that put the dream in the team. Michael Laudrup arrived from Juventus in 1989 as a bargain-basement has-been at just 25. It proved to be Italy's loss. Spain is a country where football fans are ferociously partisan, yet standing ovations from neutrals were the Dane's companion for five sublime years. The irremediably belligerent Hristo Stoichkov would be distraught if he ever received a round of applause from opposing fans, and nobody ever accused him of elegance *à la* Laudrup, but his never-say-die spirit was gloriously infectious. Three times, Barça would seal the championship thanks to Hristo's goals on the last day of the season. Yet when Barcelona signed him from CSKA Sofia in 1990, he was barely a rumour outside Bulgaria; it was Cruyff who turned a rough diamond into the European Footballer of the Year.

Unlike Laudrup and Stoichkov, Koeman didn't come cheap at £5 million, but he did prove cheap at the price. For six seasons, 'Tin-Tin's' ability to marshal an undermanned rearguard, coupled with his trademark rifled passes out of defence and unerring dead-ball accuracy, gave the team options no other player on the European stage could match. And if Koeman had kicked just the one ball for Barcelona, his European Cup-winning free kick against Sampdoria in 1992 was payback and then some. Throw in Romario, whose presence was fleeting but glorious (30 League goals in 1993/94, most of them works of art), and it's clear that initially at least Cruyff had a keen eye for talent. It was only when he lost his knack for buying the right players, and/or began to believe that his much-vaunted system was the real key to success, that things began to go wrong.

From the very beginning his talent-spotting ability was some-what hit and miss. He was ridiculed for claiming that 1990 signing Richard Witschge was the best left-sided midfielder in Europe. But not being able to dislodge the Laudrups and Stoichkovs as a teenager hardly constitutes a career-defining failure. Witschge's subsequent resurgence at Bordeaux and Ajax demonstrates that Cruyff wasn't totally off the chart in his prediction.

In other cases, mitigating circumstances were notable by their absence. The Barcelona board actually agreed terms with Romario after his explosion at the 1988 Seoul Olympics, but Cruyff said thanks but no thanks, and opted to sign his Brazilian teammate, Aloisio, instead. An accident-prone defender, Aloisio flopped at Camp Nou and was quickly bundled off to FC Porto. It took a five-year goal glut in Holland before Cruyff recognised his mistake and signed a by then considerably more expensive Romario.

And then there was the stranger-than-fiction case of Romarito. The Paraguayan midfielder was a Stateside pal of Cruyff's during his late 1970s playing days in the United States. He was hardly a household name at his peak, so imagine his surprise at thirtysomething when Cruyff swept him from his anonymity in Asunción, flew him to Spain, kept him hidden in a hotel room for two days, and then pitched him into a March 1989 showdown against Real Madrid! Heaven knows what Gary Lineker – dropped to make way for the mystery man – made of the whole affair. That game finished goalless, and after six more appearances the perplexed Paraguayan was shipped back whence he came.

Nobody at the club was going to complain about the occasional bad buy as Cruyff piled up the silverware; two trophyless seasons and several unmitigated flops would turn the tide of opinion. The already-past-it-when-he-arrived Gica Hagi spent two years either on the bench or out of position, Robert Prosinecki was presumably bought as an ornament, whilst Cruyff transformed Meho Kodro from a 25-goal striker with Real Sociedad into a nine-goal bag of nerves at Camp Nou. After Barcelona's defeat in the 1994 European Cup final, Cruyff decided to offload Zubizarreta, Laudrup, Goikoetxea and Julio Salinas, and build a new side around cut-price bargains such as Eskurza, José Mari, Korneyev, Escaich, Sánchez Jara and Cela. None of these players made the slightest impact at Camp Nou and only José Mari, now with Athletic Bilbao, remains a regular in the Spanish First Division.

Transfer travails aside, Cruyff's most persistent caprice was his inexplicable habit of playing people out of position. A memorable (bizarrely so) Spanish Cup quarterfinal at Atlético Madrid in April 1989 saw Gary Lineker confined to the right wing while *three* international wingers (Carrasco, Valverde and Begiristain) struck an unsatisfied pose on the bench. Stoichkov, Salinas and Kodro were other victims of Cruyff's persecute-the-centre-forward-by-sticking-him-on-the-wing fixation. In the 1990/91 title-winning season, Goikoetxea's excellence on the right wing gained him the

Spanish Footballer of the Year award. The next season Cruyff banished him to full-back! More recently, Portuguese playmaker Luis Figo struggled through his first season at Camp Nou. 'I'm sick and tired of Cruyff and his whims,' he moaned, a week before his persecutor got his marching orders in 1996. 'I've never played on the wing in my life before. Why does he insist on buying players and then playing them out of position? Him and his bloody inventions!'

If you treat your best players like that, they are bound to rebel in the end. Lineker, Milla, Roberto, Salinas, Laudrup, Stoichkov, Romario; the list of players who fell out with the autocratic Dutchman is endless. A major ingredient of the Cruyff recipe is charisma; as a Barça player, he was known as 'the Goal Prophet', as a coach he was simply 'the Genius'. Unfortunately, man management is not the prerogative of the gods. 'I might have got on better with Cruyff if he hadn't made life so difficult for the players I picked, especially the ones he knew I was close to,' says Spain's Javier Clemente. 'You could write an encyclopedia about the way he mistreated players. I thought he might mellow with age and after his operation [a double bypass in February 1991], especially with his son playing in the first team, but he kept on pushing people and living on a knife-edge. He got rid of the best goalkeeper in Spain [Zubizarreta] just to destroy the bridge between the players and the board. If you spend your life making enemies, it's hardly a surprise if things eventually blow up in your face.'

Michael Laudrup, as laid-back a character as they come, jumped ship to Real Madrid in 1994, claiming, 'I just can't stand Cruyff anymore.' The Dutchman's run-ins with the not-*quite*-so-laid-back Stoichkov were legendary. 'When the team wins it's because of Cruyff, when we lose, it's down to the players,' said the Bulgarian shortly before escaping to Parma in 1995. 'He can't have it both ways, it's impossible; a coach is only as good as his players. Does he think that slagging his team off in public is going to motivate us; that players take the field thinking, "Right, I'm going to show him?" If he does, he's seriously wrong. I for one can't go round all day worrying about what he thinks.'

José Mari Bakero, another player who had plenty of run-ins with Cruyff, is more benevolent. 'I think it was inevitable Johan's reign would end on a controversial note, but I still think his overall influence was positive; I for one am proud to be associated with the man who rewrote the Barcelona history books. In every situation in life, there is always a hierarchy. Barça needed someone like Cruyff, a man who was prepared to accept the responsibility that hierarchy brings and impose his character and experience on the club. People don't realise how much pressure he took off the players – in his first couple of seasons, when all the new players were still finding their way, it was Johan who absorbed all the pressure; he took all the flak on our behalves.'

Whatever his problems with more experienced players, Johan Cruyff proved a master at blooding youngsters. Before his arrival, a home-grown player in Barça's first team was an unknown species. In his eight seasons at the club, an amazing 29 players from the *cantera* made their debut, and we're not talking cameos, either. In a 5–1 victory at Real Betis in 1996, no fewer than eight home-grown players made the starting line-up and another three came on as substitutes. Players such as Guardiola, Amor, Sergi and Ferrer have been fundamental to the Barça cause, and the new wave of Oscar, Roger, Celades and, above all, Iván de la Peña promise an even brighter future. Ajax may attract more attention for growing their own, but the man who grew up on their doorstep in Amsterdam paved the way for a decade in a far more competitive environment than the Dutch League.

The cynics say Cruyff shouldn't take credit for the emergence of the home-grown players because he rarely cast his gaze beyond the first team. Admittedly, once Jordi Cruyff made the step up to the first team in 1994, Dad's seat at Barça's Second Division nursery side remained steadfastedly unoccupied, but that's surely missing the point. At Johan Cruyff's Barcelona, if you were good enough for the big time, you were old enough. Young players can hardly ask more.

Spanish football fans are not noted for their patience. Three games into the 1995/96 season, Real Madrid coach Jorge Valdano found himself roundly abused by fans who had lionised him after the club's first championship in five years the previous spring. In his last season, Terry Venables was barracked savagely after two years of near misses but no silverware. Despite his last two trophyless campaigns, the day after Cruyff was sacked in May 1996, an overwhelming majority of Barça supporters spent the game against Celta barracking President Núñez and his board. Many of those fans were genuinely sorry to see him go, others were just unhappy with the club's handling of the affair. Uncer-emoniously dumping your most successful coach ever with just two League games to go did seem unnecessarily vindictive.

When Bobby Robson stepped into Cruyff's shoes, he became the tenth Barça coach since Josep Lluís Núñez was elected president in 1978. The ensuing trophy count reads Cruyff 11, The Rest 9. In the style wars, it reads 'No Contest'. Valdano, another coach who preaches the beautiful game, insists: 'The powers that be at Barcelona hated Cruyff because they couldn't tame him. It's been an eight-year marriage of convenience. His classic Barça were a side that played for kicks, a team of great players who played with criteria, rhythm and grace; they were a side that could beat you and make you look silly in the process. If luck was on their side in those last-gasp Championships, I'd like to think it's because fortune favours the footballing brave. Cruyff takes with him the club's best-ever results, the memory of an incomparable side, and the goodwill of the masses. If it was hard to live by his side; the club will soon discover it's harder to live with his ghost.'

A ghost that bequeathed a nightmare, insist Cruyff's detractors. In Spain, a lucky person is said to have 'a flower up their bum'. According to his many critics, jammy Johan sports an assfull! If you believe the alternative version of the Cruyff saga, in eight *mis*directed seasons his Barcelona side won just one championship (the first, in 1991); the other three came gift-wrapped.

Cruyff's side did indeed enjoy an unprecedented run of good fortune; a sequence, however, not entirely unconnected with his charisma and unwavering self-belief. At times it seemed as if opposing players and coaches would visibly wilt when confronted with the invincible Dutchman. Barcelona spent two whole seasons lagging behind a past-their-sell-by-date Real Madrid side, and a third in the slipstream of a workmanlike Deportivo la Coruña. On each occasion, Lady Luck intervened on Cruyff's behalf at the death. Barça kicked off the last game of the 1991/92 season resigned to the fact that a Madrid win in Tenerife would put the title beyond them. The dramatic events on the isle are so well documented they'll never make *A Question Of Sport*. In a nut-shell, Madrid surrendered a two-goal lead as Barça simultaneously beat Athletic Bilbao and went top for the first time all season. *Campeones!* A year later, Madrid repeated their snatching-defeat-out-of-the-jaws-of-victory turn in tropical climes. Meanwhile, a grateful Barça beat Real Sociedad to secure another last-gasp Championship. In 1994, it was third time most positively lucky as Deportivo's Miroslav Djukic missed a 90th-minute penalty against Valencia. If he'd scored, Deportivo would have been champions for the first time in their history. As it was, Barcelona's 5–2 win against Sevilla meant an historic fourth title in a row for the Catalans.

Deportivo's coach in that 1993/94 season, the normally circumspect Arsenio Iglesias, spoke for a nation of dissenters during that third run-in. 'Barcelona only won the last two Championships because Madrid handed it to them on a plate. The potential of Barça's squad is immense but they only manage to win the League because of presents. It's as clear as day; if they were a well-coached team, they'd win the League by streets. Cruyff should start taking notes and go back to school to take his coaching badge.'

Iglesias' successor in La Coruña, John Toshack, is equally sceptical about the claims of the 'Dream Team'. 'A side that wins three championships in the last game of the season is not a really great one,' says the Welshman. 'Even my Real Madrid team that won the League in 1990 with six games to spare was not one of the all-time great sides, and we scored 107 goals. The Real Madrid team that won the first five European Cups, the Ajax or Liverpool sides of the 1970s, or Sacchi's Milan, that's what you call really great sides.'

And then there's what the Spanish call 'the Kaiserslautern Miracle'. Barcelona kicked off their 1992 European Cup second-round, second-leg tie in Germany defending a 2–0 lead. Eighty-nine minutes later, Cruyff's team were 3–0 down and *damn* lucky to have got the nil. Koeman's free kick from deep inside his own half was a case of hit and hope; that the five-foot-seven Bakero got his head to the ball despite being surrounded by lofty Germans was a miracle in itself; that the ball looped bizarrely off the side of his head and curled into the far corner of the net was stretching the credulity of the angels. Barça would eventually beat an overawed-by-the-occasion Sampdoria in a dour final to earn Cruyff his place in the history books. However, the fact that Sampdoria and Kaiserslautern were flying the flags of Italy and Germany that year says everything about the 1992 vintage of the European Cup.

The following year, Cruyff's defending champions were bundled out of the European Cup by a run-of-the-mill CSKA Moscow side, and in 1994 the 4–0 débâcle against AC Milan in Athens laid to rest the myth of Barcelona's 'Dream Team'. That one-sided battle of wits with Fabio Capello proved that off-the-cuff preparation was a poor substitute for rigorous professionalism. The Italians probably thought Johan's claims that he was 'a lucky fella and the Greek gods are on my side' were a case of pre-match kidology. His critics would say they were a perfect résumé of his tactics.

Whilst the Barça side was teeming with world-class players, Cruyff could get away with his extragavant tactics, argue his detractors, but his supremacy-of-the-system-over-players theory collapsed like a house of cards when he dismantled his team after Athens, and the genius of Laudrup, Stoichkov and Romario was replaced by more prosaic talents. Barcelona's 1995 Champions League defeat at the hands of a Weah-and-Ginola-inspired Paris Saint-Germain confirmed that there is no tactical substitute for talent.

Despite all Cruyff's achievements, it was an open secret that the Barcelona board, and president Núñez in particular, had been gunning for him for years, but four Championships, even if they were 'in spite of', represent a considerable baggage. However, an ignominious end was always on the cards. 'The day I leave Barcelona, it'll be in a hot-air balloon,' Cruyff was fond of saying. Twenty-four hours after authorising that long-awaited flight, Núñez launched a ferocious attack on the Flying Dutchman. Amongst other crimes and misdemeanours, he accused Cruyff of accepting commission for scheduling pre-season games in Holland and leaking stories to the press for money or favours. Johan's love of a buck is old news, though. In the end, it was his obsession with son Jordi's career that forced the board's hand.

'Cruyff's last two years were a disaster, characterised by frivolous team selection and an absolute lack of tactical planning,' says Antonio Franco, editor of *El Periódico de Barcelona*. 'Cruyff had to go because he was unable to rebuild, mainly because his hands were tied by his son. If he'd signed the kind of quality forwards Barça really needed, Jordi would have been relegated to the bench like a shot.'

Núñez picks up the theme with a vengeance. 'Cruyff made us get rid of Laudrup, Salinas and Romario so that Jordi could play, and he sold Zubizarreta so that his son-in-law Jesús Angoy [at the time approaching 30 and *still* in the nursery side!] could make the first-team squad. Earlier this season, we offered him the chance to sign Mijatovic [the 1996 Spanish Player of the Year] and Davor Suker [top scorer in the Euro 96 qualifiers], but he said it was crazy to spend five or six million pounds on them, and that he had better players lined up for far less money. I was taken aback when he handed me a list in May headed by Ryan Giggs, Steve McManaman, Robbie Fowler and Ciriaco Sforza, players who are twice as expensive and not for sale anyway. When we got in touch with their clubs, they treated us like we were retarded for being so out of touch.

'Maybe we should have sacked him at the beginning of the season when he refused to take part in meetings. How can an employee who earns one and a half million pounds a year refuse to take part in meetings? We were completely in the dark about his intentions. Nobody has done more to help Cruyff than me, and the board has always respected his decisions, however strange. We've got players at the club who have never played in their true positions and we've got youngsters whose careers are threatened because they were made to play when they were injured. Two years ago, Cruyff told me we needed to build a team for the future and asked for six new players. A year later, all six were on a list of players he didn't want!'

So there you have it. A pretty convincing case for the prosecution against Barcelona's most successful coach. In reality, Cruyff is neither a genius nor a con man. If there is one thing about the Dutchman that everybody agrees on, it's that he never changes. By that token, it was the very same Johan Cruyff who 'won' four Leagues and 'lost' another four. Despite all the errors of judgement in his last two seasons (and turning down Mijatovic and Suker when they were going for a song *was* criminally negligent), Cruyff's side were still in the running for the 1996 Championship with just three games to go. As late as March, there were even possibilities of a clean sweep. Both the 1–0 defeat in the Spanish Cup final against Atlético Madrid and the UEFA Cup semifinal loss against Bayern Munich really could have gone either way; and seven points behind champions Atlético is the kind of final margin open to any interpretation you like. (How about Atlético were awarded 10 penalties during the season and Barça one?) Whatever

Cruyff's latter-day sins, would Núñez have dared to have sacked Barcelona's most successful coach *ever* if he'd just won yet more major titles? The answer is obviously no. And whilst we're on the subject of lotteries, who knows what would have happened if Terry Venables' Barcelona side had struck lucky in the penalty shoot-out against Steaua? Maybe Seville 1986 would have marked the beginning of an era instead of the beginning of the end for El Tel. If Venables had gone on to greater glory, Cruyff might never have joined Barcelona in the first place. And coaches still claim they control their destiny?

If two of the world's most prestigious managers can produce such a topsy-turvy saga over a dozen seasons at one of the world's most powerful clubs, what the hell does that say about the rest of the men at the managerial helm? The vicissitudes of Terry Venables and Johan Cruyff at Barcelona suggest that even the top men are at the mercy of the footballing gods. After all, very little changed in their respective philosophies as personal fortunes wavered; one day they'd make the most astute decisions, the next defy logic, but hey, who cares if it's all down to luck in the end, anyway? The same whims and circumstances that dictate the fate of all managers eventually got to Venables and Cruyff as well. And it doesn't matter what your name is and where you ply your trade, if Lady Luck turns her back on you, managerial accountability eventually translates into culpability. That means *adiós*, bye-bye or *vaarwel*, whatever your previous achievements.

9 Managers and Mavericks

By Adrian Thrills

In the 1970s, they were often, usually detrimentally, called Fancy Dans. By the 1980s, they had become Wayward Geniuses. In Scotland, they were once Tanner Ba' Players, nimble operators who could turn on an old sixpence. At their ultimate best, they are the Super-Superstars that historically stamp their skills and personalities on major international tournaments.

Footballers with great flair have not always combined their inspiration with perspiration. They have not always tracked back, got 'stuck in' or adapted their skills unselfishly to whatever system of play their coach favoured. But they have turned crucial games in a fleeting moment of individual brilliance – the inspired through ball, mazy dribble or stunning shot. What they give is something that lies beyond the imagination and ability of the average professional.

A team's dependence on its most talented individuals has traditionally become more pronounced as the challenge has intensified. Historically, the higher you go in the global game – to World Cups and European Championships – the more influential your most creative attacking players become. They produce the element of surprise that can unlock even the best-organised defence.

In the five major international competitions between 1982 and 1990, the side that eventually emerged triumphant relied heavily on one outstanding individual star at the absolute pinnacle of his game. In the 1982 World Cup, it was Paolo Rossi of Italy; in the 1984 European Championship, Michel Platini of France; in the 1986 World Cup, Diego Maradona of Argentina; in the 1988 European Championship, Marco Van Basten of Holland; and in the 1990 World Cup, arguably, Lothar Matthäus of West Germany.

In each case, the supporting cast were also impressive. Each winning side enjoyed vital creative contributions from elsewhere in the team: Conti and Tardelli for Italy, Giresse and Tigana for France, Burruchaga and Valdano for Argentina, Gullit and Rijkaard for Holland, and Klinsmann and Brehme for West Germany.

If the international stage in the 1980s was set for a succession of individual greats, the 1990s have seen the pre-eminence of the team ethic. The game had already begun to move in this direction by Italia 90, and Franz Beckenbauer's winning side depended as much on collective effort and tactical nous as the occasional commanding solo performance like that produced by Matthäus in the opening game against Yugoslavia and Klinsmann in the second round against Holland.

Since 1990, the major trophies have been won by the best *teams*. In the European Championship, the victories savoured by Denmark in 1992 and the injury-savaged Germans in 1996 were essentially communal affairs in which no single attacking player left an indelible creative stamp. The Danish star in Sweden was goalkeeper Peter Schmeichel, outstanding in the final, while the most important German player at Euro 96 was the ball-winning anchorman Dieter Eilts.

And, despite the odd flourish from forwards Romario and Bebeto, the Brazilian side that won USA 94 counted more on organisation and the detailed planning of coach Carlos Alberto Parreira than those off-the-cuff moments of magic traditionally associated with the Brazilian game.

The trend in recent years, at international level, has been to tailor the talent to the shape of the team. Tactics and systems have generally been more important than players, and international squads have often been assembled with scant regard to those with the greatest individual skill.

With the onus increasingly on stopping the opposition, the more unorthodox creative player is often the first one omitted by a manager. The squads for Euro 96 were typical: among those absent were Cantona and Ginola of France, Baggio and Vialli of Italy, Matthäus of Germany and Le Tissier of England. Then there was the youthful Spanish promise of Raúl and Ivan de la Peña, unfledged talents that were kept under wraps until the Olympic tournament in Atlanta. Any one of these special players could have brought additional class, unpredictability and finesse to football's much-trumpeted 'homecoming'.

For most paying spectators – happily detached from the pressures of a managerial hot seat – such unique individuals are still the essence of the game. In our Dream Teams and Fantasy League line-ups, only the most extravagantly talented need apply. Football managers might take the gifted artisan over the exceptional artist, but fans will never tire of the mavericks.

Such suspicion of flair players was once a peculiarly English disease. The history of the England team is littered with the ghosts of talented misfits. Sir Alf Ramsey's exclusion of Jimmy Greaves from the 1966 World Cup final team had the ultimate exoneration in Geoff Hurst's thumping hat-trick for the Wingless Wonders. But the manner in which Ramsey and his successor Don Revie marginalised the likes of Alan Hudson, Stan Bowles, Frank Worthington, Charlie George and Tony Currie during the 1970s was never vindicated by the national team's achievements.

Hudson, an elegant midfielder in the glamorous Chelsea side of the 1970s, never fitted in with either the Ramsey or Revie regimes. Though originally selected by Sir Alf for the 1970 World Cup squad, he was forced to withdraw through injury and had to wait five years for his debut, eventually winning just two caps under Revie.

The first arrived in a tough but prestigious friendly against West Germany, after which his passing skills in a 2–0 home win had the Germans praising him as one of the finest talents in Europe. His second and final game came in a 5–0 win over Cyprus in which the Newcastle United striker Malcolm Macdonald scored all the England goals.

'The thing with Frank Worthington, Stan Bowles, Tony Currie and Rodney Marsh was that we could all play,' Hudson told *Goal* magazine in 1995. 'They didn't want that. They wanted hard-working players who would run their arses off. We didn't need to run our arses off. We could turn a game with skill, with an accurate pass or a chip over the top.

'If we had been picked more regularly, I'm sure England would have qualified for the '74 World Cup, the '76 European Championship and maybe even the '78 World Cup. Some people go on about the '70s being great. But on an international level, they were a disaster. It wasn't that we didn't have the players. It was that they were never picked. The emphasis in those days was pretty much as it is now. It was on selecting people who could stop others from playing.'

For Hudson and a host of other straggly-haired virtuosos of the 1970s, read the straggly-haired Glenn Hoddle in the 1980s. The supreme naturally gifted British footballer of his generation, the deceptively languid Tottenham midfielder was both a superb passer and an explosive long-range finisher. Under first the cerebral tactician Ron Greenwood and then the bruised romantic Bobby Robson, Hoddle should have racked up a century of international appearances.

Yet, despite scoring superbly from twenty yards on his first full England appearance against Bulgaria in November 1979, Hoddle was in and out of the national side until Robson made him a regular in the four years between 1985 and 1988, a period that encompassed the 1986 Mexico World Cup and the 1988 European Championship in West Germany.

Hoddle, who now picks the England squad himself, has claimed that his biggest regret in international football was not getting an extended run of games under the Greenwood tree. After his spectacular goalscoring Wembley bow, the 22-year-old sat out the next five international matches until being recalled for an end-of-season débâcle in Wrexham, where a makeshift England were humbled 4–1 by Wales. An occasional player in both the 1980 European Championship and 1982 World Cup, Hoddle held down a regular place only after England's failure to qualify for the 1984 European Championship in France. The current England manager believes his own international career might have been very different had he been given that vital run a little earlier in his career.

Bobby Robson, the England manager who eventually placed unimpaired faith in Hoddle, was initially criticised for not picking the Tottenham man more often. But he argued that he would have made him a midfield fixture much earlier had Glenn himself been constantly fit and available. Robson, vilified by the tabloid press during his eight-year stint at Lancaster Gate, was essentially a progressive coach who would generally resist a cautious approach in favour of an attack-minded one. Towards the end of his tenure, which culminated in the unlucky Italia 90 semifinal shoot-out defeat to West Germany, he often played with two skilful wingers

– Chris Waddle and John Barnes – neither of whom was noted for his propensity to track back.

But it was another precocious English enigma who gave Robson his biggest selection dilemma in the lead-up to Italia 90. The young Paul Gascoigne, like Hoddle before him, was the dynamic fulcrum of a Spurs midfield. His tactical naïveté and volatile nature, however, also made him a high-risk selection for a tournament as important as the World Cup.

In March 1990, as the build-up to Italy intensified, Bobby Robson told a gathering of national newspaper reporters that he could not afford 'to be deceived by flair alone'. At first glance, his words seemed to encapsulate the ambivalent attitude that England managers have historically taken towards their most skilful players. The implication appeared to be that footballers with flair were deceivers and not to be totally trusted.

Robson, wrestling with the Gazza conundrum, was probably just thinking aloud. A successful manager needs to strike a delicate balance between match-winning flair and an effective team pattern. Cramming a side with ten Chris Waddles plus Peter Shilton might have kept a full-time team hairdresser in gainful employment, but it would not have been much use against the Dutch team that England were due to face in their Sardinian World Cup group.

But Robson also knew that Gascoigne's effervescent talent could be his Italian trump card. Here was a player who could do for England what Maradona did for Argentina in 1986. A year before the finals, Gascoigne, struggling with a weight problem, was an outsider for the final 22-strong squad. Six months later, Robson had him inked in as a substitute. By the time the first game came around, he was a vital component in the team and emerged from Italy as the best young player in the tournament.

Accommodating maverick, often mercurial talents is arguably much easier at club level than in the international arena. The great Manchester United title-winning sides put together by Matt Busby often went onto the field of play with instructions simply to 'enjoy themselves'. And the refined Tottenham sides of the 1980s that were built around Hoddle, Waddle and Gascoigne – and the imported Argentinian invention of Ossie Ardiles and Ricky Villa – were further testimony to what can be achieved while playing with abundant flair. Spurs won two FA Cups and a UEFA Cup between 1981 and 1984, although their collection of beloved entertainers never made a serious challenge for the League crown.

Championship-winning sides in England traditionally integrate the skills of their solo stars into a team pattern durable enough to withstand the rigours of a long and demanding season. Howard Wilkinson, whose Leeds United side won the old First Division in 1992, decried as a 'myth' the idea that football should strive to be entertaining. Sport was not entertainment, argued the sage of Elland Road. It was an activity for the benefit of the participants.

Another title-winning manager of the early 1990s was Arsenal's George Graham. So laid-back was Graham as a player that he was given the nickname 'Stroller'. By the time he took up the managerial reins at Highbury in 1986, however, his philosophy had changed radically. Graham won six major honours with the Gunners, including the 1989 and 1991 League titles, and he did so with an unswerving belief that the team as a whole – rather than its gifted creators David Rocastle, Paul Davis and Paul Merson – was the star.

'The belief that no individual is bigger than the team is the one that has served Liverpool well for years,' Graham told *Goal* magazine in October 1995. 'Though there are still clubs in England and Italy who will buy a star and attempt to build a team around him, the Anfield way is still the best in my book. The greatest Liverpool sides have had genuine world class players – Hansen, Lawrenson, Souness, Dalglish and Rush in the '80s for example – all playing for the good of the team.

'The key to any signing, for me, has always been how a player will fit into your system. Most successful teams have a system and buy players to fit into it. For me, the crux always lies not in a player's individual attributes, but what he can contribute to the team. Take the overseas players who are now coming into the domestic game. There is little doubt as to their technical ability. Any doubts concern their mental and physical strength over a hard English season, where they might sometimes be playing three games in a week.

At overseas clubs, there have been many outstanding examples of coaches prepared to place more onus on attacking verve than defensive organisation. The Dutch manager Leo Beenhakker dominated the Spanish League Championship in the late 1980s with a flair-filled Real Madrid side built around the scintillating skills of the *Quinta del Buitre* – the Vulture Patrol – of Martin

Vázquez, Michel, Manuel Sanchis, Hugo Sánchez and Emilio Butragueño.

The muscular presence of somersaulting striker Sánchez notwithstanding, the quintet were hardly celebrated for their physical bite. Their ability on the ball, however, was mouth-watering, and they were a joy to behold in full attacking flow. The greatest club side of the last decade *not* to have won the European Cup, they still made a major impact on the continent's premier club competition, particularly in the 1987/88 season: in addition to eliminating holders FC Porto, they also defeated Napoli and Bayern Munich before losing on the away goals rule to eventual victors PSV Eindhoven in the semifinals.

In the early 1990s, the Parma side coached by Nevio Scala linked Gianfranco Zola of Italy, Faustino Asprilla of Colombia and Thomas Brolin of Sweden in a dizzy attack that was bolstered by the midfield artistry of Argentinian Nestor Sensini and the powerful shooting of Portuguese centre-back Fernando Couto. Though continually frustrated in their quest for the Italian *Scudetto* by the northern giants in Milan and Turin, Scala's Parma won four trophies in four seasons – the Copa Italia, Cup-Winners' Cup, UEFA Cup and Super Cup – while playing an exhilarating brand of football.

Particularly satisfying for Scala were two prestigious European victories over their major Italian rivals, where Parma displayed the full range of their extravagant technique and attacking abandon. The first came against Milan in the 1993 Super Cup final. The second was over Juventus in the two-legged UEFA Cup final of 1995, when former Juve and Italy midfielder Dino Baggio scored both goals against his old club in a 2–1 aggregate win.

When Pelé called football the Beautiful Game, he did so in an era when unfettered attacking flair enjoyed almost total ascendancy over the system addicts. And if some of the world's more cautious coaches in England and Italy were devising strategies to guarantee narrow victories or, at least, scoreless draws, the Brazilians traditionally maintained a classic philosophy: if they score three, we'll score four. It was an attitude that had brought the South Americans three World Cups between 1958 and 1970, and given the world both its finest player and its greatest-ever team.

In returning Brazil to the highest perch in world football for the first time in 24 years, however, the team's USA 94 coach Carlos Alberto Parreira opted to go against the grain of Brazil's soccer heritage. Without completely sacrificing the individual skills associated with the famous yellow shirt, Parreira won the World Cup, albeit in a penalty decider against the Italians, through organisation and planning. In the build-up to the tournament, the squad trained morning and afternoon for fifteen days, working on set pieces, corners and free kicks. Rather than play off the cuff as the team had often done in the past, Parreira prepared every detail. He also ensured that his side were among the fittest in the finals. And it worked.

'I didn't have to teach our players how to play football,' he told *World Soccer* after the triumph. 'But I did have to help them play as a unit. That can be very difficult for Brazilian players, because they are all individuals. My prime concern was to get my players to concentrate on playing without the ball.

'In the past few World Cups, we have been good when we had the ball, but not when we lost it. My concern was to organise our team without the ball. I accept that we were not the greatest Brazilian team of all time, but we had a winning mentality. And we had harmony within the squad.'

Stars or systems. Talent or tactics. Never was the debate about whether or not an international side should be built around its most gifted individuals more intense than in the prelude to the 1996 European Championship in England. Football came home in Euro 96, but some of its most exciting practitioners controversially stayed away. And for once – give or take a few token protests about Terry Venables not picking an out-of-form Matt Le Tissier – the hottest debate centred not around the English squad, but around the selections made by two of Europe's most eminent managers.

French coach Aimé Jacquet approached Euro 96 in charge of a side that ranked among the pre-tournament favourites. In a 22-match unbeaten run before the competition, France had won fifteen games and drawn seven. And they had done it without two of the biggest stars in French football.

Eric Cantona and David Ginola, plying their trade impressively in the English Premiership, were players of unquestionable international pedigree. But they, along with tried and trusted striker

Jean-Pierre Papin, were both *persona non grata* to Jacquet. The coach, who disliked the concept of players as 'superstars', had built his team's run on defensive steel and the emerging attacking talents of Bordeaux midfielder Zinedine Zidane and deep-lying Paris Saint-Germain forward Youri Djorkaeff – players who occupied the very positions that Ginola and Cantona had previously held in the French side.

Cantona had been Jacquet's first captain when he took over the national side in 1994 following their failure to qualify for USA 94. He had been, according to Jacquet, a key influence in a developing squad. But Eric was stripped of both the captain's armband and his place in the French squad after his attack on a fan in the Crystal Palace–Manchester United game at Selhurst Park in January 1995, an offence that also earned him an eight-month ban from the English game. While logging Cantona's pivotal role in inspiring United to a double win in England after his return, Jacquet opted to stick with the players and system that had served France so well in qualifying. The twenty goals that Cantona had scored in his 45 appearances for *Les Bleus* were deemed insufficient to secure him a place.

Ginola's case was slightly different. The winger had been in sparkling form for Newcastle United as Kevin Keegan's exciting side challenged, fruitlessly, for the English Premiership. But he had never been a regular in Jacquet's squad. To many French fans, he was also the scapegoat for a blunder that cost France their place at USA 94. In the last seconds of a crucial World Cup qualifier against Bulgaria in Paris, he lost possession, setting in motion a swift counter-attack from which Emil Kostadinov scored a goal that allowed the Bulgarians to steal a dramatic 2–1 away victory and eliminate the French. The fact that Bulgaria, like the Polish team that conquered England twenty years previously, went on to become World Cup dark horses and semifinalists was of little subsequent consolation.

Before finalising his squad, Jacquet watched both his exiles in England in 1996, seeing Cantona star against Aston Villa at Old Trafford before moving down to Coventry where Ginola played the following day for Newcastle. When it came to the crunch, however, neither of the senior servants made the final cut.

Though there was predictable clamour from Manchester and Newcastle for the inclusion of their heroes, Jacquet argued that he was not picking a team for the benefit of English fans. It was not just the English, however, who wanted to see Cantona and Ginola in the squad. Luis Fernandez, coach of Cup-Winners' Cup champions Paris St Germain, claimed that most French supporters also wanted Cantona in the side, an opinion backed by a nationwide poll on the eve of the competition.

But Jacquet maintained that the French had taken on another dimension without the gifted duo, and he did not wish to alter this balance. He also maintained that Euro 96 was a chance for an emerging side to gain experience. The 1998 World Cup on home soil was the real objective.

As the tournament got under way, France initially looked the part. They extracted comprehensive revenge for 1993 by beating, and thus eliminating, the Bulgarians 3–1 at St James' Park. But, after topping their group, they were unable to overcome either a demoralised Dutch team or the unfancied Czechs in the knockout stages. Two goalless draws and the lottery of two penalty shoot-outs ensued. The first, against Holland, was won. The second, in the Old Trafford semifinal against Dusan Uhrin's Czech Republic, was lost, and the French were out.

Though well organised as a unit, France lacked the fantasy, the flair and the attacking imagination that might have unlocked resilient opponents. The midfield brilliance and the Platini-inspired side that emerged in the 1978 World Cup in Argentina and went on to become European champions on home soil in 1984 was a distant memory.

Would Ginola and Cantona have made the difference? Some thought they would, although others argued the problem lay elsewhere. Former France and Bordeaux midfielder Alain Giresse believed that the inclusion of a clinical goalscorer – he cited Olympique Lyon's Florian Maurice – was all that was separating France from greater things. For Jacquet, with only friendlies to play until the summer of 1998, the real test of his theories is yet to come.

Aimé Jacquet was not the only Euro 96 coach confronted with clamour from both media and fans for the inclusion of certain players. In the Spanish football citadels of the Camp Nou and Bernabeu, the popular choices were two teenage prodigies who were beginning to make their mark in the domestic League and in the various European club competitions.

The Cult of the Manager

In Barcelona, the star was explosive young midfielder Ivan de la Peña. An impetuous player nicknamed 'Little Buddah' because of his close-cropped hair, de la Peña was already a hero to Catalan fans, despite only making his debut on the opening day of the 1995/96 season. He had marked that first game with a goal, dribbling the ball around the Valladolid goalkeeper to score audaciously. His first touch in European football was even sweeter – a right-footed free kick that sailed into the net.

Barça's great rivals Real Madrid, meanwhile, had a young star of their own. Raúl, a sublimely gifted nineteen-year-old inside forward, had become Real's youngest-ever debutant when he made his first team bow at seventeen. Described by the then coach Jorge Valdano as a player who could create 'something out of nothing', Raúl had also been enjoying a spectacular season, most notably in scoring a hat trick for Madrid against Ferençvaros in the Champions League and then netting another three for the Spanish Under-21 side against Macedonia. As with de la Peña, youthful confidence enabled him to play without fear.

Among Spanish fans, the clamour for the inclusion of the two precocious young luminaries was intense. For national coach Javier Clemente, however, qualification for Euro 96 had been achieved through team strengths and tactical adaptability rather than reliance on outstanding individual talents. Like Jacquet of France, Clemente opted not to upset the balance of team and squad. The two public favourites were left on the sidelines. With youth on their side, and places in the Spanish Olympic squad guaranteed, Raúl and de la Peña would eventually get their chance. But it was not to be in Euro 96.

'Raúl is destined to make his mark on a whole generation, and not just in Spanish football,' said Clemente. 'At his age, he's got to take things one step at a time. My job is to defend my players, so I only pick players I can defend. I wouldn't want to take a youngster like Raúl without being sure that the experience wouldn't affect him adversely.'

Going against popular opinion was nothing new to the single-minded Spanish coach. He had omitted Real heroes Butragueño and Michel from his USA 94 squad. Many Madrileños bore him such resentment that they even took pleasure in Spain's unlucky quarter-final defeat to Arrigo Saachi's Italians in Boston, a match marred by the elbowing of Luis Enrique by the *Azzurris*' Mauro Tassotti.

In qualifying for USA 94, Clemente's side had been drawn in the same group as Jack Charlton's Republic of Ireland. Spain eventually topped the section, booking their ticket to the finals with an emphatic 3–1 win over the Irish in Dublin in October 1993. Among those who was able to view Clemente's management style at close quarters that afternoon was Republic striker John Aldridge. Having also played Spanish League football, 'Aldo' was already familiar with Clemente's methods and likened them to an English approach. This was not totally surprising: Clemente, as a young coach, had studied under Bobby Robson at Ipswich Town.

'As Spanish manager, Clemente has got rid of a few players,' observed Aldridge at the time. 'The players he has left out were outstanding individuals, but they didn't really fit into a team plan. He's now got Spain playing the way the Irish do. They play as a tough unit, rather than relying on flashes of individual brilliance. They work hard and pull for one another.'

One of the virtues of a top coach is loyalty to his players and Clemente could never be faulted on that score. When choosing his three nominations for the FIFA World Player of the Year in 1996, an award scooped by Milan's Liberian striker George Weah, Clemente went for Hierro, Nadal and Zubizarreta. The players were three of the defensive linchpins of his Spanish side, a team unfortunate to leave Euro 96 as penalty shoot-out losers to England.

Not all of the game's leading coaches admired the efficient pragmatism of much of Euro 96. Former Barcelona manager Johan Cruyff, one of the patriarchs of Total Football, criticised what he called 'the cult of fear' that had enveloped football at the highest level. Citing the Old Trafford semifinal between France and the Czech Republic, Cruyff claimed that teams were no longer capable of taking a risk in order to try to win a crucial game during normal time.

The defensive outlook of the majority of managers at Euro 96 was borne out by one staggering fact: until the final, when Germany stormed back from one down to beat the Czechs 2–1, with goals from Oliver Bierhoff, no team had come from behind to win a game. Many teams were taking the field without the creative resources to chase match-winning goals when they most needed them.

Another esteemed observer, Arsène Wenger, believed that the 'golden goal' method of settling games that went into extra time was wrong. The profusion of 120-minute-long scoreless games in the knockout stage of the competition appeared to prove that players were merely trying to avoid making mistakes rather than attempting to score. It was essential, Wenger argued, that players and managers adapted to the new rules and took more risks. Only that way would the next generation of Maradonas and Platinis emerge.

Perhaps the sternest and most outspoken critic of what he termed 'the dictatorship of the blackboard' was Jorge Valdano. A World Cup winner with Argentina in 1986 and a title-winning manager with Real Madrid in Spain during 1995, Valdano was also disillusioned with Euro 96. Blaming the coaches, he claimed the tournament was intrinsically defensive and lacking in fantasy.

'Trainers are now more important than players, and that's an extremely dangerous perversion,' Valdano told *World Soccer* in September 1996. 'But talent is primordial. A good player is always worth more than a good idea. Production line players, systematic players, have now become indispensable. And players who are different, who can change a match with something unexpected, are having great difficulty in adapting.

'These players are getting increasingly less freedom to create. They are seen as a threat to an order which considers imagination as subversive. And that is why Ginola, Cantona, de la Peña and Baggio were left out. We trainers are now so careful about the insignificant details that we are losing sight of the essentials.'

Valdano's perception of where football may be heading is not particularly alluring for those seeking entertainment, aesthetic pleasure even, from the game. But the Argentinian also believes that soccer moves in cycles, and points out that the late 1970s were a wasteland for truly stellar talent before genuine greats like Platini, Zico, Maradona and Van Basten took control in the 1980s.

The same thing could easily happen again. Any one of a rising tide of new young players could be the world's next superstar. It could be Raúl or de la Peña. It could be Robbie Fowler or David Beckham, both already capped for England. Maybe one of Parma's new stars, the Italian Enrico Chiesa or the Argentinian Hernan Crespo. Possibly a Nigerian such as James Obiorah of Anderlecht or Tijani Babangida of Ajax. Perhaps the South African Mark Fish, the German Lars Ricken or Barcelona's £12.5m Brazilian Ronaldo, already the third-most expensive player ever . . .

Much of this budding young talent could flower spectacularly in the 1998 World Cup in France. That is, of course, if the trainers allow it to bloom fully. Football may be too imprecise a sport to become a science, but even ex-England coach Terry Venables has warned that it will rely increasingly on organisation, with computers used to analyse tactics. The days of coaches, like the idealistic Ossie Ardiles, simply telling a team to 'go out and play like Pelé' appear to be over.

But the modern game at its best – as played by Holland's Total Footballers or Milan's more recent sophisticates – is a delicate compromise between tactics and talent. It is a matter of balance, and some managers are in danger of falling off the tightrope. Somewhere down the line, the equilibrium must surely be restored.

10 Managing on Limited Resources

Macari, Ardiles, Hoddle and McMahon at Swindon Town
By Graham Carter

The gulf between the stinking rich clubs in the Premiership and the stinking peasants in the bowels of the Football League is huge, and growing wider every day. For most of the smaller clubs, the Premiership is a foreign country run by (and for) huge marketing machines which generate cash at a rate almost unimaginable in the lower divisions; but although competing with the Premiership giants requires massive financial investment, life in Divisions One, Two and Three is not (and never has been) about the 'haves' and the 'have-nots'.

The scale of clubs' operations outside the Premiership is largely irrelevant because many of those clubs find themselves in the same boat. When your rivals' resources are as limited as yours and you are competing on equal terms, success is achieved firstly by really wanting to raise the stakes and secondly by giving yourself an edge. It's more a question of 'wannabes' and 'don't wannabes' – and spotting them is easy because you often need look no further than the manager's office.

In the last dozen or so years, no club has demonstrated the lot of the also-rans better than Swindon Town. The Wiltshire club has shown that it is possible to rise from the terminal mediocrity that infests the lower divisions. Since 1986, Swindon Town has seen five promotions and two relegations, high-profile comings and goings at managerial level – and not one but three financial scandals which led to demotion by two divisions (later reduced to one division on appeal). It added up to easily the most turbulent period in the club's 110-year history, but it was certainly the time when Swindon left all that small-club mentality behind them.

In 1996 Swindon Town fans were celebrating the latest promotion – ironically at Blackpool, where a 1–1 draw clinched their return to the First Division. Blackpool may be the home of the biggest white-knuckle ride in the world, but, as the *Swindon Evening Advertiser* put it in a series of weekly flashbacks charting the club's recent history, Swindon Town were the ones who had just lived through the Rollercoaster Years. And the rollercoaster was driven not by the chairman and the directors, but by the managers. Ask any Swindon Town fan and he'll tell you that managers make all the difference.

Swindonians still talk about the dark days before Lou Macari was appointed manager. Until then, Swindon Town's contribution to footballing history in the 100 years since it was founded had been minimal, bordering on the anonymous. It took the club over 30 years to crawl out of the obscurity of the Southern League and they spent the next 40 years wallowing in the depths of the old Third Division. Fans from the 1940s and 1950s still recall how the Town often looked capable of reaching the heady heights of Second Division football, only to fall back out of the promotion race just when things started to get interesting. Many still argue that the prospect of leaving behind cosy little Division Three (South) with its minimal travelling expenses and its non-existent hotel budget ensured that the club never quite made the mistake of getting itself promoted.

It was the Swinging Sixties before the fans finally got their first taste of life in the Second Division, winning promotion twice in a decade that also included a fairytale League Cup win over Arsenal at Wembley. By the mid-1970s normality was restored as Town were back in Division Three again, and they even dipped into Division Four for the first time in the club's history.

Then, in July 1984, everything changed. Swindon Town got themselves a new manager in Lou Macari, but much more important than that, they got themselves a new type of manager.

The transformation of Swindon Town from rank also-rans from rural Wiltshire into a club that now expects First Division football at the very least was not brought about by any routine boardroom decision. Yes, the chairman and his directors decided it was time for a change, but only after the club's first-ever sponsors, insurance brokers Lowndes Lambert, had insisted they wanted to break the mould and bolster the club's image with a high-profile player/manager. Swindon, at this time, was the fastest-growing town in the whole of Europe, starting to think about trading in its town charter for city status and congratulating itself on being a boom town while the rest of the nation was sliding into recession all around it. The time was ripe and Lou Macari fitted the bill exactly. 'We didn't interview him; he interviewed us,' claimed the club chairman as Macari took the driving seat and set the rollercoaster in motion.

But even before Macari's first season was over, the board had grown tired of the manager and his assistant, Harry Gregg, bickering over the team's style of play and the training regime, so both were unceremoniously sacked. The board clearly hadn't read the script and after an outcry from the fans (who clearly had) Macari was reinstated, five days later. This remarkable and admirable U-turn said everything about where the club was going – and who would be leading the revolution. Macari was given a free rein but hardly any money – and he would soon prove that at that level he didn't need much. The board, bless them, clung on to the rollercoaster for dear life.

It was a huge milestone for Swindon because the die was now cast and even after Macari had conquered and left, his successors were cut from the same cloth. With the exception of John Gorman, whose appointment in 1993 was to be an understandable attempt to maintain the continuity of a successful team, all subsequent managers have been international midfielders with exceptional reputations as players who took their chance of cutting their managerial teeth at a 'wannabe' club with both hands – and succeeded.

But to understand how managers can have such an influence on not just a small club's football but its whole status, you first have to understand about life in those lower divisions. Make no mistake, in the depths of professional football in this country, mediocrity is king. We could talk about York, Cardiff and Lincoln – cities unable to produce a single team worth more than a footnote in the annals of football in this country – but they are merely the first three that spring to mind from a long list of fully paid-up members of the Going Nowhere Club. You can add plenty more names of your own.

The fact is that at the majority of the clubs in Division Two and Division Three – and often in Division One, for that matter – the trick is to avoid getting on any rollercoasters in the first place. Like any other business, and especially a small one with perhaps less than 30 full-time employees, a football club's mission is all about satisfying customers, building markets and delivering the right product. But the so-called hard-up clubs are not sailing nearly as close to the wind as they might have us imagine. In any other comparative competitive market, you might expect at least ten or twenty per cent of small businesses to go down the proverbial pan in any period of, say, five years, but how many supposedly insolvent football clubs have we said goodbye to in the last ten years?

None of them may have the potential to become the Manchester Uniteds of the twenty-first century, but most clubs in the Football League have evolved into remarkably resilient survivors. They have lived through two world wars, recessions, Tory governments and all the incompetent football authorities we could throw at them – and will probably also ride out any ripples caused by Mr Bosman and his lawyers.

The fact is that most clubs in the lower reaches of the League are doing quite nicely thank you, chugging along in the slow lane while the boy racers like Swindon risk their necks in the middle lane. Why change? Any successful business remains prosperous by cornering the market and making sure it is a fat fish in a small pond and the smaller clubs, or at least their boards of directors, have been content in the knowledge that their little industry runs on a small staff (both on and off the pitch) who demand not unreasonable wages, and this makes for very healthy economics. Steady (if unspectacular) income is guaranteed at the turnstiles – much of it up front, thanks to perennial season ticket holders – and any club can always rely on a predictable hard core of diehard fans who will put the bread and butter on the table, come rain or shine. And if some of your customers don't like your product, they're hardly likely to go down the road and sample somebody else's. Football fans provide a habitual loyalty factor that many other businesses would kill for.

Extra revenue comes from sales of programmes and burgers and by stamping the club's old-fashioned badge on everything from knickers to nappies. The sale of ludicrously overpriced replica shirts that have become a fashion accessory for every snotty-nosed schoolboy and beer-bellied former bovver-boy is not so much a spin-off as a licence to print money. Other nice little earners include the ingenious sponsorship deals now peddled by every club in the League, from the multinational companies who will pay tens of thousands to put their name across your shirts, to those fanatics willing to dip into their pockets to sponsor the reserve team goalie's shorts. But even if your little club is slow at coming forward when it comes to marketing, the bank manager still goes to bed happy when the cheques arrive for the club's share from the pools companies, TV stations and (should you be forced to improve the ground for any reason) a handy grant from the Football Trust.

Every so often every club is also guaranteed to hit the jackpot with a plum Cup draw, and its cigars all round when Manchester United or Liverpool come to town. For most clubs there is also the promise that, one day, one of the more talented youngsters on your books will attract the attention of the big clubs. With any luck you will soon have Alex Ferguson on the phone, telling you you've won the lottery.

Poor they may appear, but these comparatively tiny businesses can have very healthy turnovers and they are seemingly immune from bankruptcy because their assets in terms of the ground, the value of their players and the goodwill of their customers are strong enough to offset any temporary losses, season by season. Football clubs can even survive for no other reason than their potential to rapidly generate more income. In other words, if they fail to cash in on the sources already highlighted here and all else fails, they could go and get themselves promoted.

For many, this will certainly be a last resort because when it comes to the real world of business and economics, small can be beautiful. Many businesses would flounder under the kind of rapid and unplanned growth that a football club goes through when promoted, particularly when there is no certainty of where its market will be another twelve months down the road. It could spell financial disaster for a minnow to be suddenly launched into a sea of troubles, dominated by sharks. The rapid rise in overheads, not necessarily accompanied by a corresponding boom in income, could cripple a club. Frankly, most club directors need promotion like they need a hole in the head.

But if clubs in general don't need success on the pitch, then directors need it even less. You only have to ask yourself what makes anybody want to be a director in the first place. Chances are he's a genuine fan who is passionate about football, but essentially he's a would-be footballer who never had anything like the ability to be a pro himself and now craves the lifestyle and the buzz that goes with the professional game, even in Division Three. He is probably a moderately successful businessman with neither the money nor the inclination to become the next Jack Walker, but he is happy enough to contribute a reasonable amount – either in cash or as overdraft guarantees at the bank – in order to buy himself a seat on the board. In return he gets a special kind of season ticket that costs rather more than the standard issue but which gains him unlimited access to all parts of the ground and a degree of power, if he wants it. He loves every minute of it.

Most of what directors do, either consciously or subconsciously, is surely designed to preserve their status. If the club were to be promoted, for example – and particularly if it suddenly rose two divisions in two years – the stakes would immediately be raised and directors would be expected to dig deeper into their own pockets to maintain the club's new status. The rollercoaster begins racing out of control and the first passengers likely to be thrown out as it reaches a new peak are the directors who can't afford the new fares. You can hardly blame them for seeing to it that any thoughts of real change are nipped in the bud and that the aspirations stay well and truly grounded.

An example of the small-time mentality of your average director is highlighted in Garry Nelson's fine book *Left Foot Forward*, which recalls one director (appropriately at Swindon) who 'was in the habit of putting his head round the door and dazzling us with: "Win today, lads, and you're all on a free chicken" ' It makes you wonder how many chickens they start the bidding with these days in Premiership dressing rooms.

Small-minded the boards may be in the lower divisions, but they must also appear to be trying their best to get results, especially when supporters are paying good money to see their team lose every week. Yet when the pressure is on and the restless natives are organising sit-down protests and post-match demonstrations, change is still resisted. The board will issue the customary vote of confidence in the manager, but eventually they will have to show that they mean business by calling him into the boardroom and showing him the door. There's nothing unusual and certainly nothing brave or revolutionary there, but what the board does next speaks volumes about their true ambitions for the club.

They could promote from within, perhaps raising an unsuspecting youth team or reserve team coach to the hot seat, or they could reward a particularly loyal and devoted veteran player or former player with a crack at the job. They could even splash out on an advertisement in the *Daily Mail* and wait for a string of moderately successful lower division managers to spoil them for choice. Any one of these options might – just might – produce a dramatic change in fortunes, but, ultimately, all three plans will see to it that nothing actually changes. The names may change, but it is still in everybody's interests for the club to remain where it is, and that could even include the new manager.

A manager's position is most precarious after he has enjoyed success. You are far more secure scraping into the play-offs at the last minute and just missing out on promotion than if you move up a grade and hold a mid-table position where fans and sponsors can soon lose interest. Twitchy directors looking for scapegoats for the apparent rut the club now finds itself in (albeit in a higher division) are likely to be calling for the head of the manager to appease them.

The final and most important bar to any club hauling itself out of obscurity is the players, who (as any manager will tell you) are a breed apart. If any fan had a fraction of the pure, natural talent for the game that every single professional footballer has in abundance, he wouldn't sleep for fear of waking up and finding it's a dream. There is no shortage of fans who would sell their grandmothers for five minutes in the club's colours – and not five minutes at Wembley or the San Siro or the Maracana, either, but five minutes at Bootham Crescent or Ninian Park or Sincil Bank. If only.

Yet the ungrateful majority who actually live the life of these gods almost seem to resent it. Having ridden their talent to the heady heights of being a full-time professional, many are reluctant to work at it and, like their clubs, are happy to be underachievers, perhaps afraid of getting out of their depth. In no other industry do managers (good ones, anyway) feel the need to shout and bawl at grown men to try to motivate them into just doing what they are paid for. Football managers are in charge of highly skilled workers who have a rare talent and might be only 90 minutes from real stardom, yet so often they have to resort to treating these grown men like children. How many other professional sportsmen do you know of, including those in much less fashionable or lucrative sports, who have to be curfewed and bullied into refraining from drinking, even the night before a match?

Long after Lou Macari had left Swindon, the overriding memory of his time as manager was how he dealt with those members of his squad who lived more for Friday night than Saturday afternoon. Stories are legion of how Macari would go undercover to track down the drinkers and clubbers, and at one stage he even went public to shock and shame them into changing their attitudes. Indeed, Macari's unpopularity with certain players was already well established because of a tremendous emphasis on fitness. 'I can remember worrying midway through lung-bursting, gut-busting running sessions,' recalls Garry Nelson, 'about whether I would be able to recognise a ball again in the unlikely event of ever seeing one.'

Macari's team had a reputation for playing the long-ball game, especially in hindsight when compared with the slick-passing teams from Swindon's Ossie Ardiles and Glenn Hoddle eras, but this is as much a misconception as it is an injustice. As players later argued, it wasn't necessarily a long-ball ploy, it was just that they moved the ball forward so quickly. What Macari had done was to weed out those who were more interested in socialising than keeping their athletic bodies in A1 shape, and then turned the rest into the fittest, strongest team in the old Division Four. They were by no means exceptional players, but Macari either made the most of the limited ability of the players he already had or bought cheaply to bring players whose attitudes matched his own to the County Ground. He meant business, and once it was pointed in the right direction the rollercoaster started to climb at lightning speed. After a shaky start to the Fourth Division season which saw them drop to fourth from bottom of the League in September 1985, Swindon Town suddenly took off on a run of success that was to catapult them into the record books by the end of the season. They are still there as the only team ever to gain over 100 points in a single campaign.

All Macari really did was get that little bit extra from players who, on paper, seemed to have little to give and they were bonded by a team spirit born out of devices like pre-match training camps at army barracks – ideas that would be anathema to many players, but they produced a team that was almost invincible that season.

Money was never a driving force, even though the much-publicised and grossly exaggerated financial 'scandals' at Swindon might suggest otherwise. Irregular payments were certainly made to players, mainly to get them to sign for the club in the first place, and this was a grave error, but wages were not the spur that rocketed the club out of the basement.

Full-back Dave Hockaday, one of the mainstays of the team during the Macari reign, recalls: 'Lou had a great knack of finding players and bringing them in cheaply. He would knit us together and we would die for each other out on the pitch. It's ten years on and I still keep in touch with a lot of the lads because the team spirit was so good at the time, but it's amazing really because we got paid peanuts. People would be amazed to find out how much we were on. Lou used to think it would keep us hungry, but when I moved on, the grass was definitely greener on the other side. I think he modelled himself on Jock Stein and his authority kept him separate from the players. If Lou would say jump, we would ask "How high?"'

In fact, they jumped right out of the Third Division a year after winning the Fourth Division Championship, and were only denied the last chapter of a truly meteoric rise up to the top division by big-spending Crystal Palace in a Second Division play-off a year later. The climb had been thrilling and hair-raising, but as Macari left for the brighter lights of West Ham, financial scandals were beginning to raise their ugly heads.

There were, in fact, three so-called scandals, which all took place during the Macari years, beginning with a bet that chairman Brian Hillier had placed on the club to win the Third Division Championship. A disappointed Football Association scoured the rule-book before admitting that, actually, Swindon had broken no rules. With the second bet, however they clearly had overstepped the mark. This time Hillier backed the club to lose an FA Cup tie at Newcastle – which they duly did in no uncertain terms, thrashed 5–0. Hillier claimed the bet had been 'insurance' against expenses that his little club had incurred on the long trip north. It didn't stick and he was banned from the game for six months, later increased sixfold because he dared to appeal.

Having scented blood, both the FA and the Inland Revenue moved in for the kill, and the bloodhounds were licking their lips when they were fed further evidence of dodgy dealing. An under-hand takeover bid had been brewing at the County Ground as others tried to jump on the suddenly successful bandwagon that Macari and Hillier had set in motion. Details of under-the-counter payments to players were leaked by insiders willing to risk wrecking the club for a piece of the pie. Fans woke up one morning to find the gory details splashed across the back page of the *People*.

New manager Ossie Ardiles' style of football – and indeed his softly spoken style of management – was radically different to the gospel according to Lou Macari, but Ardiles' success at Swindon was achieved with many of the self-same players whom Macari had assembled. The new emphasis on ballwork and fancy foot-work now embellished a still fit and eager team with a midfield diamond formation and other niceties that most of their oppo-nents had never even heard of. Slick-passing, classy Swindon Town and their fans were a credit to English football, but the Football League allowed a sham of a play-off in front of a full house at Wembley in 1990 before they threw the book at them ten days later, turning the celebration of the club's first-ever promo-tion to the top division into a wake. The League's argument that Swindon had gained an unfair advantage over their penniless rivals never held any water.

Swindon's fans simply concluded that their crime was not that they had risen above their peers, but that they were muscling in on the forbidden fruit of the Premier League which the big clubs were conspiring towards. The demotion by two divisions was later reduced to one when it was pointed out that the club could win a High Court case against the League because the guilty parties had now moved on. Swindon's loyal and well-behaved fans were the ones who were punished most for the club's minor indiscretions. The penalty was still harsh.

Chairman Brian Hillier eventually went to jail for failing to declare the tax on the 'under-the-counter' payments and his six-month jail sentence for a first offence was designed to make Swindon Town as much a scapegoat for the Inland Revenue as it was for the FA and the Football League. Their biggest crime was breaking the eleventh commandment – 'Thou shalt not be found out' – and the fact that any one of a dozen or more clubs might have been the ones to take the rap instead was no consolation. The bitterest irony for Swindon fans is that subsequent similar breaches of rules by Chelsea and Tottenham went virtually unpunished.

The simple fact, though, was that Swindon Town didn't need to cook the books in order to achieve the success they had been starved of for so long. The edge they needed to climb out of their mediocrity had not been provided by ill-conceived financial shenanigans, but because Lou Macari had broken the mould and turned journeymen footballers into winners, and Ossie Ardiles followed suit. Despite everything, and although the club had almost faced financial ruin, its willingness to move on was undiminished.

After Ardiles came Hoddle, a player/manager who rebuilt another team of apparently average players into one capable of reclaiming Town's (rightful) place in the top flight, and one that was as watchable as any that had ever graced the County Ground. Hoddle, when he shook off his injuries, led by example on the pitch. While his inch-perfect cross-field passes caused the fans quite literally to gasp in admiration, something similar was happening on the training ground. Though the installation of a manager who also happened to be an exceptional player had been the original master plan, both Macari and Ardiles had marshalled their troops with considerably more success from the dugout than from the centre circle. Indeed, the beginning of Macari's team's rise up the League coincided almost exactly with his final appearance as a player/manager. But Hoddle was different. He did his talking on the field where just a little of his immense ability and reputation was bound to rub off on those around him.

Sadly, even as he was inspiring and masterminding a dramatic 4–3 Wembley play-off win over Leicester in 1993, Hoddle was preparing to leave for Chelsea. Frustrated by the need to sell key players to finance the club's push towards the Premiership, he was in no doubt that he had done all he could for Swindon Town and moved on to a club better suited to fighting the enormous financial battles of the Premiership.

Hoddle's erstwhile assistant, John Gorman, deserves more than a little credit for the achievements of the Hoddle years, but when he took the helm he was always doomed to fail to keep the club in the top division. Swindon Town simply found that the step up from the First Division to the Premiership is too great for any club and probably for any manager without multi-million-pound backing. Dogged by a need to pay substantially bigger wages and trapped into offering three-year deals to players who were never to repay their faith, the club was knocked sideways by huge staff costs. With this millstone around its neck it was sent spiralling towards two consecutive relegations. Rightly or wrongly, Gorman, who had been given the job in order to preserve the status quo after Hoddle's abrupt departure, was held responsible for the slide, and there was never any question that the club would return to the old formula of installing a big-name player/manager in his place.

Steve McMahon got the nod and he wasted no time in taking a new brush to virtually every corner of the County Ground. One of the first to go was Jan Aage Fjortoft, the Norwegian international who had found his scoring touch too late to rescue the club from the Premiership's wooden spoon but had turned himself into a scorer of sensational goals and a crowd-pleaser like no other player seen at the County Ground for a generation (Hoddle excepted, of course). McMahon's preference for workmanlike and committed (but none the less skilful) players saw virtually the whole playing staff and most of the key backroom people sacrificed in the name of change.

If some fans never quite forgave him for selling Fjortoft, and if his no-nonsense approach rankled with many who came into contact with him, most were still prepared to forgive McMahon for failing to save the club from relegation to the Second Division in 1994. In the following season, Swindon totally outclassed a division that was heaving with no-hopers and the rollercoaster was back on track.

Nobody is suggesting that Swindon Town's policy of making managers out of highly successful players is a guarantee of success, but if anybody, in any walk of life, wants change badly enough, then it will come. Bringing in men who have tasted success at the highest level – including one with a World Cup-winner's medal – certainly had the desired effect of inspiring mostly ordinary footballers to achieve something extraordinary at Swindon. The same might also be achieved at any other club with supposedly limited resources, but only if they have the stomachs for the ride.

Lou Macari and Ossie Ardiles have so far failed to achieve great success in the top division (which may or may not be significant) and we will have to wait to find out whether Glenn Hoddle and Steve McMahon will go on to be great managers at a higher level. But when they were in charge at one small club, it enjoyed the kind of success that had previously eluded it for a century. Either

The Cult of the Manager

Swindon Town stumbled on a magic formula for fighting their way out of obscurity in the lower divisions ... or that's one hell of a lucky streak.

11 Managing Home and Away

In conversation with Bobby Robson and Michael Robinson
By Jeff King

Bobby Robson has managed Fulham, Ipswich, England, PSV Eindhoven, Sporting Lisbon, Porto and FC Barcelona. As a player at West Bromwich Albion he was capped twenty times for England.

Is a manager's success born of what he does on the training ground?

It's about being knowledgeable and being able to get things across to your players. What a manager does in training – every day of the week, every week of the season – is crucial; his ability to train the players well, to inspire them, to improve their technical expertise and tactical knowledge. So much is about being fit and being able to perform over 90 minutes, so you must always have a good conditioning programme, aimed at players sustaining a level of fitness over a long period. Everything you do in training is reflected during games: you develop organisation, you foster good habits and attitude, you instil discipline; all of which you hope translates into good performances on match days. At the same time, you've got to keep your players interested. They need variety, nobody wants to do the same thing day after day; it's like eating steak all the time, after a while you get fed up with it, don't you? So you need a varied training programme; a manager's knowledge of coaching methods is very important.

As a manager, have you always been a hands-on coach as well?

Yes, I've always taken training at all my clubs. When you're appointed manager of a football club, essentially you're being appointed to get results on a Saturday; when a manager is sacked it's not necessarily because the club is being run badly off the pitch, it's because the team is failing. A board changes its manager hoping they can find someone to improve performances on the pitch; the club could be running very well. So you have to make sure you don't spend *all* your time on the side issues, and get taken away from the very thing you were contracted for in the first place, the very thing you're good at, which is running the team. It's not always easy to stick with the team, though; getting distracted is a trap that many managers fall into – and I know because it's happened to me. When I was at Ipswich, I did all the coaching but I had a million other things to do as manager as well. But it doesn't matter how well you do those other things, it'll always be the team's performances you'll be judged on. A manager should never forget that. If, for example, Blackburn Rovers are looking for a manager, it's not to run the club, Jack Walker can do that quite nicely, thank you, but to improve results.

I think English clubs will eventually adopt the European formula. Here at Barcelona I'm just the coach – all my work is with the team. It was the same at PSV, Sporting and Porto. My job is to coach, train and develop the players, and to get results. I'll choose players and make recommendations to the board, but I'm not involved in transfer negotiations. I do my negotiationg with the president; I'll tell him the players I think the team needs and what I think they are worth, the rest is down to other people.

You've been a manager for three decades. Has your approach changed over the course of the years, especially now you're working abroad?

The way you coach, whether at Ipswich or Barcelona, is very similar. The basics are the same wherever you are; you have to keep the players fit, develop their technique, you have to decide on a certain playing style and then fine-tune it, you must have a certain tactical flexibility within your overall framework – all that will never change. Tactics and styles may vary but football is always played on the same-sized pitch with one ball and 22 players. Circumstances change, though, even if you stay at the same club for a long time. I was at Ipswich for thirteen years, but in that time I had something like five *different* sides; I developed at least three special teams during that period – the players changed so the system changed. What you must always do is look at your squad and find a system to suit the players, never the other way round. There's been a lot of talk about my tactics at Barcelona [4–2–3–1], but I play a system that suits every player in the team; it suits Luis Enrique, it suits Sergi, it suits Ronaldo, it suits Giovanni, it suits Stoichkov, it suits Luis Figo, and it suits Nadal. It would be unintelligent to impose a system the players didn't enjoy, didn't understand, or weren't familiar with. So I've looked at the squad and I've decided we're going to play this way, *because we can*, because we've got these players.

Is good coaching about keeping things simple?

I know the thing at Liverpool was always about getting the ball and giving it to the nearest man and progressing from there, they did keep it simple, but again it's about the players you've got; in the Liverpool days when they had players who could dribble – wingers like Peter Thompson, Ian Callaghan or Steve Heighway – they would allow those players to have a go at people in certain positions, so it wasn't always about quick one-twos and give it and go. I initially played with wingers at Ipswich, too – I had Jimmy Robertson, Micky Lambert and then Clive Woods – but the best team I had at Portman Road was the one that won the UEFA Cup. We didn't have any natural wide-men at the club by then, so we didn't play with wingers, we played with two front players – Paul Mariner and Alan Brazil – and little Eric Gates playing as a third attacker; I developed that system to suit the players.

Does the successful manager need to be a charismatic figure?

No, I think managers are made up of all different types of characters. You couldn't say that Brian Clough was the same as Bob Paisley, in fact they were total opposites. Bob was a simple man who had gained respect, but I wouldn't say he was full of charisma, you know, he had that cloth cap and everything. His attributes were simplicity and honesty; the players respected him because he was always true to them, and he passed on his knowledge in a modest way, and they appreciated that. There is not one role model, there are all sorts of personalities who do well as managers, but there are certain ingredients every successful manager does need. It's about how you look after your players and knowing in which position they'll shine. You must be able to motivate and stimulate people, you need to be able to encourage players or get angry as the occasion demands, you must be able to criticise whilst making it clear that it's always for the benefit of the club, and always behind closed doors, never in public.

This is where the psychology comes into it?

Absolutely. You've got to know your players individually; some you can talk to regarding their game in front of a group, they're not embarrassed by it and won't feel undermined. There are other players you need to take aside and talk to personally, maybe in the confines of your office; you speak as you find and you do as you find. Alan Hunter and Kevin Beattie were both great competitors for me in defence at Ipswich, but off the park they were complete opposites. I used to fight with Alan and curse him in the dressing room 'cos I knew he'd take that away and react positively, he'd think, 'I'm going to show that bugger!' Kevin was just the opposite; he came to us as a young lad who'd not had things easy, he didn't come from a very good home, and you had to constantly encourage him and make him feel good about himself; I used to feel almost maternal towards him.

That's very important, knowing how different players respond to different situations – you can kick some players up the backside in front of everybody and they'll accept it and get on with it, but others might be a bit more soft-hearted and feel rejected by it, maybe it would affect their confidence. Whatever you say, you must *never* affect a player's confidence. Self-belief is everything when a footballer takes the field, so you must couch criticism in a way that doesn't destroy their confidence.

Working abroad, the language barrier must make it more difficult to establish relationships with players, to gauge how to treat them as individuals?

Yes, definitely, because it's not so natural to go up to Spanish players, say, and put your arm round them and chat; whereas with English players it was obviously very natural. It wasn't so much of a problem in Holland because everyone spoke English very well, but in Portugal, and now at Barcelona, it's more difficult. I still have little one-to-ones, with the help of Jose [Mourinho, Robson's Portuguese assistant]; yesterday I had a little situation with two youngsters, Iván de la Peña and Roger, who are a bit disappointed they're not playing more, but it's not so easy. Still, it's important that players know your motives for doing things, so you can't be afraid to try it.

Terry Venables would have had the same problem. One of his strengths as a manager is that he gets on so well with his players, but apparently he didn't have quite the same kind of relationship with his players at Barcelona. I'm sure that was because of the language, not because of his coaching style. If he could have conversed with Spanish players instantly and warmly the way he does at home, I'm sure they would have responded. It's very difficult, though. If you're talking to an English player you can be more subtle; if you want to criticise him, for example, you can pitch it in a way that comes across positively. That's very difficult in another language, or through an interpreter. It's probably the most difficult part of the job when you're managing abroad.

How important is it to be ambitious?

It's very important for a manager to be ambitious, and to be *seen* to be ambitious. If he wants to do well and win things, that gets through to the players; they can sense ambition, they can smell it, and if you're like that it gives them a spur, they want to show you they're winners too. Being ambitious is a big factor in motivation. The players have got to understand that you won't accept failure, that you won't accept bad performances, and that you're simply not interested in players who are half-hearted about the game. All the good managers have had a burning desire to win; British managers are certainly like that, but I'm sure it's the same the world over. If you look at Bertie Mee, at Billy Nicholson, Harry Catterick, Bill Shankly, Brian Clough, and more modern managers, like George Graham, Kenny Dalglish and Alex Ferguson, they've all been very ambitious people. And you need a special kind of desire to want to win over and over again. I don't know what the percentages are, but to defend a Championship or keep on winning things, you have to be that much better again; five per cent, ten per cent, whatever, because everybody wants to knock you off the pedestal. That's why you've got to make changes to a winning side and bring players in to try to make the team even better. It's an ongoing thing, a manager should never be satisfied with what he's got.

You've got to be ambitious in every single match, too. Barcelona played Logroñes recently and the players came off at half-time chuffed with themselves because they were 4–0 up; I said to them, 'Are you really going to be ambitious? Well, let's go out and do it again.' And they did, we won 8–0. A successful side must always want more. It's not just a question of results, either. Barcelona may be top and unbeaten, but I'll still criticise the team if the results are good but the performances are not up to scratch; but I'll stress it again, *always* in private. I've gone in to the dressing room this season and said to the players, 'Look we've won today but we've really got to play better than this.'

How important is it to be a good judge of players?

It's fundamental. If you're not a good judge of players, you'll get caught out in the end. My motto is to always spend a club's money as if it was my own, I think that's the essence of every good manager. It doesn't matter whether you're at a modest club like Ipswich or at a big club like Barcelona, you have to handle their budget with the utmost care. Here at Barcelona, I've spent $20 million on one player, Ronaldo; that's more than I had at Ipswich in thirteen years, let alone in the first year! Ipswich were never big spenders and I didn't spend much at PSV or Porto either. I can still remember how much I paid for people at Ipswich, that's how careful I was: Brian Hamilton cost £40,000, Paul Cooper, the 'keeper who played at Wembley opposite Pat Jennings, cost £23,000; they were incredible buys really . . . £23,000 hardly buys you a decent car now! On the other hand, at a club like Ipswich you've got more time; I was able to spend years building up a youth policy, but even then a football manager is constantly making decisions about which youngsters are good enough. It's still about judgement. That's tough because you can't be too sentimental; you can get too attached to players if you're not careful. People wondered why Terry Venables stuck to the same eleven players in extra time against Germany at Euro 96? Maybe he was over-loyal to his players in that situation, but you can't be sentimental.

Do you think a background as a successful player is important?

It's certainly an advantage, though there are plenty of managers – Bertie Mee, David Pleat, Ron Atkinson, John Lyall – that have had·very successful careers without being men who were great players. Look at Ray Harford, he wasn't a great player, he wasn't a player at all! And who did Roy Hodgson play for? Now he's in charge at Inter Milan. It doesn't naturally follow that a great player makes a great manager, either. Bobby Moore was an all-time great, so was Bobby Charlton, but what happened to them as managers? Jackie Charlton was less of a player but a fantastic manager. So it may not be necessary, but it is a great advantage: Bryan Robson, Ray Wilkins and Kenny Dalglish were great players and it gives them a head start in terms of credibility; if you look at the managers that are doing well now – Glenn Hoddle, Peter Reid, Gerry Francis, Brian Little – they were all very good players. If you've played at the top level it gives you a kind of instant credibility, especially when you're just starting out. In my first managerial job at Fulham, if one of the players was being overly argumentative I'd say, 'Look, I played twenty times for England, come on, put *your* caps on the table!' There does seem to be a recent trend towards top players bypassing a long apprenticeship, though. Keegan and Robson are examples, they've gone to clubs where they've had some money to spend straight away, and they've been able to buy decent players and take a short cut to success. But a lot of managers can't go into their first job at the very top, they have to start at Plymouth Argyle, or Chester, or Scunthorpe, before they get a crack at the Newcastle job.

Is that proving to be a disadvantage for the Keegans or Robsons; the fact that they haven't made their mistakes away from the limelight?

Yes, I think that's the case. A manager like George Graham, for instance, who spent several years at Millwall, would have been better prepared when his chance came. He'd spent time learning how to coach, learning how to get the best out of low-priced players, scratching around, wheeling and dealing, learning the art of football management; he'd done all that before he took a big club on. Now he's put all that behind him, so when he goes to Arsenal he ain't going to fail, he's got better conditions around him and he doesn't have to waste time learning the basics. He's a good example. Ron Atkinson spent time at Cambridge City, I spent time at Fulham and Ipswich.

How important is it to have the knack of buying well?

Your judgement of players has to be sound, that's fundamental, otherwise you'll wreck your club financially; you'll spend money, big money sometimes, on players who aren't worth it, players who don't come up to standard, so then you can't resell them without making a loss. Your eye for a player needs to be very sound. When I was at Ipswich, I never thought, 'Oh, it's the club's money so it doesn't matter!' – it *did* matter, my judgement had to be spot on, I couldn't make a mistake financially. If you're the managing director of a company and you make an investment of, say, three million dollars in a certain situation and the company goes bust, you're going to get the sack and be out of a job. The same thing applies in football – there are lots of examples of managers who have made bad buys, have wasted money, whose judgement wasn't sound. Believe me, you won't keep on getting jobs if that's the case.

That doesn't mean you shouldn't take calculated risks. At £150,000, Arnold Muhren was the biggest bargain of my career, but in those days buying a foreign player was something revolutionary. Ossie Ardiles was perhaps the first to make a big impact and then I followed with Muhren. I sold Brian Talbot to Arsenal for £450,000 and bought two better players, Muhren and Frans Thijssen, and put £100,000 change in the bank; that was a lot of money to Ipswich at the time. Talbot was a good, honest player, but he couldn't do the things Muhren could do with the ball, and Frans could run all day. I knew the Dutch players were talented, but looking back, I suppose it was a risk.

Given how unpredictable footballers are, it must be difficult *not* to make mistakes?

That's right. If you take a player from one club to another, or from one environment to another, you can never be one hundred per cent certain that he's going to perform in the same way. It's all about about seeing a player in the Third Division, and saying, 'This lad can come out of there and play for me in the top flight'; now to do that, you need a lot of judgement, and a lot of conviction. When the president of Barcelona says to me, 'Here, there are five videos of Giovanni, tell me, do we or don't we buy him?', I've got to make a decision that is going to cost the club six or seven million dollars. Just think about that for a moment; the president is saying I trust you with *seven million dollars*, that's a lot of bloody responsibility! I could say yes, and he turns out to be a disaster.

David Pleat said recently that a manager should always do his homework -- find out about a player's background, character, etc. Now Bobby Robson can look at a video of Giovanni, but you can't phone somebody in Brazil and say, Hey, what's he like, is he out on the town every night? Does it make buying players more difficult without that network?

It's definitely more complicated buying abroad. If you're buying players in your own country, you can do your homework more thoroughly. Before I bought a player at Ipswich I'd do exactly what David Pleat does, I'd investigate and I'd do my homework. But when you buy a player from Brazil, Romania, or wherever, it's more difficult, because you haven't got the personal contacts. And you can't put your trust in too many agents; all they're interested in is selling the player. So you have to be very careful who you buy. You've got to stretch your contacts as far as you can and do as much homework as possible, because you are responsible for that player, for spending that money. At a club where money is tight, you can't waste it, but I insist, even if you're at club that has got a lot of money, you've still got to spend it as if it was your own. That's how I've always operated. When I bought Mariner, or Muhren, or Thijssen at Ipswich, I had to be right. Because to us, £150,000 pounds was a *lot* of money. I had to be right.

If you're going to be a successful manager, how important is it to be lucky?

The line between success and failure can be very thin, so you do need the bounce of the ball and the ricochets, you need referees' decisions to go your way, you need the ball to maybe hit the post and go in rather than hit the post and come out. But I think basically you make your own luck, you can't win a

Championship on good fortune; you might be lucky in one match, but you won't be lucky over 42 matches . . .

Yes, but what about when two sides are neck and neck; things can still be decided at the death by a stroke of good fortune. Take the famous Liverpool v. Arsenal game in 1989; Arsenal won the League in the final seconds of the last game of the season after a ricochet dropped at Michael Thomas' feet! So both Kenny Dalglish *and* George Graham had their seasons defined by a split-second coincidence?

I was there at Anfield, I remember that game well. But as a manager you have to ignore that kind of thing, otherwise you'd go round and round in circles trying to work out what was going on – and does *anybody* really know what luck is? How do you get lucky? It's not something a manager can control, you can't go out and beg, steal or borrow it, so you're better off trying not to think about it. You've just got to hope that if your players are good enough they'll produce enough quality football and they'll get the run of the ball; if your team controls the run of the play and your players chase after every loose ball, you've got more chance of getting lucky. But yes, you can hit a shot and it'll hit a defender, come back to you and you'll knock it in, and yes, you'll think that was bloody lucky. Sometimes you need that little slice of luck.

If the referee had given handball against Maradona in 1986, who's to say what England might have gone on to do? I might be sat here talking to a World Cup winner?

Sure, nobody can say we wouldn't have gone on to win the World Cup. And then there were the penalties in the 1990 semifinal: Stuart Pearce hits his shot one way, the German 'keeper goes the other way, but the ball hits his bloody foot and goes over the bar. But even when it's close, it's not just about luck. People might say, But yes, you were lucky against Cameroon in the quarterfinals, but there wasn't much luck attached to that game, it was just a close encounter and the opposition played very well. At one stage they were better than us, but we survived and then got the two penalties – it was just a very close game with very little difference between the teams. Football is a game between two teams both doing their best to win, so you're going to get close games. Just because things are tight doesn't necessarily mean you were lucky.

Given those margins, is the best manager simply the one that gets the best results?

No, not at all. I think that's what happens, managers do get judged on their results, but there are some great managers, perhaps working at lower levels, who do a tremendous job of keeping their clubs afloat on limited resources and with limited long-term possibilities. One of my ex-players, Russell Osman, has just taken over at Cardiff. Now if he keeps the club running and out of bankruptcy, develops a youth policy, sells the odd player and makes a bit of money, picks up the odd bargain, plays good football and the club doesn't get relegated, he's doing a good job. It's not just about the Alex Fergusons of this world with the big money, playing for the Championships, having money to spend and being able to get the best young-sters. 'Cos the best youngsters will always want to go to Manchester United rather than Cardiff. So there are other good managers, people who have done a good job, with limited options and limited possibilities, and under financial restraints.

Can it work the other way round, can a team win things despite the manager?

Maybe it can happen over a short period of time, but I think a bad manager will get caught out in the end. If, at a certain club, there are a group of really good professionals, players who are driven and have ambitions within themselves, if they are good characters they can maybe get results. How long it'll last without a good manager, I don't know. Because there's no doubt, with a good manager those same players would be even more successful, and longer term. I really do believe that the manager is crucial to the team. And I'm not just saying that as a manager. I remember as a player it made a big difference to me as well. I felt much better if I had a boss I believed in and who I thought could help me improve. As a young player I liked Bill Dodgin, he was a genial character, and very fair, that's something I've tried to emulate. Later on I learnt a lot from Vic Buckingham at Fulham and West Brom. And I had a lot of respect for the England manager, Walter Winterbottom, too.

The Cult of the Manager

A good manager constantly makes his influence felt. He'll improve things in lots of different ways: he can help players individually, he makes decisions before the game – selecting the side and deciding how they'll play – that have an effect, he'll make tactical decisions at half-time, he'll see things during the course of a game, his briefing of the team before the match, his debriefing afterwards, a good manager has a big influence, there is no question about it. All the great teams had great managers. Take the Billy Nicholson team that did the double at Tottenham. Yes, there were great players, the Dave Mackays and the Danny Blanchflowers, but it was Billy who made the team grow: he really knew the game, he could talk the players' language, he instilled the discipline in the team, he dealt with the tactics – I think a good manager is essential to a club. A group of players can get results for a certain time without good leadership, but eventually that will crack. With a good manager a club can enjoy sustained success, he'll keep the kettle boiling, like the guys at Liverpool.

Can a good manager win things without the best players?

Brian Clough is an example of a manager who improved average players, even made them into superstars. Peter Reid did it at Sunderland last season, too. His players weren't significantly better than the rest of the First Division, yet they walked the League; George Graham won two championships at Arsenal but he never had the best individual players, it was all about his ability to get the very best out of people, to forge a unit that was difficult to beat. John Lyall did a great job for years at West Ham, yet by no stretch of the imagination did he have the best players – how many England players did West Ham have? – but he built sides that played attractive football, won Cups, and he kept them in the top flight most years. When I was at Ipswich, a similar-size club with the same kind of resources, I used to think, 'By God, John's doing a good job.' If a manager can really motivate players, get them to give one hundred per cent whatever the circumstances – with good organisation, a good eye for strategy, and discipline, he can make the sum add up to more than the parts.

Look at Joe Kinnear at Wimbledon. He's survived on getting the best out of his players and also on having an uncanny knack for picking up people for peanuts, not just from the lower

Leagues, but from non-League as well. Look at a club like Coventry, they haven't been out of the top flight for 30 years, so as far as I'm concerned *every* manager who has been there has done a good job. If you keep Coventry up, with no financial resources, by wheeling and dealing, and trying to build a youth policy, then that's a success. It's especially difficult in England because you're expected to do everything; on the Continent you're just coaching, you're not running the whole club, worrying about making sure it's viable and keeping it out of debt, constantly worrying about surviving.

Do players always think it's about them?

Yes, they will generally think the club is successful because of them and not the guy above them; footballers are that kind of animal, but in general they like it if there is discipline at a club, as well. They hate it if there's not a strong leader, they'll complain and argue among themselves. But a lot of players have fragile egos and don't like to praise others. A good manager, however, will always praise his players; Matt Busby would insist it was all about the Busby Babes, not Matt Busby, and you'll find most great managers will be like that.

Why do even the most prestigious managers make such obvious mistakes?

I think they can get egotistical, and maybe they'll get bad info, or not take any notice of what anybody tells them. I remember going to the 1970 World Cup in Mexico with a whole group of managers. I'd only been at Ipswich about a year and a half at the time, and Bertie Mee gave me a piece of invaluable advice; he said, 'Never forget, Bobby, leopards never change their spots.' It's the same with footballers with bad characters and bad reputations. That's one of the problems with managers; we all reckon we can make players better, we think, 'I can change him.' But the good manager is the one who passes trouble on to someone else. I'm sure that's what happened with Kevin Keegan and Faustino Asprilla; Kevin would have thought, 'I'll take a chance. If I get him out of his current situation, put him in a different environment, he'll have a new life and things will be different.' But it's always a big risk. Stick to quality and don't try and change people, that's the secret.

The Cult of the Manager

Why do managers succeed at one club and fail at another?

When you make a change from one club to another, you never really know what the possibilities are. Just because I won the Championship at Porto doesn't mean I'm going to win it at Barcelona, the circumstances are different, the competition is different. You often find out too late that what you've inherited is not quite what you expected or were promised, but if you're ambitious sometimes you've got to take a risk and start all over again.

As long as you're in a job as a manager you should have your club's best interests at heart, but when it comes to making a move, you should always have your *own* interests at heart. George Graham would have turned down the Manchester City job and accepted the Leeds job because he thought it was the best thing for George Graham, nobody else. I've turned down lots of jobs, too. And sometimes circumstances dictate things. I turned down the Arsenal job several times. I was offered it for the last time eighteen months ago, but Porto didn't want to let me go. I could have come to Barcelona a long time ago too, but I had a similar situation with Ipswich. If a club doesn't want to let me go, it's not my style to walk out on them.

Going to PSV was a key choice for me. When I left the England job I had three choices: I could have retired, that's what most people do, I could have taken another job in English football, or I could have gone abroad and broadened my experience. I didn't go looking for the PSV job, they approached me, but I had to make sure I was choosing the right club for me – they were a class set-up and I knew they were one of three clubs, along with Ajax and Feyenoord, with a chance of winning the Dutch League. So I knew there was a realistic chance of doing well. Two weeks after leaving PSV, I was offered the Sporting Lisbon job. At the time I fancied going to Italy, but Sporting are a big club and I was impressed by the set-up there.

The day after I was sacked by Sporting Lisbon I was available and ready for my next job, but there's no point being in a hurry and taking the wrong post. One bad decision and a manager's career can be finished. I turned down the Wales job, for example. I mean, how many great Welsh players are there? Then Porto came in and I knew it was the right job at the right time. I knew what their situation was, I knew I could manipulate it and get them back on top quickly. I chose to leave Porto on a high, and when I came here I knew it was going to be difficult following Johan Cruyff, it meant taking a risk. But Barcelona had gone two years without winning anything, so in another way it was a good time to be taking over. You have to remember that you never get offered jobs at the *best* possible time; when Barcelona were winning the League the job wasn't going to be available, was it? But you never completely control your own destiny. When you take over a new club it's always a lottery, so yes, you do need the rub of the green, you need to be fortunate, but again, what's the definition of luck? I apply myself and I've been successful. I'd like to think that all managers work hard; if you're lazy then you get what you deserve – nothing. Most managers are dedicated and want to do the job well, but the ones who succeed are the ones who don't despair, who keep going. It may be a cliché, but only the strong survive.

Are the most successful managerial teams precisely that?
As a manager, you definitely need someone you trust to work alongside you. At Ipswich, I had Cyril Lea and later appointed Bobby Ferguson and Charlie Woods; as England manager I had Don Howe and Dave Sexton. You need someone to bounce things off, that's very important. But there comes a time when you have to make your own decisions – you might have two opinions, your's and your assistant's, so you can't then say, 'Well, what do you think now Don?' because he's already told you! I've brought Jose Mourinho with me from Porto, he can help me at Barcelona with the language, but we're on the same wavelength as well. He's got a good understanding of the game for someone who never played at the top level; some people say that's a problem but I hope the players respect him because he's Bobby Robson's assistant. I trust him, he understands what I want, and I know if I tell him something it'll get through to the players, so I value his help.

A good right-hand man is important because maybe he can let himself get close to the players in a way the manager can't. Don Howe was great like that. If I was a bit hard on one of the players, I'd let it settle and then I'd say, 'Don go and see, say,

Ray Wilkins, tell him "Look, the boss was right, but he really likes you, he thinks you're great player, all the guys know how valuable you are" ', etc., and he'd settle any differences like that. And of course, he'd never say, 'Bobby told me to say that,' because I couldn't lose face either. In the same way, Ronnie Moran would have been invaluable to Liverpool over the years; he was close to the players, they liked him and respected him, they knew he had the club's best interests at heart. So he would be a go-between between Shanks, or Kenny Dalglish, and the players. Whatever money Ronnie has made over the years at Liverpool, he's earned it tenfold.

But there's only one manager, and he's the man paid to take decisions. Just because you're a good coach, it doesn't necessarily mean you're going to be a successful manager. Malcolm Allison was a first-rate coach, so is Ray Harford, but maybe they're not so good at managing, at judging players and making the big decisions.

Are the legendary managers a breed apart or is it just about being in the right place at the right time?

I think they're a breed apart precisely because *wherever* they go they make things happen. It's easy to say afterwards that they were in the right place at the right time, but did it look like that when Busby joined Manchester United, or when Shankly moved to Liverpool, Harry Catterick to Everton, Jock Stein to Celtic, or Bertie Mee to Arsenal? They built something, they *made* it the right place and the right time. It's always easy to say that somebody made the right decision afterwards. And it's not just about the managers who won Championships either. Ron Greenwood produced a whole school of thought at West Ham, an academy that played great football, that's what you call making a difference. I built three different sides at Ipswich, in 1975, 1978 and 1981, so it's what you do over a long period of time as well. It's about the way a manager can manipulate things and achieve success according to the aspirations or limitations of his club.

So are managers really as important as we are led to believe?

Definitely. If things are going badly at a club, the first thing that happens is a change of manager. Why? Because everyone knows the right man will turn things around. It's not always easy, because managers are so rarely given the time they need, but whatever the circumstances, by wheeling and dealing, with good judgement, by being brave, you can make a difference. If it was just about players, why would the FA bother about a coach? After all, the England manager just picks the country's best footballers – he doesn't need to go out and buy people, does he? It's what he does with those players that is important; even the best players need guidance. Terry Venables did well for England and his legacy was positive, but when he left the job, things weren't going to run themselves on their own, were they? The FA know they need a good manager.

Footballers may win games on the field, but you simply can't compare the pressure on one individual player to perform with a manager's responsibility. At Barcelona, I'm required to make decisions every day that affect the whole club; and it's about making tough decisions. I was criticised recently for substituting Pizzi [Spanish international centre-forward] in a game at Sevilla just twenty minutes after I'd brought him on. But we were in the lead, Popescu and Guardiola [Barça's midfield pivots] had run themselves into the ground, and time was running out. So it was all about securing a result. I knew I would get stick for the decision, but my responsibility is to do what I think is best for the club; football management is not a popularity contest. I sometimes wish I could swap places with my critics for just a couple of days so they could see for themselves how difficult a manager's job really is.

Michael Robinson played for Preston, Manchester City, Brighton, Liverpool, Queens Park Rangers, Osasuna and the Republic of Ireland. He is now Spain's most popular football commentator and fronts his own weekly TV show.

Are all successful managers also good coaches?
You get fantastic managers who make training sessions tremendously enjoyable and stimulating for the players, even though they might be tactically naïve; and then you get others who are tactically brilliant but go so over the top with the tactics that the players don't understand them. A coach can be very bright but at the same time very boring. You've got to remember that

most footballers have left school with little formal education, they haven't gone to university, so they're not going to understand what their manager is talking about if he goes off on a tangent. Some managers spend 24 hours a day trying to read too much into football, so they come up with ideas and football *ideology* that are very difficult for footballers to grasp.

I'll give you an example. As a nineteen-year-old kid at Manchester City, I didn't have a clue what Malcolm Allison was talking about; not a clue about how he wanted us to play. I remember he signed Dragoslav Stepanovic and made him captain, yet he couldn't speak English! He was a sweeper whose role was to surge forward from the back. When we had the ball, he'd have to knock it to Willie Donachie or Paul Power on the wing, then he had to link up with me at centre-forward; I was supposed to drag defenders out of position as he was constantly moving forward unmarked, which made him very hard to pick up . . . It also made life very hard for Stepi because after fifteen minutes he was knackered. I don't know if Malcolm ever told him to pace himself; if he did, Stepi obviously didn't understand him!

We used to have a ballet dancer who trained with us and talked about movement, that'd be say one day a week, then we had this basketball player who used to get us hopping on and off great big blocks; there was a meditating session to music, a gym and swimming instructor who'd tie us to a bed and stretch our muscles for us, and we used to go to Salford University and have our hearts strapped up and our noses plugged. When you actually sat down and worked it out, we were lucky to play football once a week. The players used to think it was absolutely ridiculous, so Malcolm certainly wasn't getting the best out of us as human beings. I'm sure most of us didn't have a bloody clue what it was all leading too.

He thought so deeply, so passionately, about football, yet he only really communicated with the players on a night out. That was wonderful entertainment. We'd all have a drink and he'd be the players' buddy. But when it came to talking about football he had some unbelievably weird ideas. I'm not saying they were wrong, but there's a difference between a manager being right, and being able to sell his ideas to the players.

Liverpool were the exact opposite, they kept it very, *very* simple, and always tremendously easy for the players to under-stand. We never stopped playing football, it was all short-sided games with the coaches running around and shouting in the background, 'give it, get it, move; give it, get it, move; give it, get it, move'. And you never really had team talks; now and again they'd just take a player to one side and have a little chat.

I was once on a run of eight games without scoring before a game against Odense in the European Cup, and I picked up the papers in the morning and they were all predicting I'd be dropped. I was the second one into training that day just after Bruce Grobbelaar, and Ronnie Moran came up to me and said, 'the boss wants to see you.' I remember walking down the long corridor at Anfield to Joe Fagan's office, thinking, 'Well, that's it, then, the papers are right, I'm not playing.' When I got into his office Joe said, 'I've got to have a chat with you, Michael. I woke up this morning and me wife was reading the papers and saying, "I see you're going to leave Michael out today, is he not playing well?" And I was really worried about that, 'cos you're worth your weight in gold, lad.' Then he said, 'Before I go and talk to the press I want you to see the team I'm going to give them.' He handed me a piece of paper with the numbers from one to eleven blank apart from number ten where it said Michael Robinson. 'That's what the team is, laddie, you and ten more,' he told me. I felt unbelievable. He then insisted it wasn't important for me to score, what mattered was to carry on the way I'd been playing because we were winning games, Rushy was scoring goals, Kenny Dalglish was playing well, and it was all working. That night I scored twice against Odense. On the Saturday we went to West Ham – they were top and we were third – we beat them 3–1 and I got all three goals. Then we played at Brentford in the Milk Cup and I got another couple, and all of a sudden I couldn't stop scoring, basically because of a guy who always kept things very simple but really knew how to communicate.

Was the secret to make each individual player feel like he had a very special relationship with the manager and coaches?
Yes, they were trying to be your friend and your confidant, but because of the way they handled it, you'd never abuse it, you were always left in no doubt who picked the team. But you'd

still feel the relationship with them allowed you to go up and say, 'Look, boss, I'm not sure about doing this on the pitch, I'm not feeling this, I'm a bit confused, guv'nor.'

When I was first discussing my transfer to Liverpool with Bob Paisley and Joe Fagan – I'd go down as Joe's first signing, it was the summer when Bob was leaving and Joe was coming in – they were baffled when I asked how I should play if I signed? *'How should I play?'* I remember them echoing the question and looking at each other amazed. 'Well, don't you know how to play? If you don't know how to play football, we're spending an awful lot of money badly here.' And I said, 'no, no, no, I mean according to the system.' 'Ah, the system,' they went. 'Now listen, Michael, we always put eleven players on the pitch so we don't start off at a disadvantage, and then this is what we try to do; in midfield we always give the ball to a red shirt, and you up front, if you can possibly kick it in the net, that'll be great. If you can't, knock it to somebody else who can. And at the back we're going to break our balls not to let a goal in. Now if we can do that all the time, and we normally do, we'll most often win. What do you think about the system?' And I said, 'Yes, but is there any more?' And they replied, *'Is there any more to football?'* So I went, 'well, not really!'

They used to make you feel that you were a great player in the best team in the world . . . until we started to win too often. Then you'd maybe get a player who was too relaxed in training or a bit over-chirpy, talking about the good press he was getting, and Joe or Ronnie would say, 'You've been reading the papers again, haven't you? Don't read the bloody papers. You love it when they write well about you, but when they don't you turn round and say journalists are a load of wankers who don't understand football. So don't read the papers.' They were very, very basic, but they always seemed to get the best out of players on an individual basis, as I said; very rarely did we have team meetings.

All those Liverpool guys had an aura about them. Is it all about charisma?

If you've got charisma, you can lead people, they'll be motivated because they wanna believe in you. Charisma helps a manager to communicate with players; footballers fall for charisma like anyone else, so they'll listen to a manager and feel motivated. I played under Joe Fagan, he was Bob's number two before that, but I remember Graeme Souness saying that Joe had been a very strong man with Bob, so the players didn't really think, Oh, things will change, 'cos Joe always used to run things, if you like. In his first year on his own, he won the League, the Milk Cup and the European Cup, and that was basically down to his own special kind of charisma; he motivated us and made us ambitious.

Every coach has their own way of doing things; it's what they believe that counts. Now you can win games by playing *catenaccio*, or you can win by playing open attractive football, there's lots of different ways of winning, the same as there are lots of different ways of preparing eggs, but they still taste all right. I don't think there's a written law, a right and wrong way of being a coach and playing football; like in any walk of life there's different styles, different ways of motivating people, and different ways to be successful . . .

Is there a wrong way of going about things?

Yes, there's *definitely* a wrong way of going about it, and again, it's all about not being able to communicate with the players, not making it clear what you expect of them. The moment that communication goes, footballers lose respect for their boss, they won't listen to him; they'll sneer at what he's got to say. That doesn't mean to say you never disagreed with or misunderstood the good managers. I was given roles to play by guys I respected and I'd say, 'I don't think I can do that.' Nonetheless you would have a try, you'd go away thinking, 'I don't know where he's coming from but I'll have a go at it'. That's different from the manager who simply turns round and says, 'You're doing it anyway.' That gets your back up, you'll talk in the dressing room about it, you'll say, 'What about this wanker?' and then you talk to other unsettled people; you don't go up to the captain or the leading goalscorer, the ones that are pleased with the manager, and start slagging him off, you do it with the other unsettled players. All of a sudden you start getting a mutiny in the dressing room; that nearly always occurs with a manager who is dogmatic, and who has failed to communicate with his players.

The Cult of the Manager

Sometimes players are happy to get managers sacked if there has been a breakdown of communication. At Manchester City, it was after we'd won a game at Arsenal, I was joking at the back of the bus with one ex-England player, and he turned round to me and said, 'Well, we've fucked that up, we've kept Allison in a job.' I was amazed, I thought it was the most unbelievable, diabolical thing I'd heard in my life, especially coming from a veteran talking to a nineteen-year-old boy just starting in the game, and not only did he mean it, but it was a great source of amusement for five or six other players around us; that was Malcolm Allison for you, him and his training methods we couldn't understand.

We weren't enjoying ourselves, we were losing, we were getting slagged off in the press, and there was a dreadful atmosphere created by a chap we couldn't understand. We thought he was completely out of his brain. We hardly played football during the week, and then when we lost he'd go to the press and he'd say, 'It's because the players were a load of crap.' He ruined Steve Daley; he was Britain's most expensive football player at the time, but he couldn't understand a bleedin' word Malcolm was saying, nobody could understand a word he was saying. He'd just walk into the dressing room after each successive defeat, pick out the most expensive player and start to slag him off. Steve ended up totally demoralised; his career was finished about a fortnight later and nobody ever saw him again.

How do managers who go abroad cope with not being able to communicate because of the language?
I arrived here without being able to speak a word of Spanish, but I think football is a universal language. Players have more or less the same problems all over the world; they've all been on a football field and been booed at, they've all been critcised and been applauded . . .

Yes, but apart from getting the tactical stuff across, it must be difficult to establish a personal relationship with players if you don't speak the same language?
It's not always necessary that the manager himself is the players' chum. I don't even know if that's a good or a bad

204

thing, as long as somebody from the coaching staff who the manager trusts can get close to the players. Howard Kendall had Chechu Rojo at Athletic Bilbao who knocked about with the players and communicated with them. Maybe Howard would invite the players to lunch sometimes at a nice restaurant and they'd all get on and he'd try and crack the odd joke in Spanish. But on a day-to-day basis, he'd supervise things from the sidelines more whilst Chechu would be moving around, finding out what problems the players had, how they were feeling about doing things. And then he'd go and sit with Howard and explain what the general feelings were.

I think it might be a problem for Bobby Robson that he hasn't got a Spanish person to relate to the players at Barcelona, the way Carles Rexach did for Johan Cruyff, that'll make things harder for him. He's brought his Portuguese assistant Mourinho from Porto, but I'm not sure if he's respected by the players. I've just slaughtered him in tomorrow's papers about the Ronaldo thing [after the Brazilian had scored Barça's only goal in a draw at Racing Santander, Mourinho had said, 'It's no good scoring a wonder goal and then going to sleep for 89 minutes']; all the pressure this lad's under, he's done nothing other than brilliant things for FC Barcelona, and when all the press are waiting for him to play badly or make a mistake so they can go, 'Blimey, twenty million dollars for that?', the first criticism he gets is from one of his own coaches! If Ronaldo keeps playing the way he is at the moment he is going to keep Mourinho in a job.

Is a background as a player important?

I don't think it's an overriding factor, but it's bloody helpful. Footballers rarely have a problem doing the basics: trapping the ball, passing it, heading it, running and moving. If they're at a top club, they've known how to do those things since they were ten. What nearly always seems to be their undoing are the psychological things, and if a manager has been a player he'll have gone through the same situations. Let's say a player is having a bad time and the crowd are getting at him; he might want to hide and avoid the ball. An ex-player will know all about that. Or a midfielder might say, 'I couldn't do that, boss, 'cos the left back ain't doing it, he's not backing me up'; it's about talking through game situations, where all those different human problems arise; fears, anxieties.

And it's not just the negative things. Sometimes players experience a kind of delirious motivation. Perhaps you're playing great and all of a sudden you get carried away, you forget to do certain things; maybe it's a full-back who's been getting down the line, he's scored a goal, he's set up two more with great crosses, so he thinks he can do it again and again. So he gets so carried away on an emotional high that he forgets the discipline element, the team framework. If the manager has been in those situations himself, he's more capable of sitting down and saying, 'Look, I know what's going on with you, I've been there, it's a bugger, ain't it?' It's the 'I remember that, I know what you're going through, son, but we've got to try and get to the bottom of this' thing. Or it could be a player has picked up a newspaper and he's been slagged off, or there's a rumour that such-and-such team want to sign him, so he comes up asking the manager what is happening. These things have happened to all football managers who have been players, so it's easier for them to deal with.

It's about understanding dressing-room tensions, too. You might have half a dozen players who are not getting a game and they're all buddies with the centre-forward; so all of a sudden he stops scoring goals because he's hanging round with these people and getting negative vibes. Managers who have been in dressing rooms a million times know the jungle; that's all about being a footballer. It's not necessarily about having been a great footballer, though. Sometimes that can be a disadvantage. We've seen great results as far as Johan Cruyff is concerned, but that's not always the case. If you've been *too* good a player, you might sometimes think that football is all about trapping the ball on the back of your neck, dribbling around six defenders and smacking it in the top corner. So you wonder why on earth the rest of the world can't do the same?

How is it that big-name players in Spain don't walk straight into managerial jobs the way they do in England?

A Spanish footballer may be more eloquent on the field, but he isn't as good a professional as his English counterpart. The English footballer really is a good, disciplined professional who works hard for his teammates, helps out around the pitch; he's not particularly tied up with his own thing, he feels like a member of a group and he's happy working in a team. In Spain, footballers are perhaps more talented so they can be less professional, more individualistic; they'll often feel that the only problem with football is 'I've got another ten I have to play with'. If you come from a background where a more collective spirit reigns, it's perhaps easier to go straight into management, because you're dealing with problems you've already given a bit of thought to. Why do I think top internationals are going into management? Because we're going through a phase where rolling up your sleeves and saying 'Aye-up lad, let's get at 'em' is no longer enough.

So it's not all about hard work?

No. You can go to football clubs where they seem to do nothing and then go to others where they run their balls off, and the successful ones are not necessarily the grafters. Training at Liverpool consisted of *nothing*, because they used to say, 'well, we're going to have to play 80 games this season, so we'll save ourselves.' Yet I went to other clubs where they ran the bollocks off you to no avail; it's about being professional and doing quality work. Sometimes footballers can be so tired after being run into the ground that they're not receptive to information; when you're running and running all the time it gets harder to control the ball and be technically at your best. A manager has to ask himself, 'Do I run them and accustom them to that pressure, or do I just work on them with the ball and try not to tire them out so they are able to do the quality things?'

Is luck a big factor?

I believe in luck. There's that much-vaunted saying, 'The harder I work, the luckier I get', but the margin between success and failure in football is so thin, luck obviously plays a big part. You can get two managers who both know an enormous amount about football: one wins the League on goal average and gets to become Manager of the Year; the guy that comes second gets a reputation as a nearly man. But how much better is the winner? Bobby Robson might say, 'if it wasn't for the "Hand of God" I might have won the World Cup in 1986,' but he won't say, 'I was lucky to beat Cameroon in 1990.' I think luck plays a big part, but managers won't admit it.

Let me put it another way; they do when they lose. It's 'What bad luck I've had there, that referee chalked off two perfectly legal goals for offside, this is disgraceful, what bad luck I'm having.' Then the next week, someone has a speculative shot, it hits a defender on the back of the neck and flies in, his team has won 1–0 and the same manager will say, 'My tactics today were brilliant, haven't we done well,' etc. So they don't admit luck plays a part unless it suits them. And luck is something managers should take into consideration even when they've won 1–0 away from home. Instead of being satisfied, the boss should maybe accept that his team didn't do that well after all and had perhaps enjoyed a massive slice of luck. He shouldn't let luck camouflage the fact that an awful lot of things went wrong and maybe the team isn't working well; 99 per cent of professional people in all walks of life don't want to recognise luck, but luck plays a big part.

Should we judge a manager purely by his results?
It's not just about results. If there's a manager who is half dodgy but gets good results, it doesn't necessarily mean the players will think he's good at his job. I'll give you an example: I played in a Queens Park Rangers side that got to the final of the Milk Cup and finished fourth or fifth in the League under Jim Smith, yet 90 per cent of the dressing room thought he was a load of crap as a manager; I thought he was a decent chap but not a great manager. There are other managers who have been considered particularly good and yet not achieved anything. I played for Nobby Stiles at Preston and thought he was brilliant; I thought Bobby Charlton was good as well, but neither of them really progressed as managers. Then Harry Catterick, who'd won the League at Everton, came to the club and I thought he was an awful manager. So maybe a team of talented players can win things with a bad manager.

On the other hand, a well-managed side can win things with mediocre players. Look at Brian Clough's Nottingham Forest. John Robertson was fat and in the reserves when Cloughie arrived at the club, John McGovern, Ian Bowyer and Frank Clark were journeymen, Tony Woodcock was struggling to make it in the reserves. Here in Spain, Arsenio Iglesias' Deportivo La Coruña won the Cup and were runners-up in the League with a team of rejects, players like Nando and Lopez Rekarte. If you're a good manager, 90 per cent of the time you'll get good results. I think it's a matrimony, it's about players playing well, but sometimes it's the managers who get the players to play well, even beyond their potential.

People say Cruyff's Barcelona were so good purely because he had the best players, but who built the team? Ronald Koeman was the only player Cruyff signed who offered guarantees. When Cruyff arrived at Camp Nou, Ferrer was on loan at Tenerife and Sergi was in nappies; now they're two of the best full-backs in the world. Nadal was playing for Mallorca in midfield or up front; now he's all of a sudden a great player at the back. He threw Guardiola in as a kid, Goiko went from the subs' bench at Real Sociedad to being Spain's Footballer of the Year, he made Bakero and Txiki into internationals. If you went to Bulgaria tomorrow and signed their leading scorer, what are you gonna get? You don't expect Stoichkov, do you? And Michael Laudrup was more or less kicked out of Italy. So is it just about the players? No, it's a matrimony; sometimes a manager can make the players.

Do the players themselves think it's all down to them?
They're like managers; it's all down to them until things start going wrong. Then they always want to talk about the way somebody else played. If I'm playing up front and we've been done 2–0 I'll be going, 'Fuckin' centre-half, what a nightmare,' and he'll be going, 'You couldn't hit a barn door, Robinson.' It's amazing how centre-halves are always magnificent centre-forwards and vice versa. Players don't like managers who take all the credit. The Barça players used to tell me, 'Every time we get done it's our fault, every time we win, Cruyff's brilliant.' But the same thing applies the other way round; when they win, players will think they've done really well – 'What great lads we are' – but when they play badly and lose, they think, 'what a wanker the manager is!'

Javier Clemente's [the Spanish national coach] motivating powers are largely about never slagging off his players. Radomir Antic [manager of 1996 Spanish champions Atlético

Madrid] is another manager who's got a really close relationship with his players. A coach who always defends his players is more likely to earn their respect. Great managers tend to have this thing where you've just been beaten after a game, the press have had their say, and you get on the bus feeling really bad for the boss, you think, 'Bloody hell, he's in trouble.' When Alan Mullery was under pressure at Brighton, I used to go on the pitch thinking, 'I've got to do the best I possibly can for this fella, he's under the cosh and we've got to find something extra for him'. I felt bad for him when things weren't going right; I used to feel the same for Joe Fagan or my coach at Osasuna, Pedro Mari Zabalza. He wasn't a great coach but he deserved better than to suffer. I felt that for Eoin Hand, the Irish manager, too. When a manager creates a sense of togetherness, footballers who should always be giving 100 per cent anyway will give 101 per cent, and sometimes that can determine that manager's future. The team will perform better and he gets to be seen in his true light. The great thing is when you get the subs feeling positive, or the players in the reserves who don't play regularly; when they like the manager then you've really got a good thing going.

Do players all tend to have the same opinion about their manager?

You've normally got several identifiable groups: there are the players who *always* like the manager or *never* like him, they tend to be groups of mates with the same opinion; then there are the the ones whose mood depends on whether they're playing or not, they'll like the manager one week but not the next; and there are the sensitive types who maybe get a bollocking in front of the other players and won't like the boss for a couple of weeks, till next time he turns round and says, 'You should all be like this lad.' For a lot of players it's up and down all the time, according to how the team is doing and if they're playing or not, or how they're playing.

If a player has a problem it's often about dialogue. You know a manager has to think of the way the whole team is playing, but if you can talk to him and say, 'I don't like my role, boss, I'm not getting the ball,' it helps. Ninety per cent of managers will say they encourage their players to talk to them all the time, although good intentions soon go out the door when things are going wrong. When they go to a new club, managers will say, 'you're all starting from scratch, my door is always open and you can always come and speak to me'. All of a sudden, he's been there six months, some players start going to talk to him, he'll finish arguing with them and bang, the door is always shut.

In general, English managers are much closer to their players than Spanish ones, though. A good manager needs to know how to appease players, to say, 'I know you've only got a marking job, you won't see too much of the ball and you're going to work your bollocks off, but you're doing a great job for the team'. And even if you say, 'But I'm not happy at all about this, boss,' he'll convince you that you're doing a good job for the rest.

It's about convincing the full-back that the goals are down to him as much as the centre-forward. Hugo Sánchez may have scored all the goals for Real Madrid, but Chendo [the club's long-serving, unsung right back] should put his name down for one or two as well; *he's* won the ball off the other side, *he's* knocked it into midfield, it's gone out wide to Michel ... *he* shimmies, *he* centres it and Hugo scores the goal – so the centre-forward's was the ultimate pass in a movement, but maybe his touch of the ball, or his nod into the net, was less classy than the rest. That's the kind of thing a good manager, a good psychologist, would use; and he'd get the centre-forward to mention it to the full-back, as well.

The psychology of a good manager is all-important. Maybe he's got a full-back who is very bad at passing the ball, but fast and good in the tackle. You don't ever mention to him that he's crap with the ball at his feet; a good manager would say to him, 'Do you know what you do brilliantly, son? You're the fastest thing breathing and in the tackle you're unbelievable ... and I love that little five-yard ball that you give to the player closest to you'.

Why do even the top managers make such blatant mistakes?
Because they start to believe their own hype. If you get to be considered a great manager it's probably because 90 per cent of the decisions you've taken have been correct, and when you get

to that level, you think it's very difficult to make a mistake. When people heap praise on a manager, he starts thinking, 'now, if I could convert Glenn Hoddle into a centre-half, a stopper, bloody hell, that would be a revelation,' or 'if I can get Romario to play right-back ...' When they get away from basics and start to believe they are always right and want to rewrite football, that's when things go wrong. It's like Fabio Capello arriving at Madrid and playing Manolo Sanchis [thirtysomething defender] in midfield, they want to write their page in the history of football ...

Liverpool managers didn't seem to fall into that trap?
Well, unconsciously they did rewrite the history books 'cos they kept on winning. The biggest question in British football for 20 years was 'What's Liverpool's secret?' But they kept on winning year to year by keeping it simple on a day-to-day basis. Winning was the only secret.

Johan Cruyff once said to me in a bar, 'I'm going to rewrite football, I'm going to play with only one defender, and he's not going to be a centre-back. I'm going to have midfield players at full-back and I'm going to play with two wingers and not a centre-forward.' I thought he was pissed! I think real geniuses can get to the point where they get sick of winning, they think, 'What I wanna do now is have a statue of me built' ... If you take Cruyff globally, 95 per cent is good to brilliant, but then all of a sudden he makes a mistake and it looks worse precisely because he is so good, even if it's a mistake lots of others make. And people say, 'The problem with Cruyff was ...' but basically, Johan Cruyff ain't got a problem. Cruyff could be arrogant but I'd be bloody arrogant if I was him. I wouldn't speak to some people!

Why do managers succeed at one club and fail at another?
It happens with players as well. There are some grounds you just never play well at, whatever team you go there with. It doesn't matter what kit you're wearing, what time you go to bed or what you eat before the game, year after year you always play crap. I never played well at Maine Road and I went and signed for Man City, that was a *real* problem! Even when I went back there with other clubs I still played crap. It can be

like that with managers, it can be something to do with the city. When you travel a bit you maybe go to cities that are falling down yet you have great times there, and you wanna go back just because it feels right, it's about good memories. That gut feeling works with managers, as well. When a manager is happy and comfortable, his mind is feeling good and he starts making good decisions.

Are the best managers one-man shows?

That changes according to the personality of the individual manager, there's not one role model. Personally, I believe in a managerial team; maybe a manager has a great brain but the communicator is his number two. The boss can sometimes have questions inside of himself so he needs to lean on somebody else that perhaps has an answer; top managers nearly always have a sounding board – Johan Cruyff had Charly Rexach, Shanks had Bob, Bob had Joe, they've all had Ronnie Moran, Clough had Taylor. I think being a football manager is one of the loneliest jobs in the world – sometimes an assistant can be just like a key-ring to have around, a rabbit's foot; sometimes the coach doesn't know that much, but he makes the players laugh and feel comfortable.

Are Shankly, Busby, Stein, Revie etc., a singular breed, or are they all totally different?

The ones you've mentioned always got on with their players, they were all communicators. According to each player, you have to give 'em a bollocking or put your arm round him. But you shouldn't confuse being able to communicate with being articulate in a conventional sense. Kenny Dalglish is still struggling with English but you end up understanding him, like Bob Paisley; 'why'eye, laddie, ehwheywhey, wheyeyeeeeeiie, laddie' – he never in fact said an actual word, or at least a word that anybody could understand, but everyone knew what he meant. Dalglish is a communicator without being able to speak; that's the charisma thing again. If there was a team meeting when I was at Liverpool, every time 'Dog's' spoke it was a load of crap – well, no, not a load of crap, he was always funny, but he wasn't like the wise, all-knowing football player. Souness was the one who would speak in the dressing room and nearly always be right, or there was Alan Hansen who always made a lot of sense. Kenny was the joker in the dressing room – well, not the joker, he was sometimes the butt of jokes, we always used to take the piss out of 'Dog's', but we all thought he was a genius; his other nickname was 'Super'. I never envisaged Kenny Dalglish being a manager, but Kenny Dalglish the man? I thought he was one of the most wonderful human beings I'd ever met. I don't know what the secret of his success is, but it might be that he's a wonderful person who everybody adores, so when he speaks, once you've deciphered it from his broad Scots into English, then you tend to take some notice of it. I think all the great managers would share that charisma and personality: Shankly, Clough, Revie, Busby, Dalglish; they've all got personality with a capital P. When they walk into a room, even without saying anything, people will stop what they're doing, and when they open their mouths, people will immediately shut up and listen. I've met all these guys, and believe me, you can believe something quite strongly, yet if they say the opposite, you immediately begin to have doubts!

Is the influence of the manager exaggerated?

Football is all about the players, but nonetheless the manager should create the circumstances where they can play and give them a safety net. But that's all a system is; it's not the determining factor, footballers are the determining factor. A manager's job is all about giving his players a north, to help then work out where they are going. He's a kind of father figure, the man who says, 'We're going to play this kind of system' and instils self-belief. I think this is what a manager can be good at.

12 The *Quote* of the Manager

Compiled by Jeff King

Nice work if you can get it?

'Managing England should be the best job in the world, but it has become a horrible job; to think of my children going into school and getting hammered in the playground because their dad is the England manager. Perhaps we should be looking for a guy who is divorced with no kids.'

Glenn Hoddle, 1994 (he's still married)

'There are two possible ways I can end this tournament. Either I shall be kissed all over my bald head or I will have tomatoes thrown at it.'

Arrigo Sacchi, before Euro 96 elimination and messy target practice

'I've never wanted to become a manager, it doesn't appeal. Frankly it is a pretty awful job, a thankless task. You get hassle every day, from players and other people who think they could do the job better than you. I look at most managers and, with the odd exception, they look permanently miserable; they're an unhappy, touchy bunch, even when they are successful. Look at Alex Ferguson. He is as successful as anyone at the moment, but he seems to think the whole world is against him.'

Gary Lineker

'I love football but I positively hate being a manager.'

Lou Macari

'Why should I blow my brains out? There are far more important things in life than football.'

Billy Bonds on managerial life at West Ham, 1992

The Cult of the Manager

'Managing was unrewarding and stupid.'

Geoff Hurst, World Cup winner and ex-Chelsea boss

'The three toughest jobs around are football managing, lion taming, and mountain rescue . . . in that order.'

Jimmy Armfield

'You work till you drop, grab a bag of fish and chips in the car, get home at ten o'clock at night, bark at the wife and kids, lie awake all night worrying, then hare back to the ground at eight the next morning.'

Terry Butcher on why he's 'finished with the management carousel'

'You can be on a beach in Marbella and you'll be thinking about formations, selections and players. Go to the theatre and you might be watching the most enthralling play, but I can guarantee any manager will be thinking about what he's going to do on Saturday.'

Steve Coppell

'As a manager you're like a prostitute. You depend on other people for your living.'

Coppell, after a dubious refereeing decision saw Crystal Palace lose to Hartlepool in the 1992/93 FA Cup

'Football management these days is like a nuclear war. No winners, just survivors.'

Tommy Docherty

'Managing a football club is a bit like having sex. You don't exactly enjoy it at the time but it's the aftermath you enjoy. You don't turn to your missus and say, "This is great," but afterwards, when you have a fag, you say to her, "That was bloody good!" '

Alan Smith on the ups and downs of a football manager

'Too many managers moan about their lot, but they don't realise that there are guys out there who'd love their jobs. It's a hard job, but it's also a great one.'

Smith, just days before being released by Wycombe
Wanderers

I'll get me coat . . .

'If you're a manager you don't have fitted carpets.'

John Barnwell, ex-Wolves, Walsall, et al.

'I told the chairman that if he ever wants to sack me, all he has to do is take me into town, buy me a meal, a few pints and a cigar, and I'll piss off.'

Millwall boss Mick McCarthy

'If he wants to get rid of me then it's time he came up to my face and called me a fucking wanker and sacked me.'

Barry Fry at loggerheads with Birmingham guru David
Sullivan

'We feel Barry has taken the club as far as he can. After three years and 61 players, we think someone else is entitled to a go !'

Sullivan finally sacks Fry

'Kristine's gone shopping as usual and I've gone to the Job Centre looking for new employment. Funny ol' game, innit?'

Fry's answerphone message on the day of his demise

'I don't understand it. We did everything right in training, but yesterday every time they came near our goal they scored. I'm very disappointed. I still think I'm a good manager.'

Torquay boss Don O'Riordan, sacked after an 8–1 home
defeat to Scunthorpe, 1995

'I don't kill managers for pleasure. The way people go on you'd think I was Dracula and liked drinking managers' blood. But if I

217

need to change coach another hundred times to get things right I will. There are always hundreds more in the queue.'

Atlético Madrid President Jesús Gil (23 coaches in eight years) gives ex-manager Alfio Basile the vote of confidence

'I see Atléctico just sacked another manager before the season has even started. He must have had a bad photocall.'

former Gil victim Ron Atkinson

'I think about the sack all the time. It's my biggest worry. Having a job like this is like loving a beautiful woman and fearing to lose her.'

Mansfield boss Andy King in 1993 (he lost her in September 1996)

'Other clubs could learn from Oldham's attitude. They have been a beacon of stability. Three managers in twenty-five years? Other clubs have had twenty-five managers in three years. They change managers like the chairman changes his vest.'

Joe Royle

A Survivor's Guide . . .

'There are two types of people who succeed in coaching: the con man and confidence trickster, or the intelligent man who builds your confidence and belief. I'm the con man.'

Malcolm Allison hits 65 and takes over at Bristol Rovers, 1992

'I think it's impossible to manage, train, and do the paperwork. Everybody has his own specialities. I don't have an office.'

Ruud Gullit on life among the West London homeless

'Me havin' no education, I had to use my brains.'

Bill Shankly

'The secret of being a good manager is to keep the five players who hate you away from the half-dozen who are undecided.'

Jock Stein

'His management style seems to be based on the chaos theory.'

Mark McGhee on Barry Fry, 1996

'I believe you have to work with your ideas, do quality work, and after that . . . hope for the best.'

Arsène Wenger takes over at Highbury

'In defence you prepare, in attack you improvise.'

Ex-France boss Michel Hidalgo

'No coach can guarantee results, you can only guarantee a way of playing. Results are in the hands of fate. It is ridiculous to pin the etiquette of success or failure on a coach just because a coin comes up heads or tails.'

Valencia coach Jorge Valdano

'You hope and you pretend you know what you're doing.'

Kevin Keegan on the art of successful management

'All you need is a team of eleven very good players that are also very lucky!'

Herbert Chapman

Secrets and Lies . . .

'I'm not a paragon of virtue, but at the moment it does seem football is devoid of almost all principle and moral standing.'

Martin O'Neill

'If I had to be holed up by terrorists for a few weeks and was allowed one companion from the football world, Martin O'Neill would be high on my list. He is engaging company, a charming companion and a brilliant raconteur. How did he finish up as a football manager?'

John Motson

The Cult of the Manager

'I admit there are times when I lie to journalists. I'll lie rather than slag off my players.'

George Graham

'Regarding the recent speculation linking me with Aston Villa. I wish to make it clear that I will not be the next manager of Aston Villa; I've had no approach from them and I've no idea what my plans are. It's time to do something different with my life.'

Brian Little resigns as Leicester manager; after four days doing 'something different' he took over at Villa Park

'I've heard it said that you can't be a football manager and tell the truth. Well, I'm going to have a go at it.'

Liam Brady embarks on his brief reign at Celtic

'If Tommy Docherty says good morning to you, you'd better check the weather outside.'

George Best

Good Fellas . . .

'Louis Van Gaal is a tough man, but at this level you don't get by with just a smile and a few kind words.'

Jari Litmanen on his Ajax boss

'He's got a very tough persona, despite the fact they used to call him Glenda.'

Peter Shreeves, Glenn Hoddle's manager at Spurs and assistant at Chelsea

'Everyone's been saying that Swindon are too nice and I'm here to change that, but I don't want people being nasty and getting booked.'

Steve McMahon, shortly before being sent off on his 1994 debut as player/manager

'At the very highest level in Europe, you take it for granted that the opposition can play a bit as well. So it's all about who's got the team with eleven players all giving one hundred per cent. If I sense that any player of mine is not psyched up and giving absolutely everything, I'll put a bullet in the back of his neck.'

Johan Cruyff motivates (!!!) his Barça troops before a
UEFA Cup game against PSV, February 1996

'You haven't got a fucking clue. I'm going to shit on your mother.'

Valencia midfielder Roberto 'trash talks' Carlos Parreira
(only a World Cup winner, after all)

'The Ray Clemence thing was stupid really. I thought he was wrong, but you can't go around taking pokes at the coaching staff.'

The pugilistic Paul Walsh repents

'The players were warming up when a couple of helicopter gunships started circling the stadium. They just strolled off as if to show they weren't frightened.'

Lebanese national boss Terry Yorath on genuine 'made men'

Eleven daft lads . . .

'My brother always said you'd have to be mad to be a football manager. What other job is there where your entire livelihood depends on eleven daft lads?'

Francis Lee on the perils of football management

'It's very tough. The team bus is more like a school outing, full of kids eating crisps.'

Former Hartlepool boss John MacPhail on the financial
restraints of life at the bottom, 1993

'When I first played for England, I used to ask the Liverpool players what they did, what was their secret? They'd say, "Five-a-sides". They wouldn't work on set pieces and that sort of thing. Liverpool never did much in training but they all knitted together well in a certain formation. When I was at United we would work on a lot of things but we always fell short of what Liverpool did. Then all of a sudden when we were successful at United, from

The Cult of the Manager

1990, I saw why. It was simply because in seven or eight places you could probably say we had the best players in those positions in the country . . . the secret of success is good players.'

Bryan Robson, 1996

'It's players, not coaches, who win football matches. The more good players a coach has at his disposal, the more chance he has of winning things. OK, a coach might be able to move his pieces around, co-ordinate tactics and encourage his players, but at the end of the day he's like a conductor; if the musicians are bad his orchestra will sound terrible!'

Hungarian legend Ladislao Kubala, ex-Spain and Barcelona manager, 1996

'I am not important. Only the players are important.'

Bertie Mee

'My job is to look for good players and put together the best possible squad. If your players are better than your opponents, 90 per cent of the time you will win.'

Johan Cruyff

'I made a number of enquiries about Eric Cantona and everyone said the same thing: "He's totally unsuitable for English football." Needless to say, I acted on that information and turned him down.'

Howard Kendall on why Everton said no to Cantona

'I socialise, I still enjoy a laugh and a beer with the players, but you have to know when to go. You need to be a little bit detached. There are tough decisions to be made at times, and they'd be even tougher if you were too close.'

Peter Reid

'Unless you employ a 24-hour detective agency for weeks you don't know a player's habits.'

Keith Burkinshaw responds to West Brom's proposals for vetting prospective signings, 1994

'There are no prima donnas, no heavy gamblers. We have a neat side, with no permed hair.'

David Pleat keeps it tidy at Luton

'Let's get one thing straight, these lads are on very good money. Quite frankly, if you have to talk about motivating a player these days, then you haven't got a footballer at all. Talk of a lack of motivation is the biggest load of nonsense in the game today. If they can't go out there in a City shirt and play for their own pride and their families, then you can forget about motivating them because they're not footballers, they're not even people.'

Alan Ball, a couple of days before getting the sack at Manchester City

'Why should I be sacked when it's the players who go out and make the mistakes.'

Vujadin Boskov, a Scudetto winner with Sampdoria

Do they mean us?

'I always disobeyed my coaches, even if it meant they fined me.'

Alfredo Di Stéfano

'I was wearing my tracksuit bottoms when Craig Brown [then Andy Roxburgh's assistant] told me to take them off. "All the players have to look the same," he told me. I pointed out how cold it was and kept them on. I don't think he ever forgave me.'

Richard Gough on his premature international retirement

'We may not be used to it, but I reckon we could do without coaches.'

Hristo Stoichkov

'The lasting memory I have of Roy Hodgson is that he always had a very runny nose.'

Bath City keeper Dave Mogg recalls his ex-Bristol City boss, now in charge at Inter Milan

The Cult of the Manager

'A lot of managers want to turn football into a philosophy, as if they had invented it. I call them professors. But in reality football is a very simple game, it always has been and always will be.'

Jurgen Klinsmann

'When I was in the Crystal Palace youth team, Alan Smith said I should forget about football and become a travel agent!'

Gareth Southgate

'It's funny how great players, the ones who tend to be the most rebellious and the ones with the most little phobias, become the most authoritarian managers. And they're especially hard on their own great players. It's like, "I remember what I was like, and there's no way you're getting away with the same!" '

Michael Laudrup on Johan Cruyff, 1996

It may sound daft, but . . .

'It may sound daft, but until we let in those three goals just before half-time I thought we were the better side.'

Marine boss Roly Howard after his team's 11–2 defeat against Shrewsbury in the 1995 FA Cup

'The aims and ambitions of players should be perroglyphic. Their objectives should have their own realisms. Why should not their realisms be to realise that their own sanity is dependent on their own strengths. The strength in this case being unwavering with regard to the execution of their duties . . . when we talk about football we would do well to consider other contingent essentials which need to be required apart from those of the technical and understanding nature. Is it conflict? Does style become a metaphor?'

Ex-Lincoln manager Colin Murphy's surreal programme notes

'The art of Being is the assumption that you may possess, this very minute, those qualities of spirit and attitude of mind that make for radiant living. It is a philosophy of being today, instead of being in a tomorrow that never comes . . . it is developing an awareness of the infinite possibilities in each magic moment. It is heeding the wisdom of the ancient Chinese seer who observed: "A journey of a thousand miles begins with a single step", and it is taking that step today.'

Current Lincoln boss John Beck inspires his team to a 2–2 draw with Exeter (what is it about the air at Sincil Bank?)

'Bora is a perfectionist. If he was married to Demi Moore, he'd expect her to be a good cook.'

American pundit Rick Davis on USA 94 manager Bora Milutinovic

'I am interested in football as entertainment. You have to play attractively. If you don't it is like trying to make love to a tree.'

Jorge Valdano (it must lose something in translation)

Blackboard jungle ...

'Talent, technique and touch equals triumph. $T + T + T = T$.'

Jorge Valdano's coaching formula

'We play head tennis and I'm just brilliant at it.'

Peter Reid's alternative; that's T for tennis

'Football is like a car. You've got five gears, but the trouble with English teams is that they drive in fourth and fifth all the time. They never use first, second and third, never build up as you should. When they crash in Europe they say it's bad luck ... it isn't; it's bad driving.'

Ruud 'BSM' Gullit, 1995

'There are lots of coaches who spend their life selling smoke-screens. Tactical systems are absolutely worthless, it's all about what the players are worth.'

Victor, 60 caps for Spain, now Mallorca coach

'Coaching is for kids. If a player can't trap a ball and pass it by the time he's in the team, he shouldn't be there in the first place.

225

The Cult of the Manager

At Derby, I told Roy McFarland to go and get his bloody hair cut; that's coaching at top level.'

Brian Clough reflects on the secret of his success

'People often say that because I believe in attacking football, my teams don't know how to defend. That's false, but even if it was true, I'd still send out teams to attack. There is a saying in Brazil – "football is like a short blanket, if you cover up your feet your head pops out, and if you cover up your head your feet pop out" – in other words, you can't have it both ways. Concentrating on defending is the coward's way out.'

Jorge Valdano

'It's easier to destroy a painting than create one.'

Glenn Hoddle seems to agree

'I'm not in the entertainment business.'

Jack Charlton begs to differ

'I was very influenced by watching Northampton when they won the Fourth Division.'

Big Jack on the roots of the Republic of Ireland's style

'If war is too important to be left to generals, is football too important to leave to football managers?'

Brian Glanville, doyen of the cynics

'The best team always wins. The rest is only gossip.'

Jimmy Sirrel

You work hard for the money . . .

'Hard work doesn't guarantee you success, but without it, you haven't got the slightest chance of winning anything.'

Pat Riley, four NBA titles as coach of the LA Lakers and a man who once fined a player $1500 for helping an opponent get up from the floor!

'Clough was very idiosyncratic; he once threatened to fire me because someone told him I was training on my day off.'

Frank Clark on life with Brian

'When I read about such-and-such player being a hard worker, I just don't want to know. A professional footballer shouldn't be anything else but fit, so there's no hard work in just being able to run. The hard work comes when you have to play with imagination.'

Dundee United boss Ivan Golac, 1994

'My electrician's exam was much tougher than this.'

Jimmy Case takes over at Brighton, 1995

The People's game?

'What do you mean by the street? Taxi drivers? Butchers? Fishmongers? Caretakers? With taxi drivers, I'll talk about cars and with butchers about meat. But I'm not going to talk to them about football because I know more about the game than all the taxi drivers, all of the butchers and all of the caretakers put together. And for that matter, I know more about football than all of you ... *journalists* ... put together. What do you expect me to do? Hold a straw poll every time I pick the team?'

Jorge Valdano, under pressure at Real Madrid in 1995, responds to suggestions that he heeds the word on the street

'It has got to the stage where I thought I was being followed in my car. There was even a threat to kidnap me and take me to the zoo, but it didn't materialise.'

Ex-Southampton boss Ian Branfoot on the fans' campaign to oust him, 1993

'He's fat, he's round, he's taken Leicester down!'

Reading fans taunt the club's former manager, Mark McGhee, 1995

'I am fat. It's difficult not to get that way with the kind of life I lead, but the important thing is that it doesn't affect my golf swing.'

McGhee takes it in his stride

The Cult of the Manager

Money! Money! Money!

'People say it's not about money? What a load of bollocks that is. Have a look at the League table, the teams at the top are the ones with money. Buying a team is not that difficult really. It's when you haven't got money that it is really hard. You're always taking chances, gambling on players and wondering if they're really good enough. It's always a gamble. If you can buy Sutton or Shearer it's so much easier.'

Harry Redknapp, a man who spent £2.4 million on Florin Raducioiu

'When I sign a player, I always arrange to meet him in a service station or a hotel, before he gets the chance to see our offices.'

David Pleat on luring players to Luton

'I've never had so much money to spend – well, apart from perhaps in a previous life.'

Ex-Middlesbrough boss Lennie Lawrence, 1991

'Four out of five ex-internationals don't do that well as managers. But one in five gets some money to spend and does.'

David Pleat

'Because of our financial situation I spent my first three months here trying to do swap deals. Funny how other managers always want to exchange one of their reserves for your best player!'

Partick Thistle manager Murdo MacLeod, 1996

'Where would you rather live? Streatham or a big place in France with loads of space around you?'

Palace boss Alan Smith explains his failure to land Swedish giant Kennet Andersson, 1994

'I was on a drip in a hospital bed and this player came in to see me. I thought he was enquiring about my health. He never even asked how I was. All he was interested in was how he stood regarding his contract. He'd even brought his agent in.'

Former St Johnstone manager John McClelland on why he quit football

'The sooner I can get rid of the agents, the sleaze and the pimps from my football club the better.'

Alan Smith, shortly before Crystal Palace got rid of him, 1994

'Dogs, worms, vermin.'

Joe Kinnear on agents, 1995

'A lot of managers rejoice in stupidity. For the very few bright ones there's an awful lot who don't bring any credit to the sport. Can you think of any other trade in the latter part of the twentieth century where they call their superiors "gaffer" or "boss". I think that's pathetic.'

Agent Jon Holmes, 1996

'All good footballers never did any work, they just played football. They became players and then you expect them to be managers and deal with multi-million-pound transfers. Invariably these guys went to a secondary modern school. On the Continent most managers have degrees before they come into the business. Rarely do you find the football side and the directors working together. There's too much suspicion between the two. You don't get much long-term planning because people have short-term agendas in order to further their own ambitions.'

Crystal Palace chairman Ron Noades

You can take the boy out of Dagenham . . .

'Terry Venables was too cheeky for my own good.'

Tommy Docherty on his youthful Chelsea skipper

'I've never come across anyone in the game who knows more than Terry. But he doesn't brag.'

Steve Archibald

'The most successful England manager of all time, that's me, came from Dagenham. Why shouldn't the next one, too?'

Sir Alf Ramsey

The Cult of the Manager

'I don't really get nervous; I suppose just before the game the butterflies go a bit, just like they used to as a player. It's different as a manager because as a player, you only had yourself to take care of, now you've got the bigger picture. It's actually ten times better when you win and ten times worse when you lose.'

Venables at Euro 96

'It makes me feel ill to hear that we have too much coaching. The sickening thing is that we have too much bad, pathetic coaching.'

Venables

'Coaches will become stronger personalities in the future. Any team game will become more and more about organisation; there'll be people using computers to look at percentages, at which part of the pitch the game is played in. If I can get three per cent on crosses, four per cent on midfield play and organise the back ... I'm not saying that this and that percentage scores goals, but if there's a way goals are scored, I'd be stupid to ignore it.'

Venables on the cybernetic future

'You play, coach, manage ... and then you die. I'm concentrating on getting out of that last one. I don't fancy someone bending over my coffin saying "Go on, my son, coach your way out of that!" '

Venables

Da doo Ron Ron . . .

'There is this champagne and nightclubs image around Ron Atkinson, but above all he loves the game and the company of football people. He's still a child at heart. In training this season, he's been everyone from Arnold Muhren to David Ginola.'

Gordon Strachan, 1996

'He loves his little cracks and keeps everyone on their toes. He's a piss-taker, basically, and it's always good in training.'

Coventry's Noel Whelan

'How can anybody call this work? People in this game don't realise how lucky they are. You drive to the ground, play a few five-a-sides, then have lunch. It's wonderful, enjoyable fun.'

Big Ron puts it all into perspective

'I always make sure I write Atkinson D. on the team sheet. Sometimes I wonder if I'm making a mistake.'

Atkinson R. on Villa's Dalian, 1993

'I just wanted to give them some technical advice. I told them the game had started.'

On why he left his seat in the stand for the dugout, just fifteen minutes into a game (Villa v. Sheffield United, 1993)

'Let's have one of those old-fashioned Saturdays where we come to a game, have a pre-match meal, get the right result and go out and have a few drinks. It seems to work better than all that tactics bollocks.'

Inspiring Coventry to their first win of the 1996/97 campaign, against Leeds

'Once you've had a taste of it you never have enough. You tell me a better way to spend a Wednesday night – under the floodlights at a cracking stadium, big game, plenty at stake. Not even *Coronation Street* is that good!'

Taking a midweek defeat against Wolves in his stride, 1996

Gorgeous George . . .

'We were surprised to say the least when George Graham said no, because 90 per cent of other managers would have been happy with what we offered. I am dumbfounded, but nothing surprises me in this game.'

Francis Lee, dumbfounded but not surprised

'Look at the successful clubs and there's usually a driving force within, a figurehead. And that's what I was at Arsenal.'

'I got this silly reputation for being tough and walking around with this cane in my hand smacking everybody. I helped players.

The Cult of the Manager

I really helped Paul Merson and his wife during all the problems they had with his drinking and gambling, even the drugs thing. It's amazing some of the things you have to do as a manager; there were times when I felt like an agony uncle!'

'I think Cantona will let you down at the very highest level. I think he let Leeds down last year against Rangers. Cantona will go missing. He's a crybaby when the going gets tough.'

GG, before they invented the phrase 'double Double'

'In our profession, there's an opposition. And in any confrontation you try to look at your opponents' strengths and weaknesses. And my philosophy has always been that you've got to know their strengths and nullify them, and then try to impose your strengths on them. It's no use saying: "Oh, they've got wonderful players. Like Chris Waddle." It amuses me when I am actually criticised for nullifying Waddle and John Sheridan. I laughed when I read Brian Glanville saying that George Graham had ruined the game! How naïve and innocent for such an experienced journalist to say that I had ruined the game. It's my job to nullify the opposition, and I thought, "I'll get some credit for it." That's when I said: "Let's just forget about the press in future and just get on with winning some more trophies." '

Reacting to negative press reaction after Arsenal's League Cup final victory against Sheffield Wednesday, 1993

'5–2 is too cavalier. I would have preferred 2–0 or 3–0.'

Arsenal beat Sheffield United, but Christmas comes too early for George (December 1991)

'Winning isn't just about pretty football. It's about hunger and application.'

'I'm not a great believer in luck, you make your own. I think it was Gary Player who said that the harder he practised, the luckier he got. We worked very hard at Arsenal. If there was any luck going I'd say it was deserved.'

'After eight and a half years they sacked me in two minutes.'

The end of Graham's Highbury reign, February 1995

King Kev . . .

'If Kevin Keegan fell into the Tyne, he'd come up with a salmon in his mouth.'

Jack Charlton, 1995

'The moment I stepped in the door at Newcastle he said I could play for England. He's great at giving confidence to people. He makes you believe that you are a good player.'

Robert Lee on the charisma of Keegan

'As a manager, you've always got a gun to your head. It's a question of whether there is a bullet in the barrel.'

'I always thought managers were more involved, but when it comes down to it, I just sit there and watch like everyone else.'

'It helps if you've achieved something in the game as a player, especially when it comes to transfers. It means that you can put your cards on the table and the guy knows who you are. I'm sure guys like Kenny Dalglish, Bryan Robson and Graeme Souness are the same – known throughout Europe and the world.'

'I think in a way the players run the club at Newcastle. I don't mean they can just do what they want. We talk. We communicate. They know what they can and cannot do. They've seen what happens when somebody oversteps the mark. The rules are there but they're not up on a wall. For instance, if anybody drank two days before a game he'd be severely punished. I give them licence to run their own lives, to be adults. In short, we put it this way: "You know what's right and what's wrong. We've got you for two hours or six on a bus, so at home or in a hotel do what you know is right." I give the players freedom and in return I get respect.'

'There are lots of presents around at Christmas, but there is also "Scrooge".'

Keegan on Newcastle's goalless bore against Leeds on Boxing Day, 1994

'Sir John Hall was a multi-millionaire when I joined. Now he's just an ordinary millionaire.'

The Cult of the Manager

'I'm in charge, not you. If it doesn't work out I know what the bottom line is. If you want to be manager of Newcastle, apply for the job.'

Keegan trys to placate fans unhappy at Andy Cole's departure to Manchester United

'If Manchester United came on the phone and mentioned Andy Cole, I'd put the phone down.'

Of course you would, Kevin

Fergie baby . . .

'We were on the eighteenth green and a man I had never met before walked over the hill and said, "Excuse me, Mr Ferguson, you are the champions. Oldham have just beaten Villa." '

Fergie finds out United have broken their 26-year duck

'I made a pig's ear out of that one.'

Taking it on the chin after Galatasaray ended United's interest in the 1993/94 Champions League

'Alex always had a hot temper. He'd have caused a fight in an empty house.'

Martin Ferguson on his fiery big brother, 1995

'Kenny Dalglish has associates, but only a few true friends. There's nothing wrong with that because, at the end of the day, you only need six people to carry your coffin.'

Fiery but not diplomatic

'That wee fat boy will never make a footballer.'

Ferguson, then playing for Rangers, on Kenny's future prospects

Ferguson: 'Five hours sleep is all I need.'
Journalist: 'Like Margaret Thatcher?'
Ferguson: 'Don't associate me with that woman.'

Exchange at 1995 press conference

Howard's way!

'I've worked for the last three England managers and I've seen what it did to them. I saw Ron Greenwood break out in sores, Bobby Robson go grey, and poor Graham Taylor double up in anguish and stick his head between his legs so far it nearly disappeared. If I was single, with no kids, it'd be no problem, but I've a wife and three children and I've seen the effect the job can have on your family. It won't happen to mine.'

Wilkinson rules himself out as Taylor's successor, 1993

'Good management is all about leadership. You need a bit of brains, too, and that's all I've got. You've also got to be single-minded, knowledgeable, determined, durable and thick-skinned.'

'I feel like Corky the Cat when he gets run over by a steam-roller, picks himself up and then someone kicks him in the stomach.'

After Arsenal knock Leeds out of the 1993 FA Cup

'There are only two types of manager. Those who've been sacked and those who will be sacked in the future.'

A week before losing the Leeds job

'Trying to sign players is like picking your way through a minefield. In negotiating the minefield you sometimes get blown up.'

'If he gets us goals we'll go out there and stand on our heads if he wants us to.'

Howard gets happy after landing Antony Yeboah in 1994

'When he couldn't have things his own way he just took his bat home. Real soldiers grab their tin helmet, their rifle and spade. They know that on occasions, they have to dig in and make the best of it. When he didn't like it, he went missing. Back home to his music, painting and poetry.'

On why he sold Cantona

The Cult of the Manager

'David Rocastle is a magnificent human being. If I had a daughter free . . .'

And getting ready to sell Rocky in 1993

'No football manager is more appreciative of how much trouble and expense the fans incur to watch football and the dedication they show. But I have never been one who can relate to fans and they find it hard relating to me. Some managers have avoided getting the sack because of the relationship they have with the fans. I'm not like that. Al Capone had more friends than I've got at the moment.'

Under pressure at Elland Road, Christmas 1994

'I'm not a politician, a social worker or a clergyman; I'm a provider of distraction and fans want to go back home happy to whatever bores the arse off them in the week.'

'All coaches want to prove something, but the amount of self-justification that goes on these days makes you want to puke. You continually come across it in match reports that are almost entirely devoted to how results were achieved. Not by the players, but the managers. It's as though some of them are saying: "This doesn't happen very often so I'd better take the opportunity of proving to everybody how good I am." '

Do I not like that?

'The more I see of Graham, the more I meet him, the more impressed I am with him. I held the view he was the best man available when we appointed him and it is a view I continue to hold . . . he's not just a manager, he's a psychiatrist who is able to think his way around matters.'

Wolves owner Sir Jack Hayward, shortly before changing his shrink

'We just lack the kind of talent that makes you go . . . whooosh!'

Taylor's verdict on his England squad for the 1992 European Championships in Sweden

'In twenty years' time, people could be saying: "Bloody hell, they had to get seven that night and Poland had to beat Holland and it actually happened. Fantastic. What was the team now? God knows, he changed it so often." '

Daydreaming before the game against San Marino, 1993

'Say hello to Graham Taylor – I feel sorry for him. I am sure he has shown in the past how good a manager he is, so there's nothing to worry about for him.'

Dutch boss Dick Advocaat celebrates getting to the 1994 World Cup finals

'Napoleon wanted his generals to be lucky. I don't think he would have wanted me.'

Taylor, after that World Cup KO

'If they sing "Turnip, Turnip, give us a wave," I'll give them a wave. I have never had any serious problems with that.'

Coping admirably with vegetable taunts, 1994

'If a journalist wrote that about me, he'd have to go into hiding.'

Jack Charlton

'I used to quite like turnips, now my wife refuses to serve them.'

On life as a meat-and-one-veg man

'He only cries at a sad episode of *Coronation Street* or Vera Lynn records.'

Lawrie McMenemy on life with Taylor

. . . *and finally, in the great man's immortal words*, 'Fucking hell's bells!'

13 Kevin and John – Newcastle United's split personalities

By Michael Hodges

We have Margaret Thatcher to thank for the fact that the north-east can be described today without including clunking pit-head pulley gears or the dark swirl of the 'Coaly Tyne'. She may seem an unlikely starting point in an assessment of Kevin Keegan's time at Newcastle United, but the lady who wasn't for turning haunts every aspect of English culture over the last twenty years. And these days English culture means football.

More pertinently, Thatcher stood guard over a revolution in British management. And that doesn't just apply to utilities, industry and insurance salesmen; football management has also changed. It was the *High Noon* of Thatcherism when Kevin Keegan went to Newcastle United as a player. The Falklands had been retaken, the miners were in the government's gun sights and Tyneside was fast heading for economic oblivion, its inhabitants as ever dependent on football for relief from grim reality. Kevin Keegan's two seasons at Newcastle United provided that relief. He not only propelled the side to promotion to the old First Division but also established a relationship with the supporters that would not only drag him back from his unconvincing decision to play golf in Spain for eight years but would, if truth be told, emotionally shackle him.

As Keegan lifted a team that boasted the delightful abilities of the young Peter Beardsley and Chris Waddle, another son of a Geordie miner was seeking his nirvana in the shopping malls of the USA. John Hall saw enough in America to realise that derelict post-industrial land in the north-east could be converted into retailing opportunity. The proof of that – Hall's creation of Gateshead's Metro Centre – was enough to convince him that the dormant but potentially massive creature that was Newcastle United and its support could also be converted into a retailing opportunity.

Newcastle has a long tradition of men who want their region to be great – the industrial pioneer George Stephenson wanted it through the railways and the municipal socialist T. Dan Smith sought it through a compromised housing and planning revolution. The Thatcherite capitalist John Hall saw football as the route to glory for the relatively small acreage known as the north-east. Implicit in Hall's campaign was his vision of the club as a regional symbol – the '*Geordie Nation*' of his dream made flesh in black and white shirts – to which end he was willing to spend. And, by 1992, he was able to.

Unless you're born into it, becoming a millionaire requires nous and vision coupled with good breaks. John Hall had all that and more. He may have overreached the limits of his own idea in trying to buy into Rugby Union and ice hockey in an area that doesn't regard football as a sport but the definition of what the area itself was, but he was pragmatic enough to realise that the football team was the key to success.

We will never be sure if it was just John Hall's money, or Kevin Keegan's ability, that took Newcastle from near disaster to the top echelons of European football. Keegan's decision to come out of his unforced and unnatural early retirement was not taken lightly. Part of his inspiration was that he had been sold on Hall's vision. Also, much as the southern-based tabloids and Sky Sports are now, Keegan was convinced of the mystical status of the Geordie fan. To put himself at their head was to accept the mantel of greatness: an irresistible proposition. But not one that can offer much hope of a normal life.

Keegan was psychologically prepared to spend his way to victory from the minute he arrived at St James's Park. Few stories provide so early in their narrative a moment of epiphany that will illustrate the themes of the tale to follow, but after Keegan had been at Newcastle United for a mere month and a half such a moment happened. Convinced that Hall was reneging on his commitment to supply cash for transfers, Keegan walked, or rather drove, out.

On a Friday before a home match against Swindon, Keegan put his assistant-manager Terry McDermott into a car and drove south. Surprised to be heading down the A1 instead of running round the Maiden Castle training ground, McDermott persuaded a still unsure Keegan to turn the car round and head back to

Tyneside. The next day, Keegan engineered a Newcastle victory over Swindon by three goals to one, but struggling with his own ability to persevere, Keegan still left. It took until the Monday morning and Hall capitulating over the telephone for Keegan to change his mind. Money, transfers, temperament, attacking football, intrigue – that is the story of Kevin Keegan's time at St James's Park.

It is the sheer uniqueness of the tale – the quality that turned a football manager from a back-page feature to front-page news in five years – that makes Keegan's example a problematic one if we want to find out anything about the nature of modern football management in what happened to him. Any insight is further hampered by the fact that the story is as much about modern club chairmen as it is about managers. Keegan wasn't brought to the club by the usual chairman gambling on a favourite ex-player to take the side up a division. John Hall had only recently achieved supremacy at the club. He had been enmeshed in an at times vicious personal battle with ex-chairman Gordon McKeag for years; now finally victorious he wasn't content with building a successful side alone. His agenda was much bigger than that. He was determined to bring eighties business practice to the running of a nineties football club, as he made clear whenever he was given the opportunity. For Hall, running a football club was '. . . like a business. You bring in your MDs for your various sections and Kevin happens to be the managing director of the football. Each week, my son, the vice-chairman and the chief executive all sit with Kevin and discuss the footballing side. I don't get involved until a decision has been made about buying or selling players.' Apart from the obvious fact that there is a vital and big gap between being a MD and a messiah, this comment is telling in that it is palpably untrue. Hall is at his sparkling best when he is being disingenuous. He cloaks his ambition in a misleadingly rational business-speak he developed in the Thatcherite wonder years he so admires, but it is a cloak, because John Hall did get involved in the decisions at Newcastle United. All of them. You don't devote your life to capturing something only to let it go once you've grasped it, and that applies especially to football clubs. In retrospect, the definition of the dual relationship was established in that first weekend of turmoil. The *modus operandi* was settled – Keegan and Hall would be involved in a partnership that was as much a struggle as it was a co-operative pact. In capitulating, Hall set a precedent that did Keegan himself no favours. From that moment on he knew if he kicked and screamed hard enough, then Hall would relent. Keegan would be working in a vacuum of absent authority, yet he left it like that and never moved to fill the space with the undoubted power of his own personality. Newcastle United became an uneasy stand-off between Keegan and Hall, made all the stranger by their constantly quoted high regard for each other.

Kevin Keegan's initial buys boded well. The very first player in was inspired and ironically cost nothing – Kevin Sheedy on a free from Everton. Sheedy was the perfect acquisition; he possessed the craft and professional insight of a man who had played the great Everton midfield of the mid-eighties, as well as, and more importantly, the gratitude of a man who thought his career was over. Sheedy fought all the harder to save Newcastle from relegation, knowing that promotion the season after would probably be his last chance to shine in the Premiership. It worked and that same first season players of similar standing joined him. Barry Venison came from Liverpool, while the defence was achored by the arrival of Brian Kilcline from Oldham. John Hall could sit back and watch with satisfaction. He had picked the right man, who in his turn was picking the right men. Newcastle stayed up.

Keegan is from Armthorpe in the heart of Yorkshire colliery territory, and although having a Geordie father was a defining part of his make-up, his Yorkshireness is even more so. Generalisations based on race or a region are often misleading and occasionally plain wrong, but Yorkshire is an exception. The defining characteristic of Yorkshire people is stubbornness.

When Newcastle won promotion to the Premiership in May 1993, Keegan's team were good enough to offer the first chance of breaking the ascendance of Liverpool and Manchester United since Leeds. Newcastle had been in this position before, but previously had been content with achieving promotion, an attitude which invariably led to relegation. Keegan, twice European player of the year and with more medals than the Grenadier Guards, had offered his resignation at the end of the promotion season. He had been persuaded to stay again, and if he was going to stay then it was to win the Championship or nothing. To do so he believed he needed Peter Beardsley. It was then that Hall the businessman faltered in the face of Keegan's ambition. Hall wasn't sure that a 32-year-old playing out his days at Everton was worth £1,400,000. As he put it himself, 'We're running a business, let nobody mistake it.' The banks on his back and a hard-gained personal empire to lose, Hall saw Beardsley as an outrageous gamble. Keegan's stubbornness kicked in – he must have Beardsley. Hall, the man who has since claimed publicly not to be involved with transfers, remained doubtful – but he had been beaten before by Keegan and he had invested so much of his personal energies in preventing Keegan's regular attempts to leave the club that now he didn't have it in him to resist. Keegan prevailed and Hall was left to recount his defeat. 'I thought Peter Beardsley was too old and Kevin said, "No he's not," and he's proven me wrong.'

He certainly did. If it had been left to Hall, a man ever-quick to peddle the platitudes of Geordie nationhood, the Tynesider Beardsley would not have returned to his homeland and New-castle would not have illuminated the Premiership, finishing third in the 1993/94 season, a feat reminiscent of Don Revie's Leeds who finished second in their first season in the top League in 1965.

From that point the Keegan story left the regional and entered the national consciousness. Elsewhere in this book you can find the chronicles of old-school managers: frank, bluff Scots and north-easterners who ran every aspect of their club and would brook no questioning of their authority. Undoubtedly, the ser-geant major approach had been effective, but by the late eighties it was simply no longer feasible – not only had the top clubs grown beyond into sprawling business, media and catering con-cerns but they were increasingly using industry professionals to run themselves. Even Alex Ferguson, a man who is often held up as the last of the Shankly breed, involved himself mainly in the team and left the vagaries of the rest of the club to the Manchester United directors. The nature of teams was changing as well. No longer were they tight-knit packs of working-class British men; increasingly dressing rooms were filled with the sound of foreign tongues. Cultural change brought, by implication, managerial change. In a game that was reinventing itself as a mixture of American family entertainment and Continental play, Keegan was the perfect figurehead of a new group of managers.

Keegan, Glenn Hoddle and Ruud Gullit have all promised to change the very core of football management. But Hoddle is grounded in his Christian faith and Gullit in an easy-going realisation of what is possible and what is likely so early in his career. Keegan was dealing with much darker forces and before long they surfaced in his public actions. The first hints came in October 1993 when he substituted Lee Clark at Southampton. Few players are as committed to their team as Lee Clark; he is the personification of the Geordie who wants nothing more from life than to play for Newcastle United. As well as that he is an excellent player. But no one, least of all Lee Clark, could understand why Keegan never gave him a fair chance. Clark was always the first to be dropped and the last to be picked. When Keegan arrived at Newcastle, one of his first actions was to take Clark out of the team. Given his background Clark was inclined to take being substituted even more personally than other players – that day in Southampton he visibly complained to Keegan as he walked off the pitch. Keegan's reaction was breath-stopping. He appeared to pull at Clark's jersey and push him backward. Managers do not do that. Even a semblance of authority is best served by waiting until they get to the dressing room where they can do as much pulling and pushing as they like.

Keegan was already buckling under the weight of his own and other people's expectations. The ivory tower nature of management is bound to create a degree of me-against-the-world consciousness in a manager, but Keegan especially was prone to it, given his personality and the situation that had developed between him and Hall. His particular way of coping was to develop relations within the squad that in time became detrimental to the overall team spirit. Kevin Keegan had his favourites – in particular, Peter Beardsley, the man who he had not only fought hard for and who was in football-speak the consummate professional, but the man who had proved him right. Likewise, Alan Shearer was upheld by Keegan as a player all the others should look up to as an example. That doesn't always go down well with professional footballers, especially those whose hard work built a team strong enough and good to be able to attract the best players in the world. But Keegan was determined that the players he bought should be seen as the best, and the more money John Hall spent the more desperately Keegan had to justify it. He developed a moral fervour, with attacking football as its driving force.

But, as recent scandals have illustrated in football all over the world, the game is not really a suitable vehicle for morality. Bill Shankly may have worn it as a badge but that was its main purpose – moral authority as an effective PR tool. Keegan himself pointed out as he was coming to the end of his tether in late 1996, 'Everyone says that Bill Shankly wouldn't work with agents now, but Bill Shankly was such a great manager, if he had to work with an agent to get the player he wanted he'd work with him.' It remains a moot point as to whether Shankly could have worked with Sir John Hall. His own chairman, John Smith, was a quiet and unassuming establishment figure, a man of the old school before that meant wearing Adidas gazelles. But one of Shankly's sharper dictums – that a manager should buy players when his team is strong not when it's weak – was to prove to be the undoing of Keegan's Championship hopes in 1996.

Nemesis came in the signing of Faustino Asprilla. The facts of what happened are ingrained in the mind of everyone who cares anything for football – yet they need repeating, if only to make them believable. Keegan's side were twelve points clear at the top of the Premiership. Newcastle may have been knocked unexpectedly out of the FA Cup by Chelsea but in the Premiership they could not be caught. Parma wanted £6,700,000 for a player no one in England, apart from Keegan, could see the point in buying. But Keegan thought Asprilla was 'a bit special' and that was enough for him. Hall, surely distraught at what was happening, watched as his manager sneaked round Italy in a transfer cat-and-mouse game that would have baffled Tom and Jerry. Eventually Asprilla arrived at Tyneside in the snow, and Hall was on television praising the vision of his manager and the talent of the totally superfluous Colombian.

Hindsight makes every management decision easy and it would be unfair to blame Asprilla's inclusion for Newcastle's collapse that season. But that's what it looked like. Keegan had put himself on the line to get Asprilla, so Keegan was going to pick him. Opposition players had no idea what Asprilla was going to do next, and he spread panic and confusion wherever he went. Unfortunately, he did the same to Newcastle United.

It is hard to resist the challenge of taking an erratic player that others have failed to bring into the fold and by dint of your own personality and efforts recast him as a successful player. Keegan is not alone in that – Glenn Hoddle has committed himself to the thankless task of converting Paul Gascoigne into a balanced human being and football player. He may have God on his side but he's up against 200 years of northern industrial-class beer culture. Keegan put himself up against a more glamorous but equally engrained culture in taking on the man with alleged cocaine connections, a penchant for nude models and all the self-effacement that playing in Serie A can bestow.

Championships are commonly held to slip away, but New-castle's was worried away. There was something certain about their demise; they themselves did not have the confidence to win it. Increasingly, John Hall became more public in his assertion of Keegan's ability, just as Keegan himself became more and more unhinged in his public pronouncements. Paradoxically, football is too involving a game to admit that you're involved in it and once Keegan had publicly confessed his passion and emotional turmoil in that corridor at Elland Road, his descent into neurosis became at once unstoppable. Giving too much of yourself weakens a manager, and draws on some internal reservoir which must remain full for football, not be emptied by public gushing.

There was no way back to personal equilibrium for Keegan without leaving the game, and there was no way to success for Newcastle – and that means the Championship and nothing else – without Keegan leaving. Managing has always been a taxing occupation. Roy Evans recently remarked, 'Being a manager puts three years on your life every year.'

Keegan's decision to escape raises questions about just what kind of man can manage a football team successfully. Perhaps it's not a job for an ex-player. As Geoff Hurst put it, right after his unsuccessful spell as manager of Chelsea, 'Playing was great. Managing was unrewarding and stupid.' But Keegan never made that difficult journey from sharing the dressing room with his mates to running them from an office. His eight-year sojourn in the golf clubs of the Costa Del Sol created the space for him to grow apart. Glenn Hoddle made the trip smoothly, as did Ruud Gullit, who learnt much from his boss's smooth progression. Some argue that Keegan's emotional unbalance was a product of his age. But Bobby Robson, Newcastle's first choice as his replacement, is 63 and his fraught prevaricating over taking the job as Keegan's successor showed him to be just as likely as Keegan to be led by his heart rather than his head when under pressure.

The Cult of the Manager

Kenny Dalglish is the same age as Keegan, and if pressure is to be discussed then surely no other manager has had to endure what Dalglish went through at Hillsborough. If there is a way forward for young managers, it is perhaps, like Dalglish, to pretend you're older than you are. Although Dalglish's enthusiasm for football still inhabits his soul, where he keeps it guarded and unavailable for comment, he has ironed it out of his public demeanour. Most criticism washes over Dalglish, but for Keegan it was an affront to both his team and himself. Keegan was battling to hold on to both a team and a dream; ultimately an impossible personal task for him. Dalglish will sit happily at the head of a club that has successfully floated on the stock exchange and in all probability win a trophy during his first season in charge. His dealing will be with Douglas Hall, John's son, as Hall Senior has chosen to step down.

Rumours abound as to why Keegan left. Only two men really know what led to Keegan's cracking point. Sir John Hall has stayed fish-faced. Keegan also holds his counsel. But those who see the most likely reason in Hall's flotation of the club are surely nearest the bone.

Breaking the north-west's monopoly on glory has involved changing the club as much as the region itself has changed. There are salmon in the Tyne now and Newcastle United are on the stock exchange. Hall and Keegan put Newcastle in the city columns and football has replaced coal as the north-east's prime commodity.

The internal tension between football and finance at clubs can be dynamic and destructive. Keegan's ability to buy his way to success was useless without the ability to knit the players together. None the less, only a fool or a Sunderland fan would doubt that he achieved much in his five years. It is partly because his achievements are judged against Hall's verbose claims for Geordie greatness that they seem lessened. That and the small matter of not winning the Championship.

14 The Legendary Managers: A Statistical Record

ATKINSON, Ron
Born: Liverpool (18 March 1939)
Career: Kettering player/manager Jan. 1971–Nov. 1974; Cambridge Utd Nov. 1974–Jan. 1978; West Brom Jan. 1978–June 1981; Man Utd June 1981–Nov. 1986; West Brom Sept. 1987–Oct. 1988; Atlético Madrid Oct. 1988–Jan. 1989; Sheffield Wednesday Feb. 1989–May 1991; Aston Villa June 1991–Nov. 1994; Coventry City Feb. 1995–Nov. 1996
Honours: Division Three champions 1968; Division Four champions 1977; FA Cup winners 1983 & 1985; League Cup winners 1994

Atkinson became Cambridge United's manager in 1974. They won the Fourth Division title in 1977. West Brom reached the FA Cup semifinals in 1978, but lost 3–1 to Ipswich at Highbury and were not helped by an injury and a sending off. Man Utd won the FA Cup twice in 1983 and 1985, beating Brighton and Everton respectively in the final. However, the club's primary goal remained success in the League, which they had not won since 1967. Aston Villa finished as runners-up in the Premier League in 1992/93 and won the League Cup, beating Man Utd 3–1 in the final with Atkinson as manager against his old club.

BUCKLEY, 'Major' Franklin Charles
Born: Urmston, Manchester (9 November 1883)
Died: Walsall (22 December 1964)
Career: Norwich City player/manager Mar. 1919–July 1920; Blackpool July 1923–May 1927; Wolves May 1927–Mar. 1944; Notts County Mar. 1944–May 1946; Hull City May 1946–Mar. 1948; Leeds Utd May 1948–Apr. 1953; Walsall Apr. 1953–Jun. 1955

Honours: England international (1 cap); Division Two champions 1912 & 1932

Buckley's sides never won a major honour yet he is one of the most revered managers of all time. Wolves came close to the double in 1939, but just missed out on both. He gained fame as a shrewd manager in the transfer market, especially during Molineux where he became the manager of Wolves in May 1927. His unique ability to turn young unknowns into stars was allowed to flourish for the next seventeen years. By the time war came, Wolves had risen from a moderate Second Division side to runners-up in the League and FA Cup.

BUSBY, Sir Matt
Born: Orbiston, Lanarkshire (26 May 1909)
Died: Manchester (20 January 1994)
Career: Man Utd Feb. 1945–June 1969, admin. manager Jun 1969, caretaker manager Dec. 1970–June 1971, director June 1971–Aug. 1982, club president Mar. 1980; Scotland national manager 1958–9
Honours: Scotland international (1 cap); FA Cup winners 1948 & 1963; CBE 1958; knighted 1968; League champions 1952, 1956, 1957, 1965 & 1967; European Cup winners 1968

Busby is one of the greatest managers, not only in British soccer, but in the world. He managed Man Utd from October 1945 until June 1969 with such enthusiasm, shrewdness and skill that he turned them into one of the outstanding clubs in the world. United's honours list under Busby is remarkable: five times Football League champions, seven times runners-up, FA Cup winners and finalists twice each, and European Cup semifinalists on three occasions, winners in 1968. United were runners-up in the First Division four times before finally winning the title in 1951/52.

United were the first club to enter European competition, against the advice of the English ruling body. Reinforced with a young Bobby Charlton, they reached the semifinal of the European Cup only to lose to Real Madrid in 1957 and AC Milan in 1958. Tragedy struck in February 1958 when the 'Busby Babes' were cut down in their prime, their bodies scattered with the wreckage of their aircraft on the snow of Munich Airport. United won the FA

Cup in 1963 and the League title in 1965 and 1967, and gained their biggest prize, the European Cup, in 1968, beating Benfica 4–1, after extra time, at Wembley. After three semifinal defeats, it had become Matt Busby's last great obsession to win this competition.

CHAPMAN, Herbert

Born: Kiveton Park, Sheffield (19 January 1878)
Died: 6 January 1934
Career: Northampton Town player/manager Apr. 1907–June 1912; Leeds City June 1912–Oct. 1919; Huddersfield Town secretary/manager Sept. 1921–June 1925; Arsenal secretary/manager June 1925–Jan. 1934
Honours: FA Cup winners 1922 & 1930; League champions 1924, 1925, 1931 & 1933

One of the most successful and influential managers in the history of the game, Chapman was a great innovator who changed the face of football on and off the field in the 1920s and 1930s. He created two successful sides at Huddersfield and Arsenal, and introduced tactical methods and many other new ideas which had a far-reaching effect on the game. In the summer of 1907 Chapman returned to Northampton for a third spell, this time as player/manager. He soon weaved his magic and Northampton were Southern League champions in 1908/09. By the time he left for Leeds City in June 1912, the Cobblers had won 102 of 196 games under his guidance.

In September 1921 Chapman was invited to become the manager of Huddersfield Town. They won the FA Cup in 1922 against Preston, and the first of three consecutive League titles in 1923/24, edging out Cardiff City on goal average. The following season they conceded just 26 goals, taking the title again. Chapman had moved to Arsenal before the start of the next season, but the Terriers still won the title. In 1927 Arsenal reached the FA Cup final, but lost 1–0 to Cardiff. The Gunners made amends in 1930 when they beat Chapman's old club Huddersfield 2–0 in the final. In 1930/31 Arsenal won the League for the first time, with a record 66 points. The Gunners, like Huddersfield in the 1920s, won the League title three seasons in succession from 1932 to 1935. Chapman died halfway through the second season but many still gave him credit for three successes.

CHARLTON, Jack, OBE

Born: Ashington (8 May 1935)

Career: Middlesbrough May 1973–Apr. 1977; Sheffield Wednesday Oct. 1977–May 1983; Middlesbrough caretaker manager Mar. 1984 for short period; Newcastle May 1984–Aug. 1985; Republic of Ireland Feb. 1986–Apr. 1996

Honours: England international (35 caps); Division Two champions 1974; Anglo-Scottish Cup winners 1975; OBE 1974

Jack Charlton decided to retire from playing when he was offered the manager's job at Middlesbrough. This was in May 1973, and at the end of his first season in charge Boro ran away with the Second Division Championship. The club won promotion back to the First Division for the first time since 1954 as early as 23 March with eight games still to play. In October 1977, Charlton returned as manager of Sheffield Wednesday. It took two years to transform the club, and he created a team that won promotion to Division Two in 1980. Charlton resigned in 1983, just after the Owls reached the FA Cup semifinals. In February 1986, Big Jack was approached by the FA of Ireland. Under him, Ireland reached the European Championship final for the first time, in 1988. They also reached the World Cup finals in 1990 and 1994, attaining the quarterfinals and second round respectively.

CLOUGH, Brian

Born: Middlesbrough (21 March 1935)

Career: Hartlepool United Oct. 1965–June 1967; Derby County June 1967–Oct. 1973; Brighton Nov. 1973–June 1974; Leeds United Aug.–Oct. 1974; Nottingham Forest Jan. 1975–May 1993

Honours: England international (2 caps); League champions 1972 & 1978; League Cup winners 1978, 1979, 1989 & 1990; European Cup winners 1979 & 1980; European Super Cup winners 1980; Division Two champions 1969

Derby won the title under Clough in 1971/72, for the first time in their history. The following season they reached the semifinals of the European Cup, losing to Juventus. Clough was sacked after just 44 days in charge at Leeds United. At Nottingham Forest he produced some golden moments for the club over a sixteen-year period, including two European Cups. Forest won promotion to the First Division in 1977, and a year later they clinched the League title. In 1979, they beat Malmo 1–0 thanks to a Trevor Francis goal to win the European Cup. A year later they confounded the critics and won the trophy again, this time beating Hamburg 1–0. Forest have played in five League Cup finals between 1978 and 1990, winning four times. The one domestic trophy that eluded Clough was the FA Cup.

DALGLISH, Kenneth Mathieson, MBE
Born: Dalmarnock, Glasgow (4 March 1951)
Career: Liverpool player/manager June 1985–Feb. 1991; Blackburn Oct. 1991–June 1995; Newcastle Jan. 1997–present
Honours: Scotland international (102 caps); FA Cup winners 1986 & 1989; League champions 1986, 1988, 1990 & 1995*
(* = Premier League)

Dalglish holds the Scottish international appearance and joint goalscoring record, and is the only player to score a hundred goals in both Scottish and English football. He has won four Scottish League titles and eight Football League titles; he also played in six League Cup finals for Liverpool and four European Cup finals, including Heysel in 1985. In all, Dalglish has won 39 medals during his career to date.

Dalglish became Liverpool player/manager in June 1985. Liverpool won the double at the end of his first season in charge; he is the only player/manager ever to achieve this feat. The Reds missed out on the double in 1988 when they won the title by nine points but lost to Wimbledon in the FA Cup final. The following year, 1989, they beat neighbours Everton in the final, but lost 2–0 at Anfield to Arsenal in the title-deciding match. In 1990 Liverpool again won the title by nine points, but lost in the semifinal of the FA Cup to Crystal Palace. Dalglish took Blackburn to their first League title for 81 years in 1994/95. Only Dalglish, Tom Watson, Brian Clough and Herbert Chapman have won the title with different clubs.

DOCHERTY, Thomas Henderson
Born: Glasgow (24 August 1928)
Career: Chelsea Jan. 1962–Oct. 1967; Rotherham Nov. 1967–Nov. 1968; QPR Nov. 1968; Aston Villa Dec. 1968–Jan. 1970; FC Porto Feb. 1970–June 1971; Hull City assistant manager

July–Sept. 1971; Scotland national manager Sept. 1971–Dec. 1972; Man Utd Dec. 1972–July 1977; Derby County Sept. 1977–May 1979; QPR May 1979–Oct. 1980; Preston NE June–Dec. 1981; Wolves June 1984–July 1985; Altrincham Oct. 1987–Feb. 1988
Honours: Scotland international (25 caps); Division Two champions 1975; FA Cup winners 1977; League Cup winners 1965

At Chelsea, the Doc won the League Cup in 1965, and took the club to their first FA Cup final. This was after two consecutive semifinal defeats in the two previous seasons. In November 1968 Docherty was lured to QPR, but sensationally quit after only 29 days. In 1975/76, Docherty's Manchester United finished third in the First Division and reached the FA Cup final only to lose to Southampton. They won the trophy the following year, beating Liverpool 2–1. It was his final achievement at Old Trafford as he lost his job as a result of an affair with the physio's wife.

FERGUSON, Alex, OBE
Born: Govan (31 December 1941)
Career: East Stirling July–Oct. 1974; St Mirren Oct. 1974–June 1978; Aberdeen June 1978–Nov. 1986; Scotland national manager 1985–1986; Manchester United Nov. 1986–present
Honours: European Cup-Winners' Cup winners 1983 & 1991; Scottish League Cup winners 1985; Scottish champions 1980, 1984 & 1985; Scottish Cup winners 1982, 1983, 1984 & 1986; FA Premier League champions 1993, 1994 & 1996; League Cup winners 1992; FA Cup winners 1990, 1994 & 1996

Ferguson has an excellent record as manager in both Scottish and English football. He has taken two clubs to success in the European Cup-Winners' Cup, one of only two men to do so, and has won every honour on both sides of the border. He was snapped up by ambitious Aberdeen in 1978 and led the club through one of their most successful periods. His record at Pittodrie attracted Manchester United, and he became their manager in November 1986. Lack of success almost brought him the sack in January 1990, but after the club won the FA Cup against Palace in a replay, his job was safe. United won the Cup-Winners' Cup against Barcelona in 1991, losing to Sheffield Wednesday in the League Cup final the same season. They won that trophy the following year, beating Nottingham Forest in the final.

Ferguson came close to being the first man to steer a club to three successive Premier League titles. After winning the League in 1993 and 1994, United finished runners-up to Blackburn by only a point in 1995. But they made it three titles in four years when they took the title again in 1996. United also won the double twice, in 1994 and 1996, the first club to achieve this feat.

GRAHAM, George
Born: Bargeddie, Lanark (30 November 1944)
Career: Millwall Dec. 1982–May 1986; Arsenal May 1986–Feb. 1995 (banned for 12 months); Leeds Utd Sept. 1996–present
Honours: Scotland international (12 caps); League champions 1989 & 1991; FA Cup winners 1993; League Cup winners 1987 & 1993; European Cup-Winners' Cup winners 1994

In December 1982 Graham was appointed manager of Millwall. In his first season at The Den, Millwall won the Football League Trophy, and in 1984/85 the Lions gained promotion to Division Two as runners-up. Arsenal tasted success at the end of Graham's first season in charge, beating Liverpool 2–1 in the League Cup final. The following year they lost 3–2 to Luton in the same final, but in 1988/89 they won the League title in memorable fashion, winning at Liverpool in the last match of the season to deny the home side victory. Two seasons later, Arsenal won the title again, leading Liverpool by seven points. Arsenal won the Cup-Winners' Cup in 1994, having won an unprecedented League Cup and FA Cup double in 1993. In 1995 Arsenal lost in the Cup-Winners' Cup final to Real Zaragoza. Graham is now rebuilding Leeds Utd, having been sacked by Arsenal in the wake of a financial scandal which cost him a year out of the game.

KENDALL, Howard
Born: Ryton-on-Tyne (22 May 1946)
Career: Blackburn player/manager June 1979–May 1981; Everton May 1981–Jun 1987; Athletic Bilbao (Spain) June 1987–Nov. 1989; Man City Dec. 1989–Nov. 1990; Everton Nov. 1990–Dec. 1993; Skoda Xanthi (Greece) 1994; Notts County Jan.–Apr. 1995; Sheffield United Jan. 1996–present.
Honours: League champions 1985 & 1987; FA Cup winners 1984; European Cup-Winners' Cup winners 1984.

Howard Kendall has been involved in three Championship seasons at Goodison Park, the first as a player in 1969/70, then as a manager in 1984/85 and 1986/87. He spent seven years as a player at Everton, becoming player/manager of Blackburn in 1979. After two blank years with Everton he was in danger of being sacked in January 1984, but held on to win the FA Cup, beating Watford 2–0 in the final. The following season Everton won the Cup-Winners' Cup, against Rapid Vienna, having disposed of Bayern Munich in the semifinals. They also clinched the League title in 1985, thirteen points clear of Liverpool, but lost to Man Utd in the League Cup final. In 1986 they were runners-up to Liverpool in both the League and FA Cup, but regained their title the following season, nine points clear of Liverpool. Since then, Kendall has managed in Spain and Greece, returned briefly to Everton and is now trying to lift Sheffield United into the FA Premier League.

MEE, Bertie, OBE
Born: Bulwell, Notts (25 December 1920)
Career: Arsenal June 1966–Mar. 1976
Honours: League champions 1971; FA Cup winners 1971; Fairs (UEFA) Cup winners 1970

Bertie Mee, along with Kenny Dalglish, Alex Ferguson and Bill Nicholson, has taken a club to a League and Cup double, but is probably the least famous of the four men. In 1967/68 Mee's Arsenal lost to a controversial Leeds goal in the League Cup final, and suffered a similar fate a year later to Third Division Swindon. But in April 1970, the Gunners won their first major trophy for seventeen years when they beat Anderlecht of Belgium in the final of the Inter-City Fairs Cup, the forerunner of the UEFA Cup. The following season was the greatest in Arsenal's illustrious history. They clinched the League title at rivals Tottenham on the Monday before the FA Cup final, which they also won, against Liverpool. Arsenal reached the FA Cup final again in 1972, losing to Leeds, and in 1973 they were runners-up in the League and semifinalists in the FA Cup.

NICHOLSON, William Edward
Born: Scarborough (26 January 1919)
Career: Tottenham Hotspur Oct. 1958–Aug. 1974

Honours: England international (1 cap); League champions 1961; FA Cup winners 1961, 1962 & 1967; League Cup winners 1971 & 1973; European Cup-Winners' Cup winners 1963, UEFA Cup winners 1971

Spurs won the double in 1960/61, the first club to do so this century, with a side still remembered as one of the greatest ever. The double-winning side won their first eleven League games of the season, and beat Leicester 2–0 in the FA Cup final. The following year they won the FA Cup again, beating Burnley 3–1 in the final. They also reached the semifinals of the European Cup, losing 4–3 on aggregate to mighty Benfica. In 1963 Spurs became the first British side to win a European trophy when they destroyed Atlético Madrid 5–1 in the Cup-Winners' Cup final. Nicholson was in the process of rebuilding the side when they won the FA Cup again in 1967, beating Chelsea 2–1 at Wembley. Nicholson's new side reached four Cup finals between 1971 and 1974. They won the League Cup in 1971 and 1973, beating Aston Villa and Norwich respectively, and in 1972 and 1974 they reached the UEFA Cup final, beating Wolves in the first, losing to Holland's Feyenoord in the second.

PAISLEY, Robert, OBE
Born: Hetton-le-Hole (23 January 1919)
Died: 14 February 1996
Career: Liverpool July 1974–June 1983 (to become director)
Honours: League champions 1976, 1977, 1979, 1980, 1982 & 1983; League Cup winners 1981, 1982 & 1983; European Cup winners 1977, 1978 & 1981; UEFA Cup winners 1976

Bob Paisley stands alone as the most successful manager in the history of English football. His Liverpool won six League titles, three European Cups, three League Cups and the UEFA Cup. Only the FA Cup eluded him. He was voted Manager of the Year a record six times. Paisley failed to win a trophy in his first season, but in 1975/76 Liverpool won the League and the UEFA Cup, the start of an unparalleled period of success for the Mersey club. Liverpool retained the title in 1976/77 but missed the double when Man Utd beat them in the FA Cup final. Four days later, however, they beat Borussia Monchengladbach to win the European Cup for the first time. In 1978 the Euro pean Cup was retained, 1–0 against Bruges in a Wembley final. The 1978/79 title success was arguably Paisley's finest as Liverpool conceded just sixteen goals all season, including only four at fortress Anfield. They took a record 68 points with 30 wins and only four defeats. Ray Clemence kept 28 clean sheets, another record.

Liverpool also took the League title in 1980, 1982 and 1983, and the European Cup for the third time in 1981, beating Real Madrid 1–0 in Paris in the final. The Reds also played in four League Cup finals under Paisley, winning in 1981, 1982 and 1983 after losing a replay to Nottingham Forest in 1978. All this came despite Liverpool having never previously enjoyed success in the competition.

RAMSEY, Sir Alfred Ernest
Born: Dagenham (22 January 1920)
Career: Ipswich Town Aug. 1955–Apr. 1963; England national manager Apr. 1963–May 1974; Birmingham Sept. 1977–Mar. 1978
Honours: England international (32 caps), World Cup winners 1966; League champions 1962; Division Two champions 1961; Division Three (South) champions 1957; knighted January 1967

Ramsey took England to a World Cup triumph over West Germany in 1966, and had earlier taken Ipswich from the Third Division to the League title in little over five years. Ipswich won the Third Division (South) in 1957, the Second Division in 1961 and the First Division in 1962, against Tottenham's defending double-winning side. Ipswich were in decline when he took up the England job in April 1963. Three years later, Ramsey had fulfilled his own prophesy and England were world champions. He was knighted for his services to the game in 1967. Ramsey's England also reached the semifinals of the 1968 European Championships, and were quarter-finalists at the 1970 World Cup in Mexico. Failure to qualify for the 1974 World Cup finals cost him his job, and after a brief spell in charge at Birmingham, he retired from the game in 1978.

REVIE, Donald George, OBE
Born: Middlesbrough (10 July 1927)
Died: Edinburgh (26 May 1989)
Career: Leeds United player/manager Mar. 1961–Apr. 1974; Eng-

land national manager Apr. 1974–July 1977; United Arab Emirates national coach July 1977–May 1980
Honours: England international (6 caps); FA Cup winners 1971; League champions 1969 & 1974; Division Two champions 1964; League Cup winners 1968; Fairs (UEFA) Cup winners 1968 & 1971; OBE January 1970

Revie was one of the great managers of his era, transforming a struggling Second Division side into one of the most powerful in Europe. Leeds were often the nearly men, but following a Second Division title in 1964, Revie put the club firmly on football's map. Leeds won the title twice under Revie, in 1969 and 1974, but were also runners-up four times during his stay at Elland Road. The 1968/69 season was a record-breaker, with 67 points won and only two defeats during the entire season.

Leeds reached four FA Cup finals, winning just once in 1972, and Revie nearly moved to Everton after defeat in the 1973 final to Sunderland. He also guided Leeds to the League Cup in 1968, and Revie's Leeds had an excellent record in Europe. They won the Inter-City Fairs Cup in 1968 and 1971, and were beaten finalists in 1967. Leeds also reached the European Cup final, in 1975, but lost to Bayern Munich, and the 1973 Cup-Winners' Cup final, where they lost to AC Milan. Revie's England career ended in controversy when, having failed to qualify for the 1978 World Cup finals, he broke his contract to move to the Middle East. He was banned from football for ten years, and although this was later overturned, he never returned to the game.

ROBSON, Robert William
Born: Sacriston, Co. Durham (18 February 1933)
Career: Vancouver Royals (Canada) May 1967–Jan. 1968; Fulham Jan.–Nov. 1968; Ipswich Jan. 1969–July 1982; England national manager July 1982–July 1990; PSV Eindhoven (Holland) Aug. 1990–May 1992; Sporting Lisbon (Portugal) May 1992–Dec. 1993; FC Porto (Portugal) Jan. 1994–June 1996; Barcelona (Spain) June 1996–present
Honours: England international (20 caps); FA Cup winners 1978; UEFA Cup winners 1981

Bobby Robson has been one of the most successful managers for the last two decades. He not only found success at unfashionable

Ipswich Town but also took England to the semifinals of the World Cup in 1990, where they narrowly lost to West Germany on penalties. He took Ipswich close to the League title on several occasions (they finished runners-up twice) and led them to the FA Cup in 1978. The 1981/82 season was arguably Ipswich's finest ever. They finished runners-up in the League, four points behind Liverpool, were semifinalists in the FA Cup and winners of the UEFA Cup, beating AZ Alkmaar 5–4 on aggregate in the final. That season, Ipswich were voted Europe's top team by the Continent's press.

In July 1982 Robson succeeded another former Fulham player, Ron Greenwood, as England manager. England failed to qualify for the 1984 European Championships after losing to Denmark at Wembley, but they reached the quarterfinals of the 1986 World Cup, where they were beaten by Argentina. The 1988 European Championship finals became a disaster as England lost all three matches, but in the 1990 World Cup they were penalty kicks away from the final. Robson left for the Continent after Italia 90, and successfully managed in Holland and Portugal before taking on one of the biggest jobs in football – managing FC Barcelona.

SHANKLY, William, OBE
Born: Glenbuck (2 September 1913)
Died: Liverpool (29 September 1981)
Career: Carlisle United Mar. 1949–July 1951; Grimsby Town July 1951–Jan. 1954; Workington Jan. 1954–Nov. 1955; Huddersfield Town Nov. 1956–Nov. 1959; Liverpool Dec. 1959–July 1974.
Honours: Scotland international (5 caps); FA Cup winners 1965 & 1974; League champions 1964, 1966 & 1973; Division Two champions 1962; UEFA Cup winners 1973; OBE 1974.

Liverpool won the Second Division title in 1961/62. They were unbeaten at home for the first time since 1905, and Roger Hunt hit a new club record 41 goals in the season. In 1963/64 they won the League title, and the FA Cup followed for the first time in 1965. Champions again in 1965/66, they lost just two of their last nineteen games and reached the Cup-Winners' Cup final, where they lost to Borussia Dortmund. In 1971 Liverpool reached the FA Cup final, losing to Arsenal, but the following season Liverpool won the title again, and the UEFA Cup, beating Borussia Mönchen Gladbach in the two-legged final. Shankly's swansong was a 3–0 FA Cup final victory over Newcastle. He handed over power to Bob Paisley in July 1974, having turned Liverpool into the most powerful club in the land. Three years later Liverpool were European champions and Shankly's revolution was complete.

STEIN, John 'Jock', CBE
Born: September 1923
Died: Cardiff (10 September 1985)
Career: Celtic player/coach 1955; Dunfermline 1960; Hibernian 1964–Mar. 1965; Celtic Mar. 1965–May 1978; Leeds Utd Aug.–Oct. 1978; Scotland national manager Oct. 1978–Sept. 1985
Honours: Scottish Cup winners 1961, 1965, 1967, 1969, 1971, 1972, 1974, 1975 & 1977; Scottish champions 1966, 1967, 1968, 1969, 1970, 1971, 1972, 1973, 1974 & 1977; Scottish League Cup winners 1966, 1967, 1968, 1969, 1970 & 1975; European Cup winners 1967; CBE 1970

Most of Jock Stein's success was in Scotland, so his record is difficult to compare with most of the other great managers. His only Football League experience lasted just 44 days with Leeds United in 1978. Stein took Dunfermline to the Scottish Cup in 1961 and Celtic to the European Cup in 1967, when they defeated Inter Milan 2–1 in Lisbon to become the first British side to lift the trophy. Under Stein's all-pervading influence Celtic won ten League titles, nine Scottish Cups and six League Cups. In 1967, Celtic won every trophy they entered, and his legacy is one that the Parkhead club are still trying to live up to even now. Stein took charge of Scotland for seven years, but died from a heart attack on the bench at a match in Cardiff in 1985.

VENABLES, Terence Frederick
Born: Bethnal Green, London (6 January 1943)
Career: Crystal Palace June 1976–Oct. 1980; QPR Oct. 1980–May 1984; Barcelona (Spain) May 1984–Sept. 1987; Tottenham Nov. 1987–July 1991 then chief executive; England national manager Jan. 1994–July 1996; Australia national manager Nov. 1996–present
Honours: England international (2 caps); Division Two champions 1979 & 1983; FA Cup winners 1991; Spanish champions 1985

The Cult of the Manager

Terry Venables became manager of Crystal Palace in June 1976. At the end of his first season in charge he had taken Palace to promotion from Division Three, and in 1978/79 the 'Team of the Eighties' were Second Division champions, conceding just 24 goals. In 1982 Venables took QPR to an FA Cup final, where they lost 1–0 to Tottenham in a dull replay. In 1982/83 Rangers took the Second Division championship, ten points clear of nearest rivals Wolves, and finished fifth the following season. Venables left for Barcelona in May 1984, and took the Spanish title at the end of his first season in charge. Barça also reached the European Cup final, in 1986, but were surprisingly beaten by Romania's Steaua Bucharest on penalties after a goalless draw. Barça were runners-up to Real Madrid in 1987, and soon afterwards Venables was back in England, managing Tottenham. He led Spurs to the FA Cup in 1991 and later became chief executive at White Hart Lane. An acrimonious split with the club's owner, Alan Sugar, led to his abrupt departure, and in 1994 Venables was appointed England manager. 'El Tel' took England to the semifinals of the 1996 European Championship, and is now masterminding Australia's bid to qualify for the 1998 World Cup finals in France.

The scoring system

	Pts		Pts
DIVISION ONE		**DIVISION TWO**	
Champions	18	Champions	16
Runners-up	12	Runners-up/promoted	10
DIVISION THREE		**DIVISION FOUR**	
Champions	14	Champions	12
Runners-up/promoted	8	Runners-up/promoted	6
FA CUP & LEAGUE CUP		**EUROPEAN CUPS**	
Winners	18	Winners	18
Finalists	12	Finalists	12
Semifinalists	6	Semifinalists	6

Overall Managerial Rankings 1888–1996

	Manager	Pts	Clubs
1	Matt Busby	306	Man Utd
2	Bob Paisley	300	Liverpool

3	Don Revie	268	Leeds Utd
4	Brian Clough	248	Derby, Nottingham Forest
5	Alex Ferguson	204	Manchester Utd
6	Bill Shankly	198	Liverpool
7	Kenny Dalglish	196	Liverpool, Blackburn
8	Bill Nicholson	192	Tottenham
9	Tom Watson	190	Sunderland, Liverpool
10	Herbert Chapman	162	Huddersfield, Arsenal
11	Joe Mercer	152	Aston Villa, Man City
12	George Graham	152	Millwall, Arsenal
13	Stan Cullis	150	Wolves
14	Ron Atkinson	130	Oxford, Man Utd, West Brom, Sheffield Wed, Aston Villa
15	Howard Kendall	128	Blackburn, Everton
16	Ron Saunders	114	Norwich, Man City, Aston Villa, Birmingham
17	Harry Catterick	112	Everton
18	Tommy Docherty	110	Chelsea, Man Utd
19	Fred Everiss	110	West Brom
20	Bertie Mee	108	Arsenal

Leading Managerial Trophy Winners

Manager	Div 1	FA Cup	Lge Cup	Euro	Total
Bob Paisley	6	—	3	4	13
Alex Ferguson	3	3	1	2	9
Brian Clough	2	—	4	2	8
Bill Nicholson	1	3	2	2	8
Matt Busby	5	2	—	1	8
Don Revie	2	1	1	2	6
George Graham	2	1	2	1	6
Herbert Chapman	4	2	—	—	6
Bill Shankly	3	2	—	1	6
Kenny Dalglish	4	2	—	—	6
Joe Mercer	1	1	2	1	5
Stan Cullis	3	2	—	—	5
Tom Watson	5	—	—	—	5

*Does not include Scottish honours

Afterword

By Danny Kelly

Something strange happened. In the autumn of 1996, Ron Atkinson was booted upstairs at struggling Coventry City. Struggling Coventry City? There must be a whole generation of West Midlands youngsters who think that's the club's actual name. Anyway, for days after Ron rumbled grumpily into his new 'job', the back pages of British newspapers were awash with awful cries and lamentations. It was as if man had been around to see the final brontosaurus keel slowly over and expire before our very eyes. The fact that most of this stuff was being written by fellows who had, over the years, benefited hugely from Big Ron's legendary hospitality and bonhomie didn't make the wall of wailing any less real . . .

Atkinson, we were tearfully told, was the last of the old school of personality managers, the final example of a genus that had included Brian Clough, Bill Shankly, Malcolm Allison, Tommy Docherty, Lawrie McMenemy, Jack Charlton, Don Revie and, rather less convincingly, John Bond. With the exception of Bond (who, with an unkindness bordering on the vindictive, kept signing his fair-to-middling defender son Kevin and thus inflicted and reinflicted on the poor lad the excrutiating torture normally reserved for the kid at school whose dad's the headmaster), these were Big Men. Big Men who didn't call a spade a long-handled digging implement. Big Men who didn't cower before agents. Big Men who courted players in motorway cafs, then paraded them in front of the fans before they'd even signed the contract (Clough once came slightly unstuck with this particular stunt; Ian Storey-Moore's triumphant whirl around the Baseball Ground was followed the very next day by his actual signing for Manchester United!). Big Men who took no nonsense from the press, the fans, the fools in the directors' box, the shiny-arsed pen-suckers at the

FA, and not, *certainly* not, from the players. Big Men with football in their veins. Big Men. Managers.

But then something even stranger happened. After a few days, this weeping and sighing over the former Mr Bojangles tailed off, to be replaced by something less sentimental and well intentioned, something altogether more bizarre. A new line of thinking emerged, one suggesting that the disappearance of Big Ron from the managerial stage (and did any manager ever more treat his chosen calling as though it were theatre, ever more love the spotlight?) was actually the end of not just the Big Men, but maybe of the whole managerial era. It was suggested that players were now so well paid and ill disciplined, playing patterns so deeply ingrained, agents so powerful, and youth (needless to say) so addled by Ecstasy, McDonald's and satellite television, that management had become an impossible task, that managers and coaches could no longer make a difference to modern football teams.

This, of course, is nothing new. Ever since craggy Scots first got the newly professional footballers of the industrial hell-holes of northern England to run along roads and beaches, people have been decrying managers, saying that they make no odds. Let's get this straight from the start; to hold that belief (and many football journalists seem, to one degree or another, to cling to it) is the modern equivalent of being a founder member of the Flat Earth Society's Particularly Convinced Branch. For proof of the influence that managers can, and do, wield, we do not need a recitation of the great Big Men and their achievements. On the contrary, if you really want to see that a manager can make a difference, just look at some of football's most famous *failures* . . .

Brian Clough's 44 fractious days at Leeds . . . Don Revie's dossier-amassing, bingo-calling, carpet-bowls-playing reign as England boss . . . Ossie Ardiles' astonishing six months at Spurs, where he not only played with five out-and-out non-tackling forwards and a pair of centre-halves still waiting for their voices to break, but, for the holding position in midfield, chose, lest we forget, his middle-aged, ball-juggling mate, Micky Hazard! . . . Malcolm Allison's second spell in charge at Manchester City, when the players were made to endure a full training session on the morning of matches and where Big Mal (Big Mal? Big Ron? What a pity there hasn't been a top-class soccer boss called

Benjamin!) would baffle his players with fancy ways that he'd picked up on his travels and which had clearly lost something in translation ... Graham Taylor's time at the helm of his country; Taylor's a decent fellow, but 'that' documentary's shot of him talking, at a moment of national crisis, to Nigel Clough in what appeared to be a form of gobbledegook understood by only one man on earth (come on down, Phil 'Yes, Boss' Neal!) will stick with him forever ... Graeme Souness's reign of terror at Liverpool, which destroyed a great club and, it's sometimes forgotten, opened the door for an era of Manchester United domination that, given the changes in the way the game is financed, may never be broken ... Arrigo Sacchi's recent stint with Italy, where a managerial genius, perhaps taking leave of his senses and believing he'd been made manager of Wales, filled his potentially wonderful team with midfield cloggers and played Serie A's leading scorer, Beppi Signori, at left back! ... Ray Harford's baleful stewardship of Blackburn's expensive menagerie ... the entire career of Alan Ball ...

The list could go on and on, but the point is made. Wherever football teams go seriously off the rails, there's always a manager, sometimes even a very good manager (Clough, Revie, Allison, Souness and Sacchi have all, in their time, been seriously successful), doing something quite startlingly, thrillingly *mad*. Or doing nothing at all. And the opposite is, of course, obvious, evident and true. Behind every great team is a manager who is *making the difference* ...

Once we've accepted that – and, I reiterate, we *must* accept it – we can get on with the real businesses of this book, of which there are two. The first is to marvel at and glory in the skills, arts, sciences, stratagems, psychologies and downright hocus pocus that managers bring to the task of turning something very simple – a collection of footballers, blokes who can run, jump, and manipulate a ball – into something incredibly, almost beautifully, complex – a winning football *team*. The other is to bathe in the warm mental waters of memories provided by managers across the years ...

I think the first time I really understood that managers actually *ran* teams, that they actually fashioned them either in, or contrary to, their own image, was in the early seventies. Of course, I'd watched, boggle-eyed, as Rinus Michels created first Ajax, and then Holland, sides that seemed to defy the laws of time and motion, which allowed, indeed encouraged, players to turn up wherever they liked on the pitch, to create shapes and movement that first baffled, then overran most opposition's lumpen, out-moded, comfortable but thick-skulled 4–4–2. And of course I loved the fact that amid that gorgeous – yes, even artistic – orange whirl, craggy, cagey old Rinus had allowed for days when the going got rough. Those early-seventies Dutch sides were the most beautiful I ever saw, but in Messrs Krol, Neeskens and Haan they had three of the dirtiest great players of all time. Magnificent, and all springing from the head of one man.

But the team that really opened my eyes to the influence of managers was an Atlético Madrid side that pitched up for a European Cup semifinal against Celtic in 1974. The game was televised and I watched – transfixed in a cocktail of fascination and disbelief – as Atlético set about a game plan that seemed to combine the manners of a whorehouse cat-fight with the fanaticism of a particularly keen kamikaze squadron. They sneered, they snarled, they spat. They kicked, they punched, they gouged. They argued, they acted, they agitated. They got sent off. By the end of the game (and this was in the pre-namby-pamby FIFA directive days when sociopaths like Tommy Smith and Peter Storey would go whole seasons without so much as a booking!) Atlético had just *seven* men left on the pitch; and, what's more, they didn't seem to give a toss. In my innocence, I was astounded, and yet I soon discovered that I shouldn't have been. A little teenage research uncovered the fact that Atlético's manager – an Argentinian called Juan Carlos 'The Jackal' Lorenzo – had a long – nay, *proud* – record of putting out teams who performed like rabid dogs. Parkhead had been no bad-hair day for the Spaniards; that was how Señor Lorenzo had coached his team to play; that was how Señor Lorenzo *wanted* them to play . . .

I was hooked. If one imagination could conceive, visualise and then orchestrate on a football pitch something as radical and aesthetically overpowering as Total Football, while another could unleash something as primal, scary and, let's admit it, downright exciting as Atlético's blitzkrieg on civilisation, and if both those minds thought that they were *doing the same job* (i.e., trying to win a football match), then football managers, I decided, were fellows very much worth keeping an eye on, pop stars in track-suits.

The Cult of the Manager

The fascination has remained. The twenty years since have filled my head with the stories of the men who mould, shape, inspire, cajole, threaten, mollycoddle, restrict, liberate, make and break football teams ... Brian Clough, late at night, insisting that his Nottingham Forest team swill their way through a lake of alcohol; next day, hung over but relaxed, they won the European Cup ... Lawrie McMenemy settling some training ground score with Mark Wright with fisticuffs in the showers, Wright naked, Big Mac(!) fully dressed ... Bill Shankly's curt team talks: 'Win!' ... Bill Nicholson solving Martin Chivers' lack of aggression by secretly telling all Spurs' defenders to kick the living crap out of the big softie in training until he damn well responded. It worked; the laid-back Chiv became Europe's best centre-forward (editor's note: Danny Kelly *is* a Spurs fan) ... Cesar Menotti smoking himself into an early grave in case his 1978 Argentina didn't win the World Cup at home, and in case the brutal military junta that ruled the country took offence at that failure. Argentina won, Cesar kept puffing, now, one suspects, out of relief rather than fear ... The wonderful Guy Roux, who's been manager of Auxerre for decades now, and whose stoic wisdom has turned a team from little more than a village into a European force ... Jack Charlton sharing a beer and a song with Ireland's hordes of supporters at Cagliari airport after the Republic of Ireland had held England in a spectacular lightning storm (especially warm, this memory, because I was there) ... Bob Stokoe's skipping run to greet his goalkeeping hero Jim Montgomerie after Sunderland had beaten Leeds to win the FA Cup ... David Pleat's even less dignified dance across the Maine Road pitch after Raddy Antic (now one of the world's leading managers himself) had saved Luton and relegated Manchester City with one late strike ... The look of pride and relief on the face of Bertie Vogts as Jurgen Klinsmann lifted the Euro 96 trophy and saved him from being the first German manager in living memory not to win at least one major tournament ...

It's another endless list. These managers made a difference. Football managers *do*. That, given that they do their peculiar thing in the century's most popular and marvellous form of entertainment, is what makes them so damn important ...

Danny Kelly